Then
One Year...

Then One Year...

History's Craziest Year as Seen by a Las Vegas Bookmaker

Chris Andrews

HUNTINGTON PRESS • LAS VEGAS, NEVADA

Then One Year...
History's Craziest Year as Seen by a Las Vegas Bookmaker

Published by: Huntington Press
                     3665 Procyon Street
                     Las Vegas, Nevada 89103
                     Phone (702) 252-0655
                     e-mail: books@huntingtonpress.com

Cover photos: Typewriter ©Eyewave | Image ©Eric Broder Van Dyke
                     Dreamstime.com
Cover design: Tanya Maynard
Production & design: Alison Holka & Tanya Maynard

The opinions expressed in this book are strictly the author's and don't necessarily reflect those of South Point, Huntington Press, VSiN, Draft Kings, or anyone else with whom Chris Andrews is associated.

Dedication

To Michael Gaughan. Exhibit A for proof that someone can be wealthy and successful, yet remain kindhearted. The best casino operator in the world, whom I'm proud to work for and call a friend, thank you for all you have done for me in my career and my life.

Acknowledgments

I have been fortunate to maintain the same friendships and business relations I mentioned in *Then One Day ... 40 Years Of Bookmaking In Nevada*. Thus, many of the people I thanked in that book I will thank once again.

Of course, Michael Gaughan, who steered our sportsbook and casino through this year of absurd difficulty, and to whom this book is dedicated. Jimmy Vaccaro, who helped me keep my head on straight through the ups and downs of our chosen business, especially in 2020. Others who were there for me are Frank Toti, Ryan Growney, Dave Jensen, Zach Franzi, Art Manteris, Vinny Magliulo, Gill Alexander, Chris Fallica, Barry and Cindy Phillips, Ken Barlor, Christian Cianci, Jeff Whitelaw, Vic Salerno, Richie Baccieleri, Nick Bogdanovich, and Roxy Roxborough.

The whole VSiN operation, particularly Brian, Brent, and Todd Musburger, Bill Ady, Matt Youmans, Ron Flatter, and Brian Rodgers.

Deke Castleman and Anthony Curtis of Huntington Press.

My children—Joe, Jacque, Christos, Johnny, and Daphne.

My South Point supervisor crew—Tom, Lou, Ashley, Nick, Joe, Iva, Anthony, Crystal, Shelley, Haley, Jeff, Shea, Kam, Doug, DW, Brian, Duane, Taira, and Damon.

South Point ticket writers—Steve, Elba, Aracely, Khristine, Therese, Alexis, Noemi, Maria, Tiare, Berta, Larreen, Larry, Ken, Cresencia, Brenda, Jae, and Gabriela.

Each and every employee and staff member at South Point.

Since the last book, we lost a few who had impacted my life in many ways. My Uncle Jack passed away at 93 years old after living a life beyond measure. My godson Danny Larsen was gone much too soon at an early age. My good friends Partick McQuiggan and Tony Stempeck also passed. And a special mention to Bill Thornton, another who lived life to the fullest, before leaving us at the age of 92.

And finally, I can never fully express my deepest thanks to my wife and partner in life, Pam, who has been with me through thick and thin. Love you, baby.

Contents

Introduction

The light at the end of the tunnel is a gorilla with a flashlight.

—Anonymous

I thought it would be fun. There I go again, thinking.

Still, it felt like a natural. Every Monday, folks from management and media to bettors and passersby ask, "How did the sports book do over the weekend?" So I figured that writing a journal describing the ups and downs of a sports book in a typical season would be of general interest. I'd start with one Super Bowl and allow readers to follow the action all the way until the next Super Bowl, peppered with stories like those that made up my first book, *Then One Day … Forty Years of Bookmaking in Nevada*. I imagined an entertaining journey through a typical year in the life of a bookmaker.

Then came 2020—a year in which nothing was typical.

Kobe Bryant's death, along with those in his party, including daughter Gianna, was the year's first event that shocked us. The day after, the L.A. Times had numerous stories about Kobe and the helicopter accident that took his life. But in the lower left-hand corner of that day's front page was a story about two southern California patients who were hospitalized with a mysterious virus. Little did we know that mysterious virus would dominate our lives in the coming year and well beyond it.

When I first contemplated writing this book, I was afraid a lot of the content would be repetitive and boring. I wasn't concerned about football season, which would bookend the timeline, but could I fill the pages with substance about the daily grind of even a major Las Vegas sports book throughout the rest of the year? Would anyone care that the Dodgers and Yankees won again and the sports book got murdered on a Tuesday in July?

Talk about worrying for nothing.

Months of racial tension, reminiscent of the protest-filled 1960s, after George Floyd was murdered by a Minneapolis police officer and months of political unrest leading up to the 2020 presidential election, culminating in the invasion of the U.S. Capitol, were overshadowed by the first pandemic in more than 100 years and its unprecedented and profound impact on everyone's life, but for my purposes, sports and sports betting. COVID-19 allowed me to keep politics out of the book, but the toll it took on the world, and myself, was anything but a consolation.

In 2020, more than a half-million people lost their lives to the coronavirus. Personally, I lost a good friend to the virus while writing this book, and I suffered through a case myself. Conversely, I had the good fortune to be alive after surviving a bone-marrow transplant in July 2019. Exactly two years earlier, doctors had given me two years to live. My time was up. It was either the transplant ordeal or my final resting place.

In preparation for the surgery, my doctor said he wanted me to take at least three months off and preferably six. My wife looked at the doctor, then at me, with an expression that clearly said, you should listen to your doctor, even though I know you won't. Only a couple of days after the procedure, there I was, working from my hospital bed. Afterwards, I had to endure a strict quarantine, then a semi-quarantine, for nearly half a year. With my personal doctor-ordered mask mandate, I looked a little weird going out in public, but when the pandemic hit our shores, I appeared to be a trendsetter, rather than an outlier.

Just as I was emerging from my personal constraints, COVID imposed global restraints and I felt like I was living through an endless loop of the movie Groundhog Day.

Conversely, again, each day in the sports betting business was a new adventure. I had so much material to work with, I couldn't wait to get my thoughts about it onto the printed page. Often, I wrote late into the night and, on more than one occasion, until daybreak the following morning. The word count grew so massive that I had to leave about 40% of it on the cutting-room floor to fit it all into the book you now hold in your hands.

Plenty will be written about 2020, the year of COVID-19. I suspect, however, that few if any other books that view the year through the particular lens of sports and sports betting will be published. I'm certainly aware that neither is the most momentous or meaningful matter in the grand scheme of things, but if the explosive recovery of both after the COVID lockdowns and shutdowns is any indication, it might be among the top priorities in the lives of many of you.

Indeed, in 2020, despite all the catastrophes and abnormalities, we managed to have fulfilling seasons in almost every sport. Though a few had to be rescheduled, the NFL never missed a game. The Kansas City Chiefs scored three fourth-quarter touchdowns to beat the San Francisco 49ers in the 2020 Super Bowl; 2021's also had outstanding drama, as 43-year-old Tom Brady won his seventh ring, his first with the Tampa Bay Buccaneers, defeating his heir apparent Patrick Mahomes and the defending champs. LeBron James won another ring, this time with the Lakers. Coach Nick Saban won his sixth college football National Championship with Alabama and seventh overall. Major League Baseball had a shortened season, but the favored Dodgers, with a payroll rivaling the GDP of a small nation, won the World Series. The Tampa Bay Lightning won another Stanley Cup to establish themselves as one of the NHL's premier franchises. Okay, there was no NCAA Final Four, the Kentucky Derby was run in September instead of the first Saturday in May, the Masters Tournament got moved from April to October, and most games were played with no fans in attendance. But we got through it all and enjoyed remarkable theater and heroic efforts, just as we always had. And the betting scaled the peaks and plumbed the depths for the players and the sports book, as it always does.

So if anyone says nothing good happened in the year of COVID, that's just not true. Let this book help you remember the best parts, process the worst, and relive a most memorable year.

Chapter 1
January 19-February 3, 2020

"When men plan, God laughs."
—*old Greek proverb*

Sunday January 19, 2020:
NFL Conference Championships

I thought I'd fucked everything up.

The Kansas City Chiefs beat the Tennessee Titans 35-24 in the 2020 AFC Championship and the 49ers won big over the Green Bay Packers in the NFC. Both results were favorite and over, usually a death knell for bookmakers. And sure enough, everyone I know in the business got murdered with those outcomes. We wound up losing a little over $100,000, including $80,000 on the 49ers futures. All things considered, though, I wasn't too unhappy. After a little maneuvering on my part, the worst-case scenario wasn't nearly as bad as it was at first. It could have been disastrous and some of my compatriots in the business had a very bad day.

But Super Bowl LIV was now set, 49ers vs. the Chiefs. Both teams looked terrific to me, so I opened the game pick 'em, with a total of 52.5.

Monday January 20, 2020

It's been all Chiefs and over. By noon today, it was Chiefs -1.5 and 54.5.

1

This afternoon, I wrote our first bet on the under after 75 separate bets on the over. I still have a lot of old-school football in me. I know the game has evolved quite a bit, particularly in the last couple of years. But to me, football starts at the line of scrimmage and that was where the 49ers held the advantage. Still, I didn't have a preference yet, though if this number kept heading up, I'd start leaning toward San Francisco.

In addition, the first round of props went up today: alternate pointspreads, alternate totals, team totals, first-half, second-half, quarters—all good props. Then the stupid shit, like the coin toss, overtime, safety, and two-point conversion.

We've done pretty well on the props in the past, but they're not just gravy. I know guys who've made a fortune betting Super Bowl props. I've tried to learn from them and go in with the sides they like. A lot more props were coming in the next few days. I hoped to have a full prop menu up by Friday. A week from Friday, we'd put up some cross-sport props. They're total bullshit, but the media loves them. Sometimes you just have to play the game.

The public loves this time of year. There's a buzz in the air. Everyone has an opinion on the game and some of the player props. It's all anyone talks about.

I couldn't wait until it was over.

Welcome to the world of a bookmaker.

Tuesday January 21, 2020

Last night, I went to dinner at Michael's, the gourmet room at South Point, with Roxy Roxborough, his wife Alise, and my wife Pam. Great meal, but even better to sit for four hours and reminisce with my old pal.

At dinner, we ran into my former coworker, Nick Bogdanovich. He now runs the bookmaking end of William Hill. He told me they got murdered on Sunday. I hate to say (or more accurately, I hate that I love to say) that it made me feel good. We lost "only" $100,000. William Hill, with more than 100 locations in Nevada and many more nationwide, must have lost a fortune.

Nick's official title, Director of Trading, makes me cringe. It's a European term that's been jammed down our throats by these foreign outfits that have been taking over our business on the national landscape.

I don't care for the European bookmakers' business model. Their huge straddles on betting lines are advantageous to the house, but horrible for customers. They're also infamous for throwing out winning players. Once they're in a jurisdiction, they try to create a monopoly, so bettors have no choice to go anywhere else. I have no love for William Hill (although I do love Nick), but at least they book their action nationwide using the Nevada model.

We took a big bet this morning, $55,000 on the 49ers money line +105. Other than that, the money flow on the Super Bowl pointspread, money line, and total has slowed. It will be nothing more than a drip for the next couple of days. Bettors want to see where the line is going to settle before they make their commitments. The props are a different story. As soon as we post them, the players start firing.

Thursday January 23, 2020

We opened a massive number of Super Bowl props today. My cousin Zach, who has always been pretty good with the props, helped me. So it was Zach and I against the world. We wrote about $150,000 in the first 25 minutes, all at $2,000 a whack. The guys who bet into me are some of the sharpest in town. I hope I can maneuver the action enough by Sunday to actually need some of the same sides these guys are on.

The last couple of years, we've had as much action on the

props as on the game itself. We've done well with them, but it's definitely a challenge.

The Westgate, known for props more than anywhere in the industry, opens theirs tonight at 7 p.m. That means another round of action for all the arbitrageurs. I'll be home, so I hope the crew can handle it. If not, I'll be getting some calls. Like I said, these two weeks are a pain in my ass.

Friday January 24, 2020

This morning, a customer at the Rampart bet $115,000 to win $100,000 on the Chiefs money line, so far the biggest bet we've taken. I moved the juice on KC a nickel, from -115 to -120. I'm reasonably sure I'll get a pretty big chunk of it back when the public and sharp bettors bet the 49ers money line. Before that bet, I was about $30,000 high on the 49ers between the money line and the small pointspread of Chiefs -1, but now, of course, it's turned around the other way. It will change quite a bit between now and game time.

We filled out the last of our Super Bowl props today. We won't add any more until late next week when we post the dreaded cross-sport props. Those are always a little tougher, because you never know who'll get injured or just sit out a game, which has become the norm in recent years.

Rufus Peabody, one of the sharpest guys in the industry and probably the top prop guy in the business, came in and gave a boatload of action. If Rufus does well, which he usually does, I hope to do well, too.

Young bookmakers and even some old ones should take note: We don't throw out winning players. We appreciate the information they provide with their action. With an event this big, we do our best to go into the game needing the same sides they need. I know that's not the European model, of throwing out any and all winning players, but it's mine. Our win percentage might not be as high, but this is the way to win money. The hell with the percentage. That's not why we're in business. We're here to make money.

Remember, too, we're part of a casino. We want to boost traffic. We want to keep our existing customers, create some new customers, and in the end, make a little money. I've always been able to do all three.

Saturday January 25, 2020

With the accumulation of action, I moved the Chiefs from -1 to -1.5. I finally surrendered on the total, going from 54.5 to 55. I thought 55 would be a trigger point for under bettors, but we took a mere nickel on the under in the first hour. I'm still getting heavy action on the over at this price. I was the first to go to 55 and a few other sports books followed. I know I'm patting myself on the back, but our line gets as much respect as anyone's.

By the time I went home, we had even action on the total at 55. It looks like the number—for the time being, anyway.

Sunday January 26, 2020

The news was dominated today by Kobe Bryant's death in the helicopter crash. All others on board, including Kobe's daughter Gianna, also perished.

I'm not a big NBA fan and wasn't a particular fan of the Lakers or Kobe, but I did appreciate his greatness, so about 10 years ago, I made it a point to see him before he retired. I met Jimmy Vaccaro and some other friends at the arena. Today, Jimmy and I reminisced about that trip; we also remembered watching Kobe's father, Joe "Jelly Bean" Bryant, play when he was in high school.

Kobe had a long-running dispute with Shaquille O'Neal, stemming from their time together as Laker teammates. From what I've heard, Shaq made the first move to put the past behind them when they played against each other on Martin Luther King Day. Shaq approached him in warmups, shook his hand, and said, "Dr. King would want us to be friends." Of course, I'm paraphrasing and only repeating what I've heard, but kudos to both of them for being big enough to put their differences aside. Maybe they weren't close friends afterward, but they were no longer enemies.

Shaq and Kobe were like John Lennon and Paul McCartney—terrific on their own, but together John and Paul were the greatest of all time, and Shaq and Kobe came close enough.

Yes, it's a cliché, but life is precious. Enjoy every sandwich.

Even all of us jaded bastards in this industry are too shocked by the Kobe news to do much today and that includes the Super Bowl.

Monday January 27, 2020

Kobe Bryant's death is still dominating the airwaves and the minds of sports fans. The tragedy has cast a pall over the whole country, the sporting community in particular. Eventually, we'll get back to normal, as we always do, but it'll take awhile.

Our price fluctuated all day between the Chiefs -120 (49ers even money), Chiefs -122 (49ers +102), and Chiefs -125 (49ers +105). We didn't book a lot of action, but I was testing the market to gauge support and resistance. By tomorrow or Thursday, I'll switch to a dime line (10¢ straddle rather than the 20¢ in the examples), which is much more enticing to the bettors. I've done it the past couple of years. We give up some of our edge, but make it up in volume.

Wednesday January 29, 2020

One fairly big bet today. Joe Maloof, of the famous Maloof brothers, bet $35,000 on the 49ers +1.5. I know the Maloofs (Joe,

Gavin, and George) a little and they all seem decent, good guys you can have a beer with. At one time, they owned the Sacramento Kings, the Palms in Las Vegas, and other business interests; they're also minority owners of the Vegas Golden Knights. I sat once with George and Joe in their box at a VGK game.

Still getting flooded on over bets. I went back again from 54.5 to 55. That was the tipping point earlier. Hopefully, it will be again.

Thursday January 30, 2020

We went to a dime line this morning, Chiefs -117/49ers +107. It didn't take long to get some big play. After 20 minutes, we took $50,000 on the 49ers. I moved the money line to Chiefs -114/49ers +104 and since the pointspread was so close, I moved that too, from Chefs -1.5 to Chiefs -1. Not long after, a different guy bet us $40,000 on under 55. I moved the total back to 54.5, but we still needed the game total under for a ton.

The action really started picking up today. I don't know if the dime line had anything to do with it, given that the game is just four days from now. Either way, we booked a bunch of bets between $2,000 and $10,000.

The prop action also picked up. We limit them to $2,000 and I honestly didn't know how many limit bets we took. Plus, we had so many plays between $100 and $1,000, I couldn't keep up. I went through all the props this morning. I do that every morning, just to make sure I don't get caught by surprise from an accumulation of smaller bets adding up to the equivalent of a big bet. But that doesn't happen too often.

Tonight, Roxy Roxborough hosted his annual pre-Super Bowl dinner. In attendance were Vic Salerno, Jay Kornegay, Nick Bogdanovich, Tony Sinisi, Mike Knapp, and David Purdum. All of us have spent our whole lives in the business. Jay and Nick were the youngest, both around 56. David was the one exception; at 46, he was easily 10 years younger than anyone. David is one of the few media guys who really understands our business. Plus, we all trust him.

We had a good time sharing old war stories. Some of them were even true.

Friday January 31, 2020

First thing this morning, we took a $75,000 bet on the Chiefs -1. It was still early and I was expecting more big action, but that would no doubt be dwarfed by what we got on Saturday and Sunday.

We started seriously charting all the possible what-ifs. By doing that, you can see if you're booking the game properly. You can't improve every possible scenario, but the overall picture should get progressively better. I've done it for years to make sure I'm following the right procedures and disciplines. We'll continue it from now until kickoff.

Less than 48 hours until this is all over.

Saturday February 1, 2020

At 11 a.m., we took $190,000 on the Chiefs -1.5. I just left the spread where it was. We already had the highest money line in town—actually, the world—on the Chiefs. We'd taken in $30,000 on the 49ers' money line in the past two hours, so I was content to leave it where it was and see what happened.

By 5:30 p.m., I finally had to go to Chiefs -2 and Chiefs -120/49ers +110 on the money line. I'd tried to be patient, hoping people would take the 49ers +1.5. We had a lot of takers, but not serious enough money to make a difference.

Michael Gaughan was in the sports book for a while today and told Vinny Magliulo and me to take our wives to dinner at Michael's. The South Point is hosting a Super Bowl betting seminar tonight, featuring Brent Musburger, Jimmy Vaccaro,

Matt Youmans, Vinny, and me. The wives already had plans to come see us, so it didn't take much to convince them to have dinner with us at one of Las Vegas' top restaurants, especially with Michael picking up the check. We made reservations for 6:30, so I stuck around until then to see where the action took us.

I got awfully lucky hooking up with Michael Gaughan. I worked for him at the Barbary Coast in 1980. I didn't realize it at the time, but he was quite young for a casino owner, in his early 30s. By now, the years have caught up with us both a bit. We've both lost some hair and gained some weight. Michael has become very wealthy, with the reputation for being the best casino operator in the world. If anyone has the Midas touch, it's Michael. His knack for the business notwithstanding, he's also absolutely brilliant. You'd never know it to look at him. I couldn't remember the last time I saw him in a tie or his shirt tucked in, for that matter. He's as happy eating a hotdog from the sports book cart as he is a gourmet meal in the finest French restaurants. I see a lot more of him in the sports book watching the games than at meetings. We've booked some pretty big losses, but he never calls me on the carpet for losing. In fact, he usually just jokes with me; he loves to bust balls. I don't think we could ever come close to losing enough to affect the bottom line of the casino or him personally.

Besides all his success, he's one of the most generous guys you'll ever meet. Some employees at South Point have been with him for more than 40 years. Friends of mine who don't know him are surprised I don't have a contract. I've never asked for one. I just trust him. He spoils the hell out of Jimmy Vaccaro and me. Even before I worked for him, I always joked that I knew one billionaire who took my calls. When he asked me in February 2016 to come work for him again, fortune smiled down on me.

After dinner, I made my last check at the book. Overall, we were slightly ahead for the day, even though we lost $44,000 when Lamar Jackson was named the NFL's MVP. We knew it was coming, so I'm glad it came on a day where we had a bit of a cushion.

One of my top supervisors, Ashley Eck, had been running the what-ifs for me all afternoon and evening. We were slightly improving our positions, but it looked like we still needed the 49ers for a substantial sum. It was still about 16 hours until game time, though, and a lot could and would change in the meantime. I went home to watch "SNL" and try to get some sleep.

Sunday February 2, 2020—Super Bowl Sunday

Well, we finally got here. And what a day.

We opened at Chiefs -1.5, total 54, Chiefs -120/49ers +110 on the money line. From there, we went as high as Chiefs -2 on the pointspread, then down to -1.5, then down to -1, where it closed. The money line inched down from -120 to -118 to -116, then -114, where it closed. The total also dropped, from 54 to 53.5, then 53. At kickoff, the only combination that could hurt us was Chiefs and over. In the last few hours of betting, a flood of play came in on the 49ers and under, though not necessarily in combination. There were still plenty of parlays with both teams to over the total.

We won the coin toss when it came up tails (we always need tails).[1] But we lost when Patrick Mahomes scored the first touchdown running the ball. The first quarter ended with the Chiefs up 7-3. We lost on the total (they'd bet us under 10.5), but won on the side (they bet the 49ers to win the quarter).

We had so many props, I could never keep track of all of them along the way. I just hoped that at the end of the day, we held our percentage of the huge handle.

Oh, Jesus. Kyle Juszcyk just scored the first 49ers touchdown, costing me another $11,000. Fuck! The early props were

---

[1] I have a story about how stupid it is to bet the coin toss in my book *Then One Day ... 40 Years of Bookmaking in Nevada.*

terrible. Chiefs and 49ers tied 10-10 at the end of the first half. So far, not so good.

After we put in the props for the first quarter, second quarter, first half, first touchdowns, first scores, and many others, we were stuck $100,000. I'd been telling Michael and anyone else who'd listen that the props were anything but automatic. Yes, we did very well in the past, but that wasn't indicative of future results. Right then, we were struggling, hoping to break even by the end of the game.

At the end of the third, I still hadn't put a dent in the prop loss and I was officially getting worried.

The Chiefs looked like they were completely dead before Patrick Mahomes led them to two fourth-quarter touchdowns. The 49ers did their share to blow the game; up 20 to 10, they quit running the ball and Jimmy Garoppolo couldn't carry the team when they needed him. Kyle Shanahan, a young coach I really like, was at the wheel of an offense that went away from its strengths in the final minutes, just as he did as offensive coordinator of the Falcons in Super Bowl LI when they blew a 28-3 lead before losing to the Patriots 34-28.

We were still grading the props, so I still wasn't sure how it would play out. The game itself, though, ended in a perfect scenario. Players liked Chiefs and over or 49ers and under. With a final score of Chiefs 31 to 20, it looked like the best possible outcome.

We finally got all the props done. Like everyone else in the industry, whatever isn't directly part the game itself gets thrown in the prop pile. We had a nice cushion with the futures and the parlay card did well, so the prop figure looked good. I knew, however, that it was a little deceiving. The game props we put up over the two-week period were actually a very slight loser. The final figure, however, looked fine.

At the end of the day, we made $480,000—one of our biggest days in my four years at the South Point. Some of the larger joints would scoff at that figure, but they have multiple hotels on the Strip or many popular locations around Vegas. I was very happy with the win, though the handle was less than I expected.

I talked to Michael Gaughan after the game and he was overjoyed, not only with the result, but also the number of customers who came through the doors to bet and stay for the party, plus the service we provided. The winning figures made him even happier, no doubt, but he was most pleased about the other stuff, the things in our control. God bless him. He's one of the few guys in his position who gets it.

Even though we had a record day, I was still a little unhappy with how I handled the props. Tomorrow, I'll start sifting through the auditing reports to see what we can do better next year. I often think of the old Steeler's coach, Chuck Noll, a student of philosophy, who said, "You never get there, you never arrive, you never turn the corner." This was after he'd won four Super Bowls and probably had the greatest football team of all time. I've really tried to live my life that way, although God knows I've fallen awfully short of where I would like to be. I wish Noll had written a book. He really was a sage. Nonetheless, I'll sleep well tonight.

Monday February 3, 2020

We spent the day going over the Super Bowl figures: which props got bet, which prices were good, which ones weren't, etc. I told my supervisors what I was looking for. We got the process started, but it takes a while to finalize our complete betting autopsy. Of course, we have almost a year to process the results and we know some won't apply to next year's game unless the exact same two teams are in it, but the exercise still has merit.

Now that football season is over, I can take a look at the entire picture. The handle was way up, especially at the counter. The straight bets weren't up to the hold percentage I wanted, but the overall win percentage was fine. The college season was very good and I was happy with that figure, but I could still see a few things we needed to improve on.

Shortly after the draft, which is being held in Las Vegas this year, I'll put up next NFL season's first week. Not long after that, I'll post season win totals. We already posted the future book for next year's Super Bowl.

After the NCAA basketball tournament, I'll get to work on college football. In the past, we've been first to post the first week of college football, games of the year, and season win totals for the entire FBS. We missed it last year, as I spent four months under doctors' care for a bone-marrow transplant. More on that in the next book. Right now, I plan on enjoying a few extra days off lounging on a California beach. I let Michael know that after today, I'd be out of the office until Saturday.

Chapter Two
February 22-March 9, 2020

"It was the calm before the tempest."
—*The Dumb Knight*

Saturday February 22, 2020

Tonight is the Tyson Fury-Deontay Wilder heavyweight championship fight in Las Vegas. When I first got to town in 1979, it seemed like we had championship fights every few months—like having a few extra Super Bowls a year. Some of the lighter weights were just as big, with boxers like "Sugar" Ray Leonard, Tommy "Hit-Man" Hearns, "Marvelous" Marvin Hagler, and Roberto "Hands of Stone" Duran. But the heavyweights still held a special allure and the champ was thought of as the "Baddest Man on the Planet," Larry Holmes, Muhammad Ali, Mike Tyson, George Foreman, Ken Norton, Riddick Bowe, Evander Holyfield, and Lennox Lewis among them. And that was just after I got to Nevada.

Fury-Wilder is a rematch after their first fight, which ended in a draw. The action paled in comparison to the fights from the old days, but it was still a big event at a slow time of year. As we often do at South Point, we tightened up the line, moving the ordinary 20¢ line to 10¢. That brought in relatively high volume, but still nothing like the old days.

Fury won on a technical knockout. After Wilder went down a few times, his corner threw in the towel to stop the fight. Wilder himself objected; as the defending undefeated champion, he wanted "to be carried out on his shield," to quote him. I didn't blame him. Managers are a lot more careful now than they were in the old days. But never underestimate the heart of a champion.

In basketball, one guy came in and bet a money-line parlay on the game between San Diego State (undefeated and #4 in the country) and Gonzaga (one loss and #2 in the country) for $28,000 to win $18,000. Gonzaga was only -185, but San Diego State was -1250, which made it look like a sure winner. Guys like that figure we're giving away free money. Jimmy Vaccaro and I love to take these chalk parlays. We hear a bunch of shit from others, even some members of our crew, who think we are just giving away money. We're not. It's sports. Anything can happen. San Diego State and Gonzaga both lost.

Friday February 28, 2020

Michael and I had a bit of a disagreement today. Guess who won?

Out of all of our many phone accounts,[2] about 20 wise guys, the sharpest of the sharp, were beating the hell out of us. We do some things other sports books don't. Our limits are fair, all our straight pointspread bets are -110, and we don't throw people out for winning.

Michael didn't want to ban them from betting; he just wanted to close their phone accounts—they'd either have to come into the casino themselves to bet or post a runner in the sports book. Having to be here physically stops them from seeing the moves on the Don Best screen that gives them real-time betting lines from all over the world. It also prevents them from knowing exactly what number we have, because of the time lapse, and

---

[2] Most of us in the business call them phone accounts as a carryover from the old days. Everything mobile is actually bet on the app. Old habits are hard to break.

assuming they're trying to get down all over town. Meanwhile, if they post a runner here, that guy isn't working for free. His wages or commission cut into their profits. Michael argued that closing the sharps' phone accounts would increase our phone-accounts' bottom line and raise the overall win in the sports book.

I most certainly agreed with him on the first point, but disagreed on the second. In the first place, the phone limits are pretty low for the sharp players. From the wise guys, in the NBA, we take $5,000 at the counter, but only $1,000 on the phone. For college basketball, it's $2,000 or $3,000 (depending on the school) at the counter and $1,000 on the phone. This way, we manage the sharp guys, knowing exactly who they are, and use their information to our advantage. If they start sending in runners and beards, we never know who's who and how much to respect the play. It's a battle I've waged my entire career—with mixed results.

I showed Michael that the worse we do with the sharp players (meaning they beat us), the better we do overall. That's indisputable. The numbers prove it. We take their action and move the line accordingly, so the rest of our customers bet into a much tougher line. This past year, we had the worst year ever against the phones (which triggered Michael's action), but had the biggest bottom line ever in the sports book. Since I'd been hired as director in 2016, we'd won a few million dollars on the phone, but it was definitely not an equal percentage with the rest of the sports book. I still think we were handling the action properly, but in all honesty, it could have been handled even better. That's on me.

In the end, it was a fight I couldn't win. Sitting at lunch with Jimmy and me, Michael came down with the order. I've seen him lose his temper a few times (not many), but this time wasn't one of them. He was stern, adamant, immovable, but definitely not angry. He just wanted to get his way and he got it.

By the time the lunch meeting was over, he was laughing, slapping us on the back, and busting our balls. On his desk, his name plate reads, "Dictator."

On his business cards, it's "Benevolent Dictator." That's a lot closer to the truth. And it's one more reason why I love the guy. Even when I think he's wrong.

Sunday March 1, 2020

A bit of a tweet uproar erupted after we closed off the phone accounts. Naturally, Twitter was a wellspring of misinformation. The word was we banned a bunch of players, we were lowering our limits, etc. Unfortunately, the vitriol was directed at me. After a myriad of comments, I had to reply.

"Let me set the record straight. No one is banned. All those players are welcome. We're a casino. The limits are higher at the counter and we want people to come into the sports book." Short and sweet. Direct to the point. It stemmed the tide of negativity.

I fought Michael on his decision, but I certainly respect it. He's made a lot more good decisions than I have. I hope it all works out and I'll do my best to make it so.

Monday March 9, 2020

The college basketball tournaments have gotten underway. There were a few last week and the bulk of them start today and in the next few days. I haven't kept up nearly as much as I have to, so I have to get up to speed by Sunday, when the NCAA tournament matchups are announced.

For the past two years, the South Point was the first to open numbers. We take $10,000 a rattle, so it's no small thing. The biggest and sharpest players in town are lined up against us.

The way we do it is Vinny Magliulo, Richie Baccellieri, and I are all in my office at the sports book. We all have our power ratings and as soon as the matchups are announced, we come up with our numbers. I look at all three and make the final decision on how we'll open. From there, my crew handles the bookmaking until the matchups are completely announced. Then I jump in and see what kind of action we've gotten and make any necessary adjustments.

The actual process of making the numbers isn't that hard. You simply subtract the underdog's power rating from the favorite's and, voila, there's the number.[3] The hard part is making the power ratings. There are various methodologies, which is why there's betting. If everyone thought the exact same way, why would anyone make a bet? The same goes for the oddsmaking/bookmaking side. I need various opinions that I respect, so I can put together my numbers.

We're all not going to look at teams the exact same way, which is good. We all keep different ratings, so we all have different numbers. That's the only way to do it. I need various opinions, because it's the three of us against the world. We've done well over the years. If it were just me, the world would be a huge favorite.

Meanwhile, in the bigger picture, the coronavirus is becoming big news. By the time this book goes to print, we'll have a lot more answers, but right now, China has essentially quarantined about 50 million people, Italy about 15 million. It's starting to affect sports worldwide. Italy, Greece, and a few other countries have banned events with large numbers of participants, including sports. Some events are taking place, but with no fans allowed.

---

[3] The way you make numbers using power ratings is essentially nothing but addition and subtraction. If team A has a rating of 90 and they're playing team B with an 80 rating, team A would be a 10-point favorite. If team A is 76 and team B is 73, team A is a 3-point favorite. It's nothing more than that. Of course, you better have the right power rating to begin with or your number is going to be way off. And you'll get your ass kicked.

Closer to home, the tennis tournament at Indian Wells, considered the fifth largest tournament in the tennis world behind only the four majors (Wimbledon, U.S. Open, French Open, and Australian Open), was supposed to start today, but it has been completely canceled. As of now, that's the only American event directly affected. College basketball tournaments are just getting under way and baseball season is starting in a few weeks. At this point, we have no idea what's going to happen.

We do know that reaction to the virus has rattled the travel and hospitality industries. So far, I haven't heard of any major strategic changes in Las Vegas, just individual properties dealing with cancellations. I just heard from our casino host, Dave Jensen, that we've had a large number of cancellations for our big March Madness event. In the past two years, we've written more than twice as much business on the NCAA tournament than we have on the Super Bowl. So this is a huge deal. If it gets any worse, well, we'll have to deal with it. It won't be pleasant.

On a personal note, I have to be extra careful. When I had my bone-marrow transplant, the only way it could take was to virtually eliminate my immune system. Even before this virus, I had to be diligent. I have a station at the front counter where I prefer to work, as well as my office in the back. Since returning from my transplant, I've worked out front minimally, sticking close to the office. Though I have all the necessary screens and all, I like to see the action at the counter and I feel much more out of touch in the back. Now, I really have no choice. They estimate the death rate to be about 3.5% to 4% and I'm definitely among the most vulnerable. If you're reading this book, I probably lived long enough to finish it and get it published.

I hope they get this thing under control. If it's as contagious as the ordinary flu and those mortality rates are accurate, that means about 400,000 people will die. That's just in the U.S. Who knows what the numbers will be worldwide? We all have friends and family, and even if they're complete strangers, this will be an epic disaster.

Chapter Three
March 10-31, 2020

"The future has a way of arriving unannounced."

—*George Will*

Tuesday March 10, 2020

The coronavirus continues to wreak havoc on the world in general and the sports world in particular. Italy totally quarantined the entire country late yesterday and canceled all soccer matches, something it hasn't done since World War II.

The Ivy League canceled its basketball tournament and Big West teams will play with no fans in the building. Santa Clara County deemed that all crowds be limited to 1,000 people or fewer. That includes the NHL's San Jose Sharks, who ordinarily draw 20,000 fans to a game.

The NCAA conference tournaments are under way, with a few wrapping up today. One guy gave us $46,000 in action on teams to win their individual conferences, a couple favorites and a couple long shots. Hopefully, we can beat him on a few.

My alma mater Robert Morris defeated St. Francis for the Northeastern Conference Championship and will be going to the NCAA tourney, probably as a 16 seed. Go Colonials!

Horse racing got another black eye today with the indictments of two top trainers, Jason Servis and Jorge Navarro. Servis trained Maximum Security, which finished first in the Kentucky

Derby before being disqualified, and the Saudi Cup, one of the world's richest races. They each had tremendous success claiming horses and moving them up quickly to much higher classes. It always smelled fishy, but quite a bit is fishy in that racket. I'm not overly familiar with the indictment, but the word is that it doesn't look good for them, and even worse for racing.

Wednesday March 11, 2020

The coronavirus is still dominating the news. The NCAA announced they will play their entire tournament in arenas with no fans. Some family and key personnel will be allowed. That's it.

The CBI, a secondary tournament, has been completely canceled.

The NBA will decide soon, maybe tomorrow, it they'll play in fanless arenas, delay the season, or implement some other measures.

There are other cancellations and adjustments, but I can't even keep up with them right now.

Michael is still on my ass over these phone accounts. I closed about 20 more today. We have runners and movers at the counter and new people opening phone accounts. Previously, we knew exactly who our customers were. Now we have no idea who's who or what's what. We're totally shooting in the dark. I hope I can make this work. If not, I hope this book sells. My novel, too. I don't have the money to retire yet.

Thursday March 12, 2020

Things are happening very quickly. There are big question marks next to virtually everything, not just sports.

Every major basketball conference has canceled its tournament. The NBA and NHL postponed (not canceled, at this point) the rest of their regular seasons. NBA players have been diagnosed with the coronavirus. Rudy Gobert of the Utah Jazz,

NBA's Patient Zero, went out of his way to touch all the microphones, tabletops, and papers as a joke. Some joke. I'm sure he's not the only caveman who thinks the virus is nothing and if he were to get it, he'd be fine. He probably will be, but some he passes it on to most likely won't.

Another Jazz player, Donavan Mitchell, also tested positive. He spent the earlier part of the day at a local high school. Good on him for doing community service. Unfortunately, it could wind up a disaster.

Gobert apologized for his actions today. I don't want to be too hard on him. He's a young guy who's been an athlete his whole life, thinking he's invincible. He probably learned a valuable lesson. Hopefully, from his example, others have too.

Right now, we're looking at work schedules for our employees. We're trying to take care of people the best we can, but there's not much work to give them. Of course, the full-timers get top consideration. If NASCAR runs and there's a golf tournament, we'll try to figure as many betting possibilities as we can around those events. Currently, the byword is "uncertainty." No one has any idea what might happen next.

This afternoon, the NCAA canceled the whole megillah. The XFL canceled, too. I thought that asshole Vince McMahon, the XFL owner, might have tried to play their games. He treated all his wrestlers at WWE like shit, so why would he take the high road with football players or fans?

This is a once-in-a-lifetime event.

Friday March 13, 2020

More cancellations. I thought NASCAR and the PGA might go ahead without the fans in attendance. Drivers are in a car alone and golfers can easily stay away from the others in their group. Nonetheless, the powers that be made the decision. The PGA also delayed the Masters, traditionally in early April. No new date has been announced.

Jimmy Vaccaro was going to wait until after the Final Four to begin his yearly trip back to his hometown of Trafford, Pennsylvania. I think he'll just head home now. I hate not having him around. Besides his friendship, I often need his advice on big issues. Even though nothing is going on in the fields of battle, plenty of decisions need to be made.

For example, each year, we post our baseball season-win totals with the stipulation that if you make a bet, you have action no matter how many games are played. We implemented this a couple of years ago when a legendary Las Vegas scumbag claimed that his bet was no action after the Cubs played a game that was ruled a tie. We had to fight it out with Gaming and since it was total bullshit, we won easily. Most sports books have a clause that stipulates a minimum number of games played, usually 160 (of a scheduled 162), but we just dropped the clause altogether. Of course, we never envisioned a pandemic of this proportion canceling seasons across the board. As of now, we haven't heard of any major adjustments to the MLB schedule, but it would be shocking if they don't make some sort of arrangement, considering what all the other leagues have done.

I'll go in and see Michael this afternoon, just to update him on everything that's going on in our little world. He has much bigger problems than the sports book right now, but I still want to let him know I'm available if needed. Otherwise, I plan on staying home, considering my highly compromised immune system.

Saturday March 14, 2020

I talked to Michael and our GM Ryan Growney yesterday and they agreed that we should just cancel our baseball season-win totals. The rule states, "Once the season starts, you have action." Since the season has yet to start, it gives us the right to cancel.

I might have pulled the trigger a little too early, but I'd heard from a few players that our rules would really screw them.

Then Ryan Growney called me into a meeting with Michael, Jimmy, Tom Blazek, and racebook director Mary Jungers. Michael wanted to carve a path forward for our departments. I was confident he wouldn't shut us down, but I wanted to have a plan in place that would keep as many people working as possible. I started looking to see what I could find to bet on. We came up with Australian rules football, Australian rugby, and Russian hockey.

I attended Aussie rules football games when I was in Australia and almost became dingo food.[4] It's a terrific sport and if people get a chance to watch it, they'll really like it. The game is really violent and I mean that in the very best way possible. If you like hockey, you'll probably like Aussie rules.

Speaking of hockey, the Russian hockey league, the KHL, is probably the second-best league in the world. The Swedes and Finns might take exception to that, but it's highly competitive with up-and-coming potential stars and some fading NHL stars who still have some life in them.

After meeting with Michael, we figured out a way to keep all our full-time employees on the payroll with all their benefits intact: We cut them all to four days a week. It was a workable solution with the world crumbling around us. The part-timers, unfortunately, are left with no work. I feel for them, but at this point, there's nothing I can do.

On a personal note, because I'm extremely vulnerable right now, Michael doesn't want me coming in to work. I can do everything from home. He said he'd fire me if I left the house. I know he's mostly joking, but message received. I'm pretty relieved. I want to keep the boss happy, but I also have to worry about my health and my life. I'm the perfect candidate to die

---

See my first book for this story. It's pretty hilarious—and scary.

from this virus. My immune system has come back some, but it will take two years to come back completely.

Monday March 16, 2020

The NFL year started today. That means free agents can now sign with new teams. Two big trades happened: Stefon Diggs went from the Vikings to the Bills in a trade that makes sense for both teams and DeAndre Hopkins was traded by the Texans to the Cardinals. This one made no sense at all.

Bill O'Brien is the coach and general manager of the Texans. I have a soft spot in my heart for O'Brien. He took over as full-time coach of Penn State after Joe Paterno got fired. He left after two years, but kept the program more than respectable when it looked like a sinking ship. I never liked these one-man coach-general manager situations. It works extremely well with Bill Belichick for the New England Patriots. However, it has never worked anywhere else at any time. Belichick is one of a kind. You can't emulate him, though many have tried.

Tom Brady was the big name in free agency. Speculation about his eventual team is intense. The Titans were seen as a major player, but they re-signed their incumbent quarterback, Ryan Tannehill. I have a hunch the market for a 42-year-old quarterback might not be as robust as Brady and his representatives think it is, even if he is one of the all-time greats.

Tomorrow morning, I'll put up season-win totals for the NFL. It's way too early, but I have to give our customers something to bet on and keep our ticket writers employed.

Tuesday March 17, 2020

I didn't put up NFL season-win totals.

Nevada Governor Steve Sisolak closed all casinos and all other non-essential businesses due to the coronavirus. We thought it might be coming, but hoped it wouldn't. I can't argue with the logic. Right now, we have to stop this virus as best we can. Unless you work in one, casinos aren't all that essential. I'm not sure how long we'll be closed. The order right now is for 30 days, but that's the best-case scenario. If this thing gets worse, it will get extended.

Sports worldwide have virtually shut down, though a few things off the radar might offer some athletic competition. Nonetheless, we're completely closed, including the phone app, though I've heard William Hill and Circa plan on leaving their apps open.

Wednesday March 18, 2020

Tom Brady left the New England Patriots, with which he went to nine Super Bowls and won six, to go to the Tampa Bay Buccaneers. The Bucs coach is Bruce Arians, who made his bones in the league as a quarterback guru. Brady isn't what he was a few years ago, but the Bucs are loaded with talent at the skill positions, which Brady didn't have in his last year in New England. Tampa lost seven games by one score or less with a quarterback who threw 30 interceptions. Good lord, if they could just protect the ball a little better, they could have won at least three of those games and could have been knocking at the door for a playoff spot. Every other aspect of that team is solid, from coaching and skill positions to defense. Brady could turn the team around quickly if he has anything left, which I think is likely.

In other quarterback news, Philip Rivers is going to the Colts, Nick Foles to the Bears. The Colts see Rivers as a big improvement over Jacoby Brissett. I'm not so sure. They really miss Andrew Luck. I do, too. I don't know if the Bears are planning to start Foles or hoping he can push their young quarterback, Mitchell Trubisky, to the heights they expected when they made him the number-two pick in the draft. There is a lot of potential on that team. We'll see if quarterback play is the missing ingredient.

In coronavirus news, Kevin Durant of the Brooklyn Nets was diagnosed with the virus. A number of Ottawa Senators also tested positive. The count is now up to seven NBA players and four in the NHL.

Michael Gaughan took very good care of his full- and part-time employees. He doesn't want us telling anyone what he's done, so I'll keep it to myself. But I just want to say I'm perfectly happy with how he has handled this. No big surprise.

Friday March 20, 2020

"Your phone is dinging," Pam said as she jabbed me awake. "Someone is trying to get hold of you."

My first thought was it was a friend from the East Coast, three hours ahead, who was in on a text-message thread. He probably forgot it was only 6:30 a.m. in Las Vegas.

"Did you hear about Patrick McQuiggan?" It was a text from Ron Flatter, a member of the VSiN team. Ron is one of our top horse-racing experts, with a long career in the races before and during his stint at VSiN. Patrick was the in-house handicapper at the South Point.

"What?" I answered. This couldn't be good.

"I learned last night that he was found dead here in Las Vegas."

Fuck me. My first thought was it was the coronavirus, but he had no signs of it. His death was rather sudden, also. We'll have to wait to find out for sure.

Patrick was a happy, personable, gregarious guy. He was a man who truly loved his job and the life he was leading. He was on the air in Las Vegas for years as a handicapper. He gave seminars at South Point before the big races, as well as shared his knowledge and selections with anyone who asked him. His slogan was, "I'll see you in the cashier's line!"

As a pari-mutuel race book, the South Point isn't rooting for our customers to lose. In fact, it's much better when they win. We make money on the handle. The more our customers bet, the bigger our cut of the pie. The more they win, the more likely they are to bet in higher amounts. That's why it made sense for us to have an in-house handicapper. It's the one place in the casino where it actually helps the house if the player beats the game.

I enjoyed discussing horses with him, both today's selections and the history of the sport. He and I had become friends since I came aboard at the South Point. We'd done some radio shows, podcasts, and seminars together. I will greatly miss Patrick McQuiggan.

Boy, when things go bad, they really go bad.

On orders from the governor, we completely shut down the sports book today. We'd left it open for cashing tickets and phone-app customers taking money out of their accounts. By our reckoning, staying open was within the governor's guidelines, but evidently, he disagreed. It was no real benefit to us; we were just providing a convenience to our customers. Anyone coming into the sports book or the casino for any reason was screened at the door by security.

Saturday March 21, 2020

One of the vestiges of sports normality closed up shop today, the Australian Football League. All that's left is Australian Rugby and that probably won't make it past another day or so.

I can't argue with it. Aussie rules played its last few games with no one in the stands. It was like watching a practice session. No sense risking people's lives for that. No reason at all.

Monday March 23, 2020

The last betable event I knew of, the Australian National Rugby League or NRL, was suspended overnight. We had a little action on it, but not much. We're completely closed right now anyway, but we still had results to enter.

Tuesday March 24, 2020

Today, the 2020 Olympics in Tokyo were postponed until 2021. Canada and Australia had already indicated that they weren't sending any of their athletes. There'd have been a host of problems were the games to continue. Besides the virus itself, which is certainly a huge issue, the athletes couldn't train properly. It really was the only possible decision.

At the management meeting this morning, Michael further reduced some of the departments that had remained open. There's still some talk of the governor allowing casinos to reopen on April 15. However, Michael thinks May 1 is much more realistic. Regardless of who says what, we really need to listen to the doctors and scientists. None of us knows right now where this thing is headed.

Friday March 27, 2020

Kirk Herbstreit, the county's top college football color announcer, said today he can't see how the college football and NFL seasons can be played this year. First of all, I hope he's wrong. But what really bothers me is Herbstreit has always been seen as a voice of reason. He played college football and has been involved in the game for over 25 years. When he makes a statement like this, it's not one to be taken lightly.

The cases of coronavirus are still on the upswing. Until we reverse that, we can't make any reasonable predictions on when it will subside. Scientists are still in disagreement when that will happen. In fact, many are not even harrowing a guess.

I've been optimistic we'd get back to relative normalcy by fall, but now I'm not so sure. In fact, I'm getting really scared. It would be devastating to our business. But people's lives have to come first.

Sunday March 29, 2020

It's amazing we're only a little more than two weeks into this coronavirus shutdown. It feels like it's been an eternity, but it's just getting started. Nick Bogdanovich told me William Hill is writing business on Russian ping-pong. Russian fucking ping-pong. He shared some of the numbers with me and they're incredible. People, Americans no less, are actually betting this shit. I can't believe gamblers are so desperate.

Nick predicted that things would be normal in sports by July 1. I would have, too, except for Kirk Herbstreit's statement the other day, which has me shook. I really hope he's wrong. But every day that goes by, things look worse and worse.

Watching some of the Sunday morning news/interview shows, the consensus is things are still getting worse. In this country, the number of cases is doubling every two or three days—the death rate as well.

Monday March 30, 2020

Wimbledon has been canceled. The tennis championship wasn't scheduled to start for three months, on June 29. Maybe they know better than I do, but it seems like they had plenty of time before a decision needed to be made.

A well-connected source told me today he's afraid the college football season will be canceled. That would be disastrous, but it falls on the heels of Herbstreit saying the same thing. This source had heard a coach say that he wouldn't feel right bringing in a bunch of kids to live and sweat together without a vaccine.

I was checking my journal entries. Three weeks ago today, the world started going crazy. Twenty-one days. It feels like eons. Somehow, we'll get through this, but there will be plenty of collateral damage, including a large number of fatalities. This is as close to apocalyptic as I ever want to get.

Tuesday March 31, 2020

More scary predictions about football season came out today. Chris "Bear" Fallica was on Gill's "It's A Numbers Game" this morning, warning about the college football season. Some coaches and administrators are saying teams will play only conference games with no fans in the stands. Since they're primarily schools, it would be impossible to keep the players in a bubble; inevitably, they'll be involved with the general student population. Some of the bigger universities have more than 40,000 students. A virus would run rampant through that population. Even if the mortality rate is 1%, that would be several hundred potential deaths. It's obviously completely unacceptable for parents to send their children to school under that circumstance.

Michael Gaughan called me this morning, making sure I'm staying home. In turn, I checked on a few of my people today, too. So far, everyone is doing okay.

I don't know who said it first, but a few people on Twitter wrote some slight twists on the old saying: "Thirty days hath September, April, June, and November. All the rest have thirty-one, except March, which has eight thousand."

Boy, it sure feels like it.

Chapter Four
April 1-24, 2020

"Yesterday, all my troubles seemed so far away."
—Paul McCartney

Wednesday April 1, 2020

The NFL's attorney announced the league is planning to release its schedule on May 9, play a full 16-game season, and have a playoff tournament in the usual format. Man, I hope so.

Thursday April 2, 2020

The Brookings Institution came out with a report today, stating that Las Vegas will be the American city most impacted economically by the coronavirus. That makes sense for the broad local economy and the casino industry in particular. However, I have a feeling sports betting won't suffer nearly so much.

People are dying to bet. They want to bet on anything that will give them that tingle. The first day the major sports are up and running, we'll see a flood of business. Currently, 10 million people nationally have filed for unemployment (holy shit!) and our local economy is obviously as bad as any. So the handle per customer will necessarily be low, but folks want to be in action. They'll try to win back some of the money they lost while sitting at home. We'll write more $10 parlays than any time in history.

In the Great Recession, the one part of any industry that

didn't suffer was sports betting. Dinner might consist of dog food on saltines, but even those people will find money to bet with, that I can promise you. The same thing will happen this year, as soon as they have something to bet on.

By the way, today is my birthday. Not that anyone should give shit, but a year ago, it didn't look like I would make it to 64. And here I am. It's not the most joyous of times, but there's a lot for me to be thankful for. And I'm doing way better than most right now.

Saturday April 4, 2020

Today would have been the NCAA men's basketball semi-finals, the first day of the Final Four. If only.

Donald Trump met with the professional sports commissioners today, saying he wanted them to get back to business as soon as possible. Sounds good, but let's make sure it's safe for everyone whenever it happens. We can make up for a lost sports season. We can't make up for a life that's lost. In this case, it could be many lives.

Later in the day, California Governor Gavin Newsome said he doesn't see Trump's plan coming to fruition, certainly not in his state. California claims three NFL teams, five MLB teams, four NBA teams, and three NHL teams, plus four PAC-12 schools, three Mountain West schools, and many other smaller institutions with football teams. Newsome would most likely have more direct influence over the schools, but he might also have the power to stop any large gatherings, including pro sports.

Nevada Gaming today okayed taking bets on NASCAR virtual racing. What? Taking bets on fake racing? What have we come to?

I haven't heard that I doubt Michael will want to book this stuff. he will, but his son Brendan is a NASCAR driver, so who knows? I hope not.

Monday April 6, 2020

Today would have been the NCAA men's basketball final. What could have been? We'll never know.

I produced the first draft of my college football power ratings. Caesars put out season-win totals and conference-championship futures. I didn't want to be caught unawares. I'd done some preliminary charting, so a lot of the groundwork has been laid. There's a long way until we start the season, so I'm sure some refinements will be in order.

Caesars has a contract with ESPN; otherwise, I don't think they'd ever put out those numbers. First, a lot of people are wondering if we'll even have a college football season. Secondly, if there is a season, we don't know how it will shape up.

A rumor came out this afternoon that MLB is working on a plan to schedule all games in Arizona for the season. Florida was considered, but the powers that be decided against it. Arizona has far fewer cases of the coronavirus than Florida, which has handled this crisis horribly.

The plan sounds feasible from a pure baseball-playing perspective, with plenty of ballparks to host the games. However, some other considerations include unbearably hot weather and the monsoon season in Arizona for another. Plus, what will the players union have to say about all the ramifications? Some superstars with contracts in the hundreds of millions might not want to be away from their families for up to six months. Guys on minimum salaries might not have a choice.

Tuesday April 7, 2020

There's already some pushback on MLB's plan for playing all games in Arizona. At best, we'll have a shortened season, at worst, no season at all. I'm hoping we have a season, somehow, some way. Baseball can be a pain in the ass for bookmakers, but now I really miss it.

In the UFC, Dana White is making plans to secure a private island where he can hold fights. He hasn't said how often or what island, but it sounds like they'll be held fairly frequently. It's generally thought that the UFC treats its fighters poorly, including low pay for all but the top stars. I doubt any of them have options, like resuming their law practice or going back to being bank vice presidents. The UFC has them over a barrel. A paycheck for themselves seems to be their main concern. This would just be one more feather in their cap. White sounds more like a Bond villain every day.

All that said, we would write a ton of action on the UFC. The sport is brutal, much more so than boxing, but that doesn't seem to bother too many bettors. I don't think this is the greatest idea, but if it's on an island, I guess they aren't hurting anyone but themselves.

Thursday April 9, 2020

Today would have been the first round of the Masters Tournament and the first day of the Stanley Cup playoffs. The Masters has been rescheduled for November, but I don't know if the NHL playoffs will be held this year. And you can throw the NBA playoffs right in with the Stanley Cup. I'll keep hoping, but every day makes it a little less likely.

Friday April 10, 2020

First thing this morning, Dana White canceled the fights scheduled for April 18. ESPN, which was going to carry the fights and has been a major supporter of the UFC, pressured him into the cancellation. Even yesterday, White was adamant that the fights would go on as scheduled; the word is he was strong-armed by the network.

College football coaches are now saying they need their players in camp by July 15 for the college football season to come off as planned. That's a little more than three months away. Right now, that looks optimistic, but possible.

This morning, the XFL informed all of its employees, including the players, that the league has been shut down. Nothing has been clarified beyond that, but most are assuming that this is the end of the XFL.

A Japanese official announced that at this point they couldn't be certain the Olympics, originally scheduled for June 2020, could even be held by next summer.

Right now, there are so many cross currents, so much confusion in the message, that I don't know what to think. Dr. Anthony Fauci said the virus will set the timeline. I think that makes the most sense. I just hope it's quick.

Monday April 13, 2020

Today, the XFL filed for bankruptcy. What a shame. I really thought they had some good ideas. There were plenty of flaws as well, as any new enterprise will have. But it had a good chance of surviving as a minor-league stepping-stone to the NFL. The XFL won't be the last business to go belly up. Bankruptcy lawyer is looking to be a thriving career choice right now.

On a bright note, Germany's top soccer league, the Bundesliga, announced it's aiming for an early May restart of league play. Germany has handled the coronavirus better than any country in the Western world. The Bundesliga figures to be ahead of all the other major pro sports leagues. The plan would be to play in stadiums with no fans allowed. That really hurts, as Germany has the highest attendance of any soccer league. They're working out some revised television arrangements to lessen the projected cost of losing the rest of the season, which would be about $800 million. I hope they make it. I've seen some of their games. It's a terrific league with some world-class athletes.

Wednesday April 15, 2020

Today would have been the final day of the NBA season. Instead, we're left wondering if there will be a final day, or play-offs, or if next season will start anywhere near on time.

In baseball, today would have been Jackie Robinson Day, celebrating the day Jackie broke baseball's color barrier. When I was growing up, a lot of the best players in baseball were black: Willie Mays, Hank Aaron, Bob Gibson, Willie McCovey, and of course the Pirates' Roberto Clemente, Willie Stargell, Al Oliver, Al McBean, Bob Veale, and many more. With Dock Ellis taking the mound one day, the Pirates were the first team to start nine black players.

Nowhere near as many black players are in the MLB at this moment. It really starts when black kids are growing up; they play a lot more basketball and football. I can't help but think about collegiate third-string running backs and guys at the end of the basketball bench who are obviously athletic and would have had the skills to play baseball if they'd picked up the game at an early age.

Years ago when I had my own website, I wrote an article that Doug Glanville should be made Major League Commissioner once Bud Selig retired. Glanville was a former player, an Ivy League graduate, a baseball announcer and entrepreneur. He was also black. It would have been a great statement to make for any professional sports league, besides the fact that he was well-qualified and I believe would have done a terrific job. A black commissioner would have brought a lot of interest to young athletes who were choosing a sport to play.

I don't want to pretend I'm some great moralist or civil rights pioneer. I'm not. I just want to see sports thrive on all levels. That means getting great talent wherever you find it. And right now, we're missing out on a lot of athletic potential that isn't even thinking about the game of baseball.

Back to Jackie Robinson, he was the right guy at the right time. Branch Rickey, the Brooklyn Dodgers' general manager, wanted someone who was strong enough to take it, but also had enough will to endure it without charging the mound every time a pitch was thrown at him. It was a delicate balance and Jackie was the guy. Baseball historians have done a much better job than I can to document breaking the color barrier. Read up on it from one of them if you're interested.

Another interesting note is that the NFL actually broke its color barrier the year before. It's somewhat lost to history; at the time, baseball was the country's biggest sport by far. It was most certainly the National Pastime, while football was way down that list. What pro football did should not be so easily forgotten.

Sunday April 19, 2020

There has been nothing new in the world of sports for days. Meanwhile, frustration is growing among those who need to go to work to pay their bills and the business owners who rely on them for making money. Most rational thought is on the other much more cautious side. Whatever is decided will determine the path of this country and the world for years to come.

Monday April 20, 2020

Michael announced furloughs for all of our full-time hourly employees today. The part-timers were already furloughed. It was a tough decision; he knows many people's lives are in his hands. He doesn't take that lightly. The way he did it, the employees will actually benefit financially until July 31. After that, it's anyone's guess. I can't imagine we won't be open by August 1. I wasn't furloughed; no salaried employee was, although we did take pay cuts.

I called our top-line supervisors today. They were all happy with the way the furloughs were handled.

Still nothing positive to report as far as beating this virus. Some folks are getting anxious and attempting to force politicians to open up their jurisdictions. However, the majority of Americans, 66%, are fine with the restrictions. I realize the economy is important, but more so than life itself? Some people evidently believe it. These protestors should take a stroll through an ICU before hitting the streets. They might have a different perspective. COVID isn't a cold, it's not the flu, it's not even pneumonia. Damage to the heart and lungs can last a lifetime. We haven't peaked yet and we as a country haven't handled this well. The entire world has about 160,000 deaths, while the U.S. has more than 40,000—25% of the deaths with only 6% of the population. If we open things up too early, we'll invite a second wave. A second wave will devastate the economy much worse than what we've seen so far. Yes, I'm very afraid.

Tuesday April 21, 2020

Rob Gronkowski, the future Hall of Fame tight end from the New England Patriots, was traded to the Tampa Bay Buccaneers. He'll be united with his former quarterback, also a future Hall of Famer, Tom Brady.

The news moved the betting markets, but just a little. I can report only what happened to others, since we aren't open. For those that had Super Bowl futures up, the odds dropped from about 17/1 to 14/1. NFC odds went from about 8/1 to 7/1. In this case, perception isn't reality in terms of performance on the field, but perception is reality as far as betting action goes.

Gronk's last year playing, 2018, was not a Hall of Fame performance. You could see he was a shell of himself. If the year off helped him physically, Gronk could be a huge addition to the Bucs offense. Brady's QBR in key situations, third downs and the red zone, was about double when Gronk was on the field with him. But football ages you quickly. I've seen this go both ways. Some guys come back rejuvenated and some are washed up with nothing left. Time will tell. Count me among the skeptics.

Of course, one of the underlying themes is how both players want to finish their careers without Bill Belichick as their coach. Belichick has had unparalleled success in this league, but he's not fun to play for. He doesn't take that as an insult, but as a badge of honor. Playing careers are brief. If it's worth it to you to play for a chance to win the Super Bowl, then it's worth it to play for a coach like Belichick. Most players think it is, at least until they get to New England. Afterwards is debatable. But the organization has six Super Bowl rings. That's nothing to sneeze at.

One of the things I think has been underreported is the fact that New England's offensive line last year was not nearly as good as it had been. They had tremendous success over the years protecting Brady and opening up holes for the running game. Last year, the focus was on the lack of skill-position players around Brady, which was true, but the poor play of the offensive line was at least as important. If the Bucs want to have success with their new lineup of future Hall of Famers, they'd better beef up the front line.

Wednesday April 22, 2020

At yesterday's management meeting, Michael mentioned a reopening plan put forth by the Wynn. He subsequently got a copy of the Wynn memo and sent it out to the managers. I read most of it and it seems sensible, with a lot of protection in place for staff and customers. Everyone's temperature will be taken on the way in. If it's over 100.4 degrees, they'll be sent to the nearest health-care facility. Every other slot machine will be shut down; only three blackjack players will be allowed at a table, all spaced with social-distance considerations; the other casino games will follow suit. South Point won't use it exactly, but will most likely take parts of it for a blueprint.

On CNN today, Las Vegas Mayor Carolyn Goodman said Las Vegas should open up with no social distancing and be the control group for the rest of the country. I guess she figures that if a bunch of Las Vegans die, we'll know opening wasn't a good idea. Well, I can pretty much echo the thoughts of just about everyone I know in Las Vegas, by telling Mayor Goodman, "Don't count me as part of your control group."

Thursday April 23, 2020

The NFL draft is tonight. I have a couple confessions to make.

First of all, I barely give a shit. I had to pretend like I do, because it was the only real content on VSiN that had anything to do with sports betting. Second, I'm glad we weren't open to take action on it, because every year that we did book it, we got our asses kicked. And that's been the industry consensus. This year, with the draft scheduled to be held in Las Vegas, we would have gone overboard putting up props and gotten our asses kicked even worse. Las Vegas sure could have used the 700,000 visitors anticipated to come to town for the draft. But not this year. That mass of rabble would have brought the pandemic and spread it throughout the country and beyond. We dodged a huge bullet there.

Nonetheless, this year's draft should have enormous ratings, because there's such a huge appetite for anything with sports-related drama.

Friday April 24, 2020

The NFL draft set a viewing record for the event. I had a hunch it might. The appetite for sports in insatiable. This wasn't even sports, just sports related. And yes, I did watch.

The only real drama of the night was when the Green Bay Packers took Jordan Love, a quarterback out of Utah State. Love was relatively unknown to casual football fans until the combine this year, where he wowed the scouts. He's a talented kid, but threw way too many interceptions. The reason, or excuse, was that he was on a mediocre team. That made him force throws into coverage just to try to stay in the game. Although the scouts liked Love, he was seen as a gamble. The Packers took it. They even traded up a few spots in the first round just to make sure they could nab him.

The real drama, however, was that the Packers were 13-3 last season. They lost to the 49ers in the NFC championship or they would have been in the Super Bowl. Their current quarterback is Aaron Rodgers, one of the all-time best and a certain Hall of Famer. Rodgers is getting a little long in the tooth, but the consensus was the Packers just needed some help, either offensive or defensive, to make enough of a difference to get them over the top. By drafting a quarterback in the first round, they did nothing to give Rodgers the immediate help he and the Packers need for that extra push. It seems like the Packers have given up on winning another Super Bowl with Rodgers. If he gets that message from management, he'll look to join a team that believes it's just a top-notch quarterback away from being a serious Super Bowl contender.

Which team? For Rodgers to go to the Chicago Bears would rip the hearts out of Packer fans. If Drew Brees retires at the end of this season, as expected, the Saints would also be a fit for Rodgers. I could see the Colts souring on Phillip Rivers after a year. Who knows? I would have never dreamt Tom Brady would be wearing a Buccaneers uniform this year, either.

Chapter Five
April 27-July 22, 2020

Woody Allen: "What are you doing Saturday night?"
Girl: "Committing suicide."
Allen: "How about Friday night?"
—Dialogue from Play It Again, Sam

Monday April 27, 2020

Things are breaking today. Michael wants to open up our phone accounts next week. Tom Blazek is working on a potential schedule for employees and I'll attend to some events we can put on the board. Michael still wants me to stay home, which I can do; I have a computer hooked up to the system at work. But I kind of wanted to go in. I was in quarantine so long with my bone-marrow transplant, then I had all of about four months out in public (in which I still remained in solitude as much as possible). Now, after another month of extreme isolation, I'd like to see some new faces. Oh well. I know he has my best interests at heart and I can't knock him for that.

We have a UFC event May 9, so that will bring in some action, then NASCAR will announce its schedule. I'll put up some NFL props like MVP, Rookie of the Year, and Defensive Player of the Year. We already have Super Bowl and Conference futures up; they just need updating. I'll leave the divisions off until I know what the NFL has planned. They might revise their whole playoff structure, but I'm reasonably sure they'll keep the conference structure intact. I'm also not messing with season-win totals. The last thing I want to do is take in a bunch of money just to give it back.

Jails are a breeding ground for COVID. As a result, judges are letting out many non-violent criminals. Billy Walters, the most successful sports bettor of all time, is one of those being released early. Billy got sent up for insider stock trading, nothing to do with betting on sports. I knew Billy a little; We had a lunch and dinner together with our wives. He's very personable, but he's bet with me for years and has taken plenty of money out of my pocket. Nonetheless, we always got along well. I certainly had respect for him and he at least pretended he had some for me. He went up on a federal rap, so he was supposed to do every day of his time. With the pandemic, they made an exception. I'm glad of it. No matter what he is or isn't, he's one of us. Not many in my crowd would have been eligible to be one of the twelve apostles. I'm not particularly crazy about prison in general, anyway. If he's still betting, if he does come in, I'll keep him strictly to the limits. I'd rather go to dinner with him.

And let him pick up the check.

Tuesday April 28, 2020

It looks like we'll be opening up the sports book next Wednesday. We'll have two guys working Sunday through Friday and three on Saturday. I'll be watching the action from home.

I have to work on a few things before we open. Today, I'll get to the third draft of my college football power ratings—all the while hoping we have a college football season. Tomorrow, I'll switch to the NFL. It's nice to get a firm date on the next step. Even though it feels like we're crawling to the starting gate, we'll do that before we walk and we'll most likely walk a while until we can run once again.

Wednesday April 29, 2020

In my first draft of NFL season-win totals, I got four different lines, a couple of which had been bet into already; I also added some of my own opinions. I put them up; not putting them up would leave me at a disadvantage. I really think it's premature, but what the hell. If everyone else has them, I guess will, too.

For something unique, I'm putting up team matchups. Every team in the NFL will be matched with another. I made them across conferences and with some sort of drama (or perceived drama) attached. For example, the Bucs vs. the Packers, featuring two of the best quarterbacks of the past decade or so, both a little past their prime, but still among the league's top echelon. Also, Pittsburgh vs. Philadelphia (the battle of Pennsylvania), the Rams vs. the Chargers (battle of L.A.), Jets vs. Giants (New York), Texans vs. Cowboys (Texas), and more that I thought would garner some intrigue.

In the next day or so, I'll work on similar matchups with quarterbacks (touchdown passes or passing yardage), running backs (strictly yardage), and pass receivers (probably yardage, but maybe total receptions).

I'm really anxious to get started. I manage to keep busy reading, writing, and binge watching some of the great television shows that are coming out. (It all started with The Sopranos.) Nonetheless, I'm ready to get back to what I do. Oddsmaking and bookmaking.

Thursday April 30, 2020

We're still on track to open next Wednesday. I finished all the NFL props. Since I don't want to open them where it's just me against the world, I sent them to my cousin Zach, Vinny Magliulo, and my old partner John Falenski. Johnny might be out of the business, but he's still one of the sharpest handicappers I know. He had a great season last year and has kept up with his work this year, even though the NFL season is just an ambiguity at this point. I'll get input from them and put my final decisions up by Wednesday.

On a sour note, the Bundesliga is pushing its season restart back at least a week to May 15.

But NASCAR and the UFC are still a full go. I hope all this isn't too early. Today was the highest number of reported coronavirus deaths yet in this country.

On a very personal note, my son Joe was mugged last night. A couple of teenagers sucker-punched him from behind and stole his phone. He got knocked out. Fortunately, the security guard in the apartment complex was right there and immediately called the police. They in turn called an ambulance and took him to the hospital. He suffered a broken nose and broken orbital bone.

He was sent home this morning, but he will have surgery early next week.

Joe has a spinal deformity and is obviously physically disabled. To jump him like that is far beyond mere criminal behavior. Joe, the security guard, and another witness think they can identify the culprits. They need to be severely punished. What the fuck is wrong with people?

Saturday May 2, 2020

Today should have been Kentucky Derby Day. Usually, it's one of my favorite days of the year. This year, except to walk the dog, I never left the house. The Derby will now be run the first Saturday in September. That makes it a whole different race. The mile and a quarter is tough for three-year-olds when the race is run early in the season, but by September, they've matured to the point where many can get that extra eighth of a mile that makes a good horse into a great horse.

They did run the Arkansas Derby today. Usually, it's about

a month before the Kentucky Derby. They split it into two divisions. I hate when they do that to such an important race. Pick the top horses that meet the conditions and the rest, well, sorry. Wait for some lesser race; this one isn't for you.

Bob Baffert had the big favorites in both divisions and won them both. Baffert is a great trainer, no doubt, but he also gets the best horses in his barn every year. To get to this point, he had to build his reputation, which he did with continuous success. Still, at some point you have to wonder if some lesser-known trainer with lesser horses who can train them up to compete in big races isn't really a better trainer. Hard to say. It's like asking, is Mike Krzyewski really a great basketball coach or does he just get the best players? You've got to give credit where it's due. Getting the players is part of the game. Just like getting the best horses is. As a bettor, I don't particularly like Baffert; you can never catch a good price with him. And he wins a lot of races with the favorite. I like to play price horses and it's hard to bet on or against Baffert when he has the big chalk. I do use him in some exotics, but so do most players. Once again, that knocks out the chance of catching a decent price.

One more thing about Baffert. He trains horses to go right to the front, then gradually extends the distance of their races until he finds their limit. He never trains for the turf, only for the dirt. That speed style of training has always worked particularly well at tracks in California, which has had tremendous racing with big purses, the best jockeys, and some of the country's best barns. With that style and success, he built his reputation.

That style doesn't work on the turf, where closing speed is much more important. I also don't think that style would work nearly as well at New York tracks, where conditions play more fairly to front-runners and closers.

Yeah, I know, gamblers always have something to piss and moan about. Including me.

Monday May 4, 2020

We started getting ready to open today. I got my work computer up and signed on to the system for the first time in years. At least it seemed like it was that long.

We'll have a menu similar to other sports books. We also wanted to put up some unique betting options.

All sports books will have season-win totals. Of course, they'll all have their own numbers, so we'll be a little different too. But all the other offerings will be ours alone. I think it will bring in some business. Now I just hope we have a football season.

For some reason today, I keep thinking about what the great and quotable Yankees manager, Casey Stengel, used to say: "Never make predictions. Especially about the future."

Wednesday May 6, 2020

We opened up today with a drive-thru for deposits and new-account sign-ups and guess what? That's right, we had technical issues. Nonetheless, we had a terrific response to the offers we posted. In my first call at, we already had 50 cars lined up. I know at one point in the afternoon, we still had 20 cars in line. I'll get a figure tomorrow on how many new accounts we opened and how much money was deposited.

Our NFL props were met with lots of comments, no action, and quite a bit of publicity. I knew the media would love it. Writers are starving for content right now and they'll play up anything they find interesting. If you strike a chord with them on anything related to the NFL, they beat it to death.

After we opened, Michael was elated. The sports book doesn't contribute a whole lot to the casino's bottom line, but it does mean quite a bit to the casino's reputation and its public perception. That's more important to Michael than whatever money we can net.

Two of my friendly competitors, Westgate and Circa, copied

the South Point with drive-thrus. I don't blame them; I'd have done the same. And they are my friends. I'm just glad we got the jump on them, because they're also good competition. I'm sure they'll get the jump on me with something else. It keeps us all on our toes.

Thursday May 7, 2020

James Franklin, Penn State's head football coach, had an interesting comment today. He thinks conferences should play their games, even if some schools within the conference might not be allowed to by their states' pandemic rules. If that were to occur, there'd have to be some sort of financial consideration for the schools unable to participate. Otherwise, the competitive balance within the conference would be completely upset.

Major colleges insist that they need football. That and basketball, they claim, pay for all the other sports. While that's true, it's only because they've set it up that way. I went to the Ohio State website and looked up the athletic department. I chose them because they perennially have national championship football teams and are usually a threat to make a run at the NCAA basketball championship. That, and I hate them (I'm a Penn State fan). They have 646 people listed with a phone number, email, or both as members of the athletic-department staff. The department has revenues of more than $200 million and they'll damn well make sure they spend every penny of it. As a matter of fact, their bottom line actually showed a loss of $5 million. They need that money, because they make sure they need it. I refuse to believe all those people are earning their keep. There has to be some serious redundancy.

As a contrast, I looked up Princeton University, an Ivy League school, but one that's had competitive athletic teams throughout its history. They had 258 people on their athletic-department staff. They have more sports (31) than Ohio State (29), but don't carry the fat of that bloated Big 10 outfit.

Finally, I looked at two smaller schools. Wisconsin-Whitewater, which has won six NCAA Division III football national championships, has 106 people in its athletic department and 17 varsity sports. Washington & Jefferson, another Division III college in western Pennsylvania, has 78 staff and 21 varsity sports. Don't fluff off W&J so quickly. They played in the 1922 Rose Bowl.

Friday May 8, 2020

First thing this morning, we put up NFL lines for opening week of the regular season. A couple of lines were out there before ours and we didn't want to stray too far from the market, but I did put my opinion into our numbers. One thing I noticed was, according to my ratings, teams are getting the full home-field advantage in the number. I completely disagree with this on a few counts.

First, I don't know if fans will be allowed to attend the games. I believe the hometown crowd influences the refs and affects their calls on the field. It's not supposed to and they swear it doesn't, but one or two key calls from the refs in a game can influence the outcome, or at least the pointspread.

Second, the home field doesn't mean as much on Week 1. The road team has had plenty of time to prepare. They aren't coming off a tough game in the middle of a tough travel situation.

Third, the home-field advantage has been eroding over the past few years. You can trace it back to Bill Walsh, the former coach of the 49ers and multiple Super Bowl winner in the 1980s. Walsh's influence on the NFL has been as great as anyone's in the Super Bowl era. He's largely credited with how today's offenses are schemed. But he also taught his teams how to successfully navigate the perils of the road. NFL coaches have had his theories passed down to them like a king endowing his first-born prince with knowledge of the empire. I shaded almost every line toward the road teams. We'll get the answers to my theories in a few months.

The action picked up today. Lots of small stuff, but we did get a $3,000 bet on the NFL. This is just a precursor to tomorrow, when the UFC gives us our first real action in weeks. I might even be excited.

Saturday May 9, 2020

It felt good to be back to bookmaking again today. I wish I could have produced some better results—we wrote $158K and eked out a measly $900—but that's the way it goes. Seven favorites and only two underdogs won. And in the fight where the one dog won, we needed the favorite. I know, I whine like all bookmakers. If I don't, I'm afraid they'll take away my union card. It's a miracle we won a dollar, let alone $900.

The action was pretty steady all day. Michael and Frank both hate the UFC, so we don't want any big action. The limits were set for a nickel, which sucks, but the way the system works, the bets just go through without any need for approval. I've been in situations where we've gotten beat up by a few bets on the same side all going through at once. It's bad enough in the major sports, but they'd kill me if we got clobbered like that in Ultimate Fighting Championship.

On the plus side, since we opened up the drive-thru on Wednesday, we've taken in more each day; today, we almost doubled that first day. I told those involved that we'd write more little action than ever before. That's exactly what happened today. Don't think I'm a genius. I've just been around a long time. A long long time.

As far as opening and operating, I think South Point will be okay. But we'll have a hard time meeting the pre-pandemic revenue figures. If people aren't working, they won't have money, especially disposable income. I have a feeling it's going to be a rough couple years ahead for Las Vegas. Fortunately, South Point isn't nearly as dependent on out-of-town tourist business as the Strip. That segment of the market is really going to struggle.

Sunday May 10, 2020

Another UFC event is scheduled for Wednesday. We'll open that up today. The Bundesliga is also scheduled to reopen this coming weekend, but that still might be delayed; two players on one of the teams tested positive for the virus. Nevertheless, we opened odds for each game in their return week, so I'm keeping my fingers crossed it goes off without a hitch.

We also opened the PGA Championship and the rescheduled Masters Tournament. Tomorrow, I'll put up odds on each NFL team to make the playoffs. There will be a two-way price; customers can bet yes or no on every team. We're getting a little closer to normal every day. I'm trying to keep a good thought with all of this, desperately hoping it doesn't backfire.

Monday May 11, 2020

We started writing a lot of action this morning, on season win totals, upcoming UFC matches, NFL week one, and NASCAR. Action won't be a problem, though the amounts will be dismal, but that's to be expected with the unemployment rate reaching record levels.

Today, I have to take my son Joe to the hospital to see if he needs surgery after the mugging What a freaking world.

Tuesday May 12, 2020

We put up odds for the NFL MVP rookie of the year. We also posted odds to win NASCAR's Darlington 400 and 25 individual matchups for the race, which will be run this Sunday.

Right now, we're putting up almost anything we think people will bet on. But I'm not putting up Russian and Ukrainian table tennis or South Korean or Taiwanese baseball. Michael would murder me if we got our asses kicked in those sports and I wouldn't blame him one bit.

Wednesday May 13, 2020

Today, we're writing a lot of business. Pretty remarkable for a Wednesday, but right now nobody knows what the hell day it is anymore, so I guess I shouldn't be so surprised. Most of the action is from exactly the kind of customers we want. I always said a lot of the things we do at South Point won't necessarily get us national media exposure (although we do get plenty of that), but we take care of the customer, the regular guy, the working stiff who wants to get decent value for his betting dollar. I honestly believe we do that as well as anyone.

On a broader sports scale, there are some glimmers of good news. The baseball owners made a presentation to the players for an 82-game schedule, teams playing only division opponents, and a 14-team playoff system. The proposal also includes a stipulation where the two sides will split the revenue 50-50. Of course, the players have yet to agree and one of the key sticking points is what exactly counts as revenue? They also want to play more games, meaning a reasonable number of double headers. More games mean more money for the players. The owners have already agreed to expanded rosters, which should make the union happy. There is also some question as to how this will affect a player's status for seniority and the ability to get free agency or arbitration. If they can get a deal hammered out in the next three or four weeks, we could see the start of the season on the 4th of July. Wouldn't that be appropriate for the great American pastime?

The top players in the NBA had a video conference call yesterday. They all want to resume the season. Even if they have an abbreviated end to the regular season and start the playoffs, I think it would be terrific for betting action. The NBA players union and management seem to have a better working relationship than any of the other leagues. Those relationships could crumble in an instant with a contentious issue, but here's hoping they figure something out quick.

And Gary Bettman, the NHL commissioner, said signs are in place for a return to action for the remainder of the hockey season. Details are very sketchy at this point, but as long as they have the Stanley Cup Playoffs, I'll be happy.

These are all positive signs, but Paul Finebaum, a leading voice in college athletics, made the point that they need a Plan B. What will happen if a player tests positive? What if a bunch of players test positive? If colleges open their campuses, what will happen if a student gets the virus? What happens if students die? Students dying due to the virus will open lawsuits that will make the Penn State-Jerry Sandusky fiasco look like a jaywalking ticket.

Whether the powers that be want to admit it or not, a lot of people are dying. The U.S. is up to 85,000 fatalities from COVID, with no signs of a letup.

Thursday May 14, 2020

Tom Blazek was in the coffee shop today, the only restaurant open at the South Point, when he got a call from Michael wanting to know how we did on the UFC fights. When Tom gave him the figure, +$20,000, Michael and the whole table of executives let out a shriek of joy. Michael happened to be in the coffee shop himself, with Ryan, Frank Toti, Greg Fisher, and a few others. Michael and company didn't realize Tom was sitting on the other side of the room. Tom made it sound pretty funny and the execs were actually embarrassed. A win of $20,000 is a pretty measly figure to get excited about, but it was the first positive contribution to revenue in months. It's all a matter of context, I guess.

Michael extended our hours, which wasn't a big deal in itself, but it did allow me to bring back three more employees. There won't be a whole lot for them to do, but at least they're getting a paycheck. Good on Michael.

Saturday May 18, 2020

Today had the feel of a real Saturday.

On the horse-racing front, Santa Anita opened yesterday and Churchill opened today. We aren't booking either one in Nevada right now, because of some contractual shit those two tracks seem to put us through every season, but at least they're open.

More good action on the NASCAR race tomorrow, but we screwed up something. We put up as many matchups as we could, but didn't disallow parlays using the same driver. In other words, you could parlay Bush over Hamlin to Bush over Harvick to Bush over Logano. Obviously, if Bush beats one, he has a good chance of beating the others. That's just one example of many. We caught it, but a few got by us before I noticed it. Let's see if we can get lucky and win them. the bettors aren't guaranteed to win these parlays, but if they do, they get paid a lot more than they should.

Favorites went 6-4 in the UFC. We did okay, but I thought we'd do a little better. Oh well, we ground out a profit, wrote a ton of business, and signed up a bunch of new customers today. Considering the circumstances, that's a pretty good day.

Brent Musburger, in one of his many past lives, worked with the beautiful Phyllis George Brown, who passed away today. Phyllis was a former Miss America, married the governor of Kentucky, and more important in the world of sports, was the first female co-host of a national-network sports-pregame show. The lineup consisted of Brent, Phyllis, Jimmy the Greek, and Irv Cross. It set the standard for all pregame shows that followed. Phyllis opened the door to the women of today who find themselves in front of the camera in what had always been considered a man's world. I never met Phyllis; I only knew Brent's stories about what a beautiful person she was. RIP Phyllis.

Sunday May 17, 2020

I knew we were behind the 8-ball with the NASCAR fuck up. One guy beat us out of $700, so it could have been much worse, but a lot of other nickel bets beat us too. As it was, we lost a little less than $4,000 for the day. The golf was okay, the Bundesliga was okay, our downfall was the NASCAR. Not for much, but when it's the only game in town, you want to win at it.

Tuesday May 19, 2020

Some more movement on the pro sports front. California, New York, and Texas have all declared the professional leagues can begin operations in those states. It will start with training and when they do play, the plan is for no fans to be present.

The NFL is still maintaining the mantra that they will start on time and play all the scheduled games with fans present. Quite a few doubters remain, but until they announce otherwise, that's the story and they're sticking to it.

The NHL is looking at nine locations to hold their games in a continuation of the season. They've been relatively quiet so far. I'm hoping they've been making plans behind the scenes.

The NBA has never really waivered, as a league anyway. They have every intention of finishing the season. There have been rumblings from some players and even some owners that they should just pack it in. I have a feeling they'll get it done somehow.

Baseball has been saying for a couple days they would like to get a deal in place to open July 1 or July 4. The MLB players union is particularly strong, so that's a hurdle. The million-aires don't want to take it in the shorts for the benefit of some billionaires unless they get their fair piece. I don't blame them.

In NASCAR Xfinity race today, the Darlington 200, we booked a little action, just enough to keep a few diehard racing fans happy. At least two more supervisors returned to work this week. Once we open, hopefully on June 1, a total of eight supervisors and eight ticket writers will be back. It'll be nice to see them all behind the counter.

The race got rained out, postponed until Thursday. So no real events today. I'm getting tired of the same goddamn report every day.

Wednesday May 20, 2020

The Darlington 400 ran today. My 50 matchups were an awful lot for a race like this, but I'm trying to force all the action I can out of this limited schedule. We did some business, mostly small stuff, and made a couple of bucks.

I talked to Brendan Gaughan, Michael's son, who is now primarily a former NASCAR driver. He announced his retirement, but he'll drive in a few races this year. I asked him to help me if he sees anything in the matchup prices that looks weird. Don't worry about a nickel or dime difference, I told him, just anything major. I could use his help; the prices I'm looking at are all over the place and I don't know enough about the sport to have any significant insights. Besides, I like Brendan. He's a good kid. He might be the son of a billionaire, but like the rest of the family, he's pretty down to earth.

Friday May 22, 2020

The NBA is still moving forward, at least according to reports. An anonymous owner was quoted as saying there should be basketball in 6-8 weeks. I'll take it.

The rumors are getting stronger that the NHL is close to a deal. The word is there will be a 24-team tournament to vie for the Stanley Cup. That number doesn't fit perfectly for a seeded tournament, so evidently, I'm not aware of other stipulations. About the most official word I've seen is from the Penguin's player representative Kris Letang, who tweeted out that the league and the players' union have reached a deal. Now the lawyers go to work and if they can keep from fucking the whole thing up, we should have hockey sometime in the near future.

Saturday May 23, 2020

Today, the report is the NHLPA has voted to agree to the 24-team playoff format. The top four teams in each conference (as determined by points percentage) receive byes through the play-in round, but they play three in-conference games during the play-in round, with the results somehow contributing to the seeding in the second phase of the playoffs. The 5th- through 12th-seeded teams in each conference then play a best-of-five series. After the play-in phase, 16 teams remain and the post-season finishes with four best-of-seven series.

I can see why they did it this way. Although 24 isn't a perfect tournament fit, everyone wants to involve as many teams as possible. The word is the NHLPA team reps voted 29-2 in favor of accepting. My guess is the two no-votes came from teams left out of the playoffs. Just a hunch.

As soon as I saw a rough draft of how the NHL planned to pull this off, I reopened my NHL futures, conferences, and Stanley Cup. I'm sure everyone will just look at them for a while instead of betting, but at least they're up.

Sunday May 24, 2020

Fun day. Well, not in the Bundesliga, where the favorites keep winning. So we started out the day down a couple of thousand. Other than that, we had a chance to write some good action on a couple of entertaining events.

The first was the golf charity event with the proceeds going to COVID-19 relief. The contest featured Phil Mickelson and Tom Brady versus Tiger Woods and Peyton Manning. We opened Tiger and Peyton as a -200 favorite. I think the price was good, but all the money showed on the underdog, which was no surprise. As they teed off, we needed the favorite for a change. Nothing too serious, just a lot of little action adding up to a couple of thousand on each side. What really came to light for the world to see was just how funny Peyton Manning is. He really stuck it to Tom Brady. It's always funnier when guys punch up instead of down and Peyton doesn't have a chance to punch up against too many quarterbacks, but Tom is one. Maybe the only one. Whatever that "it" quality is, Peyton has it. The episode of "Saturday Night Live" he hosted was an absolute classic, particularly the film of him playing football with kids. His regular show on ESPN, "Peyton's Places," is terrific. Pam makes me record all of them. I think she'd like to run away with Peyton. Who could blame her?

TNT also did a terrific job on the broadcast, miking all the players so we could hear the interchanges. With the coronavirus still restricting caddies and crowds, it was just the four contestants and the announcing team. Very entertaining.

The other event today was the Coca Cola 600, the longest NASCAR race of the season. Again, lots of little action. We had some matchups worth a couple of thousand and had to sweat a few guys to win the race.

Monday May 25, 2020—Memorial Day

I have fond memories of my father on this day. Every year in Chalfant Boro, he was honored for being the first in his hometown to volunteer for the service after Pearl Harbor. The town celebrated with music, what you might call a parade, and a couple of Little League games with an all-day cookout at the ballfield. Pretty cool for such a little town, and of course it made me especially proud that my father was at the center of it. It's been 50 years since he passed and I still think of him often.

Tuesday May 26, 2020

Governor Sisolak of Nevada held a press conference today, outlining the protocols for reopening casinos. I think we're on track. Tomorrow, we have our staff meeting to nail down final details. Right now, we're looking at a June 4 opening.

We have some NASCAR truck racing, Bundesliga, Australian (National) Rugby League and Aussie rules football (AFL). We're scraping the bottom of the barrel, but people want action. And I have to say, those are two pretty darn good sports. They're just not common to the American sports scene.

I had a doctor's appointment today. I was hoping to get the nod to go to work, but he said no. I can keep working at home until I have my bone-marrow biopsy in July or August. I'm not particularly looking forward to that (painful as hell), but if that's what I need to go ahead with my life like I want to live it, bring it on. A little morphine and I'll be fine.

Wednesday May 27, 2020

It looks like Jimmy will be heading back to his hometown, Trafford, about 30 miles outside of Pittsburgh. With all the crap that's gone on this summer, he hasn't been able to leave. Some states have no-travel restrictions in place and he was afraid of getting stuck. But now that things are loosening up a little, it's time. This is a big move for him. He says he'll give it a month or two. He'll realize that his life is either in Vegas or Trafford.

I love Jimmy like a brother. I'll miss him awfully bad if he really does stay in Trafford, but he's 75. I want him to be happy. Either way, I'll talk to him often. I haven't made a big move at South Point without running it by him first. And that won't change.

Years ago, the initials WWJD were floating around, standing for What Would Jesus Do. When I was running Cal Neva, my credo was WWJVD, What Would Jimmy Vaccaro Do.

Jimmy is as sharp as a bookmaker can be, but he also has a big heart. He gives the players every break in the book.

I'm the same. Some of my employees think I let people take advantage of me. I cut a lot of people a break. A few have gotten the best of me. But guess who wound up with money? Maybe not at the end of the day, but definitely by the end of the year.

I used to kid Jimmy about who paid more losing tickets to customers with a beef, him or me. I paid more tickets, but he paid more money. My mentor at Cal Neva, Warren Nelson, had a saying: "Always bet on the butcher." The lamb might get away once in a while, but your money should be on the butcher; he'll get that lamb sooner or later. In fact, Warren wrote a book, his oral history, called Always Bet on the Butcher. If you like this book and my last one, his is worth a read.

There are some great gambling sayings out there. Though this one's more of a general business saying, Warren told me, "If you're gonna be a prick, be a big hard one. Don't be a little soft one."

From legendary oddsmaker Bob Martin: "You want to take your customers to the cleaners. You just want to do it one shirt at a time."

My favorite of all time came from a sports bettor, Nervous John, well known in Reno in the '80s. One day I saw him in the sports book and asked him, "How are you picking them, John?"

"I'm picking them right. They're just playing wrong."

I almost fell on the floor. That's the greatest gambling statement I've ever heard. How many of us bettors have felt that way? I'm guessing 100%. I just never heard it expressed so accurately. Shakespeare couldn't have said it better. Or Damon Runyan.

Thursday May 28, 2020

Since Governor Sisolak made it apparent that casinos can open on June 4th, I've fielded a rush by the media to find out the details. One call I took was from Patrick Everson of Covers. A good guy from a good outfit, he wanted to know if the hot dog cart will reopen with the casino? Well, shit, I didn't know.

A little back story. Michael started selling hot dogs—no drinks, no chips, no nothing else—out of a cart near the sports book when he owned the Barbary Coast. He charged 50¢. People loved it and the guy selling them made a fortune in tips. Almost everyone told him to keep the change of half a buck or at least tossed him a quarter. Michael wound up having a hot dog cart in every casino he opened. Eventually, he had to raise the price to 75¢, then $1.25 (making it an even dollar would deprive the employee of tips). At South Point, it's one of our most popular amenities and Michael is particularly proud of it.

Anyway, I called Michael and told him how the media and a slew of my Twitter followers wanted to know about the cart. He laughed about as hard as I'd ever heard him laugh and believe me, he has a hell of a sense of humor. Then he paused and said, "Damn, I don't know! I better find out." He called me back about 20 minutes later. "Of course, we couldn't open the joint without the hot dogs!"

Well, suffice it to say, he made hundreds, if not thousands, of hot dog aficionados happy. The tweet I sent out was viewed by more than 23,000 people in the first seven hours. I'm going to bed now, so it will be more than that by tomorrow. It's the simple things in life.

Friday May 29, 2020

Nothing going on in sports today, but in the country? Holy shit!

The U.S. has been a virtual powder keg the last few days. Several Minneapolis police officers have been charged in the murder of George Floyd Riots exploded in cities throughout the country, including Las Vegas. Athletes white, black, and otherwise spoke out uniformly to express their disgust at the killing of George Floyd.

We have 40 million people unemployed, 100,000 or more victims of the coronavirus, riots all over the country, and a particularly contentious election coming up. If we don't wind up in a civil war, it will be a miracle.

I'm going to bed. The news is wearing me out.

Saturday May 30, 2020

We had the biggest one-day handle since the shutdown today, ith action on the UFC, Bundesliga, and NRL. That was the good news. The bad news was we got our ass kicked. The UFC was the big guilty party. The other two were winners for us. I'm happy for the handle, but pissed at losing like we did. Nothing disastrous, but when it's the only game in town, you just want to win.

Sunday May 31, 2020

Bristol Motor Speedway hosted the Food City 500. Brad Kesilowski took the checkered flag in a typical close finish. We made a bit from a pretty good handle. It was nice to finish the month with a plus, booking nothing but NASCAR, UFC, Bundesliga, and a few total outliers.

The MLBPA made an offer to the owners. It sounds reasonable to me, but I've heard that some owners would rather shut down for the entire season. If they don't put together a deal, they should combine their skills and write a treatise, "How To Ruin a Sports League."

The George Floyd protests are continuing.

The world is pissing me off.

Monday June 1, 2020

We started out in a hole today with the Bundesliga and never climbed out. The NASCAR race, the Cheddar's 300, wasn't particularly kind to us either. Unfortunately, NASCAR is one of the (many) sports and betting markets I don't know all that well, while the bettors who do really know it. It's been a little frustrating, but considering what's going on in the world, my problems don't amount to a hill of beans, to quote Humphrey Bogart in Casablanca.

Which reminds me: another night of watching the country burn.

Tuesday June 2, 2020

Casinos are supposed to open on Thursday. With the George Floyd chaos continuing, I'm not sure it'll happen. This morning, I talked to Dave Jensen, head casino host at South Point, and he assured me the plan is still in effect to open the casino Thursday morning at 8 a.m.

There was some quiet movement in the NBA and NHL resuming play. It looks like deals will be made, though details are still being hammered out. What the hell is going on with baseball is a different story. They appear to be throwing out one suggestion after another, leaking it to the press, and seeing how the public accepts it. They could really use some direction from a strong commissioner, but they're not getting it.

I talked to Jimmy this morning. I don't think he's happy in Pittsburgh. I think he'll be back in Las Vegas soon. I sure hope so. I need someone to help me keep my head on straight.

Thursday June 4, 2020

Las Vegas is reopening today. The D, owned by Derek Stevens, opened last night at 12:01 a.m., the very first minute allowed. A few others opened early in the morning. South Point is opening this morning. We expect some crowds, though there still won't be much to bet on in sports. I went in last night to check out the setup. I honestly believe we're doing everything possible to stay safe. My biggest regret is that I didn't invest in plexiglass, because it's everywhere in the casino and probably the rest of the country in any business that has such close contact with the public.

I went back in for lunch today: two hot dogs. Damn, they were good.

We opened up betting on the bull-riding event being held at South Point. I've got an Italian guy in New Jersey, originally from Staten Island, who bets this stuff. Yes, a city slicker, Christian Cianci, guiding me on my bull-riding odds. What a strange world we live in.

I expected something official from the NBA, but never heard a thing. The NHL is getting closer to finalizing their playoff structure, but nothing concrete yet. Baseball has their thumbs up their asses. There goes the National Pastime. Boxing, horseracing, and now baseball: all afterthoughts to the American sports fan. It's a new century, boys and girls.

Friday June 5, 2020

The NBA format for the remainder of the season came in. Twenty-two teams, broken into the traditional conferences, will vie for 16 playoff contenders. Games will restart on July 31, which seems like plenty of time to get their ducks in a row. Today, we reopened the NBA futures odds to win the championship. The Lakers are the favorite, no surprise, followed by the Bucks and Clippers. I think you can get 15-1 in some spots (not mine) on the Celtics and if I were a betting man, I think they'd be worth a shot.

The NHL won't totally complete the season. That much we know. As a result, they'll seed the teams like they did in the past with the four division winners getting top seeds. I decided to pay those teams as division winners and refund the rest of the action. It cost us a little, but I think it was the only fair thing to do and the positive publicity we got out of it was worth it.

The bull-riding community beat me out of about $800 today. Damn. It always happens on the sports I know nothing about. Oh well. Eight hundred bucks won't kill us.

Wednesday June 10, 2020

We had a NASCAR race tonight, the Blue-Emu Maximum Pain Relief 500. And yes, that could be NASCAR playing Mad-Libs just to fuck with us. Nonetheless, we made a few bucks on the race.

We have some major golf this week with the Charles Schwab Challenge at Colonial. All the big boys are in the lineup. With golf being the biggest major sport this weekend, it should bring in some real action and high viewer ratings.

Some grumbling has emerged among NBA players about the league's plan for finishing the season. The problem is these guys have to commit to being completely quarantined, maybe a long while. We've all been dealing with uncertainty. Bookmakers are no exception. Here's one more thing to keep me awake at night. I'm taking bets on this stuff and I have a feeling someone, somewhere, somehow is going to catch me by surprise.

Friday June 12, 2020

We had another bull-riding event at South Point today. I couldn't find any prices, so my New Jersey buddy Christian and I (mostly him) put together a betting menu. We had some action on it and later, some other outfit put out some numbers. Let's see how it goes. It's maybe a few thousand at best either way, so not that big a deal. But when you make prices, you always want to win.

I also bought a barbecue, charcoal, none of that pansy-ass propane or pellet stuff. Wood and charcoal. Like the cavemen. And I put it together. By myself. So, I made bull riding prices in the morning and put together a barbecue with my own two hands in the afternoon. Next thing you know I'll be hunting wild game and skinning bear for my clothing. I'd say I'm almost like a real man, but let's not get carried away.

Saturday June 13, 2020

We made some decent money on the bull-riding yesterday. Not much, but it was good percentage out of a better handle than I expected. Today, Christian and I made the prices. Again, we wrote some business and won a little.

The UFC wasn't so good for us. It was a lousy card and most of the action came from the sharp guys. Same with NASCAR. We had one lousy race and just a little business, all from wise guys. For the day we lost. Only a bit, but it was our first losing day in a while. We can't afford to have too many with such little action right now.

Sunday June 14, 2020

We zigged and zagged all day with NASCAR, soccer from all over the world, and Australian rugby. Fortunately, golf pulled us out for the day when Daniel Berger, whom I never heard of, won the Charles Schwab Challenge at Colonial. None of the bettors had heard of him either, because we had almost nothing on the guy. He beat Colin Morikawa in a one-hole playoff to close our day with a nice plus figure.

The coronavirus is still here. The states that have reopened are seeing a resurgence of cases. The U.S. now has over two million cases and 115,000 deaths. The protests and the reopening are seen as the major causes. Texas, California, Florida, and Arizona have seen the biggest increases. This thing is far from over.

Baseball continues to fuck up everything. I don't know all the issues, but it looks like tremendous greed on both sides.

In news later in the day, it was revealed that a number of major league players have tested positive for the coronavirus. One of them was Ezekiel Elliot of the Cowboys, one of the best running backs in the game. The report is that he's doing well. Others on the Cowboys and Texans have also tested positive, but their names aren't being made public. Many more are coming. This is strictly empirical, but from my observation, the younger, healthier, and richer people are more likely to ignore wearing masks and following safe-distancing protocols. That will include a whole bunch of athletes.

Friday June 19, 2020

COVID is still with us and affecting sports in a big way. The Tampa Bay Lightning had to close their training facility when some of their players tested positive. In college football, 23 Clemson players and 15 Texas players tested positive. All major league baseball facilities were shut down for a deep cleaning after five Phillies and three staffers tested positive. One more strike against baseball having any season at all.

Since we're doing some business on both Korean and Japanese baseball, I can't help but think how badly baseball blew it. Had they figured this stuff out early, they would've had the attention of every sports fan in America. Instead, they'll be resigned to second-tier status. It will still be popular, but people will follow hockey, golf, and UFC as much as baseball.

Saturday June 20, 2020

The Belmont was the big event of the day. Tiz The Law went off as the 4-5 favorite and won by 1½ lengths; he was never really threatened by Dr. Post, the runner-up. I had a win bet on Dr. Post, who I think will be a terrific horse in the very near future.

I hit the exacta and trifecta, so I had an all right day.

In sports we had UFC, NASCAR, soccer, Japanese baseball, Australian Rules football, golf, and bull-riding. The handle was terrific and the win was even better. It was the second biggest bottom line we've had since the lockdown—by my count, Day 99 without major sports. At any other time, it would have been a nothing day.

I sat with Michael and Frank Toti yesterday and they were both very happy, first with the sports book and second with the casino overall. I can help the casino a little by bringing in customers. But mostly I have to take care of the sports book. What we're booking is not in our wheelhouse, so we're playing very conservatively and holding our own. And until regular sports come back, that's what we are going to continue doing. Michael is happy. Frank is happy. That makes me happy.

Tuesday June 23, 2020

Late today, the baseball owners and the MLBPA finally reached an agreement to bring back baseball. They start on July 23rd or 24th, play a 60-game schedule, and have a playoff just like in the past without any rule changes. It should be exciting. The intensity will be like a playoff series from day one. Even the worst teams in the league will be in the hunt, at least for a while. I just wish they could have gotten this done weeks ago. More will come out in the future, but it looks like Scott Boras, the biggest baseball agent, had a lot to do with the delay. Whatever got done looks like it took Boras's approval.

I say this as a casino executive, a former casino owner, and a bookmaker: I could never be greedy enough to be a sports agent.

Thursday June 25, 2020

The NFL's traditional opener, the Hall of Fame game, has been canceled. It's just a preseason game, so it's hard to take too much out of that, but it's certainly not a positive sign. The two teams, the Steelers and Cowboys, will be featured in next year's opener, unless there's a nuclear winter or intergalactic aliens enslave us, that is. After all this shit, who knows?

Friday June 26, 2020

The NBA announced its return. Play will begin July 30 and the schedule is aggressive. Players better be in shape or some will really drag in the fourth quarters. They didn't have much choice. All these leagues will have a vigorous timetable with a short calendar. I'm sure hockey will do the same when they announce their revamped schedule.

Reports are coming out about the first round of COVID tests conducted by the NBA. Of the 302 players tested, 16 were positive. That's a little over 5%, pretty close to the natural average.

In other coronavirus headlines, it's now spreading rapidly again in many states. Florida and Texas have closed all bars, effective immediately. Arizona and California are also among the states with the biggest spikes.

Florida presents a big problem. The NBA plan to restart the season is to have all the teams and personnel in Orlando, right in the heart of one of the worst hotspots. Some players are now balking at the return. Florida is also home to seven major college football programs, three in the Power 5 and four in the Group of 5; it's one of the most fertile areas for producing college football players.

Texas has 11 Division I football programs, five in the Power 5 and six in the Group of 5. Texas is also probably the number-one recruiting area for high-school football players.

I haven't heard much about high-school sports scheduled to start in the fall. How this will affect seniors looking for scholarships, I don't know.

As a country, the United States experienced the highest

number of new cases yesterday, over 40,000. We now have 2.4 million cases and more than 124,000 deaths.

Like I wasn't aggravated enough, we got murdered in the fucking bull riding tonight. I might have to start drinking again.

Saturday June 27, 2020

Today we had the biggest handle since the virus hit. Tons of action on UFC, golf, soccer, auto racing, bull riding, Australian football and rugby, Japanese and Korean baseball. That's the good news.

The bad news is we got beat up. Bad.

I don't know when this losing is going to end, but I hope it's soon.

It started early with soccer. We battled throughout the day and pulled ahead in the afternoon with some good NASCAR results. When the UFC got going, we had a good chance to make some money. Unfortunately, it wasn't to be. The handle was fantastic, but the fighters zigged and zagged.

I saw some touts on Twitter late in the night bragging about what a great day they had. Don't I know it.

Sunday June 29, 2020

News flash: We won today!

Oh my goodness, were we ever due. Again, we started in the hole, but slowly climbed out. Dustin Johnson won the TPC golf tournament, which was a real good result for us. We also did okay on the matchups. The final results of the night were in the NASCAR race, won by Denny Hamlin. The winner was good for the future book, but we also killed them on the matchups, a huge surprise. We've been putting up a bunch to get all the action we can, but we haven't won much. Today we did. Hooray.

Tuesday June 30, 2020

With the NHL and NBA restarting and MLB starting, there figured to be some flies in the ointment. Today some announcements came out about who won't return—or start the season—for their respective teams. The Nets' DeAndre Jordan tested positive for the coronavirus and will remain at home instead of going to Orlando for the restart. Jordan is a relatively big name, but his team is going nowhere. That makes five Nets players who won't be with the team. The loss of Kevin Durant and Kyrie Irving had been expected. The Nets didn't have much hope to begin with; now they have none.

Avery Bradley of the Lakers dropped out earlier. The Lakers lack depth, so any starter leaving is big. The Lakers are the favorite for the championship. I'm not so sure they can overcome this.

Various reports have NHL players testing positive for the virus. Some are reporting 15 players, others are saying 26. No names have been released yet, nor is anything final as to what city they have chosen for the hub or hubs for the season's completion.

In baseball, the Washington Nationals have two key players who will sit out the season, Joe Ross and Ryan Zimmerman. Mike Leake of the Diamondbacks will also sit out.

Wednesday July 1, 2020

The NFL announced today that teams will play only two preseason games instead of four, one at home, one on the road. I can't think of anything else good that came about because of this coronavirus, but this is one.

The NHL announced its hub cities. The Western Conference teams will play in Edmonton, the Eastern Conference teams in Toronto. Good. Canada has handled this virus much better than the U.S. Plus, hockey is still Canada's game.

The betting news of the day was someone hit multiple parlays at the MGM on South Korean baseball. Early in the day, the

MGM itself posted the biggest ticket, a 10-team parlay that paid $137,000. All in all, the bettor won over $250,000 on about 50 separate wagers. Nice handicapping, right? Not really. All the bets were past posted. The MGM had the wrong start times for the Korean games and this guy took advantage of it.

There will be a fight with Gaming and don't assume the player has no chance of winning. They probably have a house rule that says, "Any bets written after an event has started will be void." That might not mean a thing. Let me tell you a little story.

When I was the sports book director at the Golden Nugget (which is described in my first book), we post tournament odds that were adjusted daily; this is common now, but not nearly so much in 2004. Going into the final round of the 2004 St. Jude's Classic golf tournament, David Toms had surged to an 8-stroke lead. Toms was a solid pro and the field wasn't particularly strong. So we didn't post an updated odds board for the tournament winner, although we did have other props for that final round. But we failed to lock out the St. Jude in the computer before the final round. A bettor came in late in the day, took Toms multiple times, and beat us out of $47,000. We discovered it and immediately voided the tickets. We had the rule that any bets made after the start of the event were void and we believed it offered us protection.

The bettor came in to cash his tickets. We explained our stance to him, he said nothing, and left. Just a brief little note, if you have a dispute of $500 or more, you must inform Gaming immediately. Since the customer said nary a thing, we didn't know we had a beef.

Well, he called Gaming. It was pretty cut and dried what happened, But Gaming ruled in his favor. We couldn't believe it.

Part of their ruling was that since we updated the odds after every round, how was he to know this one was off the board? Well, it was clearly "off the board" and marked "closed." We just forgot to lock it out of the computer.

I think the MGM past-poster has a hell of a case. How was he to know this wasn't the live betting line? That particular betting proposition has exponentially gained a large portion of the betting market. I have a feeling he'll say that and wind up getting paid.

Friday July 3, 2020

Another nothing day in sports, but a lot to report on.

Late yesterday, FedEx, which paid in excess of $200 million to the Washington Redskins for the naming rights to their stadium, made a formal request that the team change its name. The team's majority owner, Daniel Snyder, has said repeatedly he will never ever change the team's name. In my humble opinion, I find Snyder to be a thoroughly despicable human being. His evil deeds are well documented and you're welcome to look them up for yourself. (It won't take an exhaustive search.) The only thing that might surpass his loathsomeness is his greed.

FedEx made it clear that they wouldn't renew the naming rights when they come due in a couple years. As much as Snyder loves his favorite team's name, I have a feeling he loves his bank account even more.

Nike, which sells God-knows-how-much NFL merchandise, removed all of Washington's team paraphernalia from its website.

With the threat to Snyder's bottom line and the current mood of the country, if a name change is ever going to happen without new ownership, this is most likely the time.

I don't want to pretend I'm any kind of marketing expert, but to me, the team would sell a ton of paraphernalia with the old name before the change took place, then sell another ton with the new name. Every team in all major league sports and college has multiple jerseys, all in the name of marketing. This would be a steroid-induced version of the same thing.

In college football, sports author and radio and TV personality Paul Finebaum, who is a voice of reason, gives the season starting on time less than a 50% chance. Finebaum reminds us that the decision lies in the hands of the presidents. Of course, sports are a major part of their operation, but the schools are much bigger than that. Running them involves the teams, coaching staffs, administration, students, faculty, community, the alumni, vendors, and so on. Most of these folks came up through the education system. Sports isn't number one on their agendas. I hope my daughter can take her classes online this coming semester. How many parents feel the same way? I'd bet a lot of them.

Yesterday, the U.S. had 50,000 new cases of the coronavirus, the highest one-day total so far. Conversely, deaths have been dropping. The number of cases is a leading indicator. Deaths are a lagging indicator. We are going to have another crisis in the coming weeks and months.

Saturday July 4, 2020

No MLB today. Boy, did those guys blow it.

Instead of America's pastime to celebrate Independence Day, we have European soccer. It's better than nothing, but somehow, I don't see Leverkusen becoming America's team.

We did have a minor league NASCAR race, but no other live sports. Sad.

Speaking of baseball, as many as 35 players have now tested positive, including a cluster of 15 on the Atlanta Braves. The U.S. is still setting daily records for positive tests and athletes are just a part of the populace. We're having a lot of trouble just reaching the starting gate.

Mike Trout, the best all-around baseball player since Willie Mays, expressed concerns about playing in this abbreviated season. His wife is expecting a baby and he realizes the potential health risks.

Former NASCAR multi-champion Jimmy Johnson also tested positive and will miss tomorrow's featured race.

Monday July 6, 2020

Today, Patrick Mahomes signed the biggest contract in sports history. NFL contracts can be a little funny, because of the incentives and lack of guarantees, but this should be $450 million over 10 years. It could come in a little higher, upwards of $505 million. That's an awfully big contract, but the kid has had as good a start to his career as any quarterback in history.

Baseball announced its schedule today. The league will begin play on July 23. So many questions remain, it's hard to believe this will go off without a hitch. A number of players are expressing their concerns, some threatening to sit out the season.

It never ends.

Wednesday July 8, 2020

The Ivy League canceled all fall sports until January at the earliest.

In my world, Ivy League football doesn't mean much. We don't take action on it and the only players I know about are the few who make it to the NFL. In major college football, a coaching job in the Ivy League is often a stepping stone to bigger jobs. And in the minds of most college presidents, an Ivy League presidency is the pinnacle of their profession. So don't be surprised if a large number of college presidents join the Ivy League in this move.

Ohio State and North Carolina State shut down practice due to positive tests. A few MLB teams have also interrupted their training camps for the same reason. This is the tip of the iceberg. The virus is still on the upswing throughout the country.

Thursday July 9, 2020

It didn't take long. Today the Big 10 announced only interconference sports will be played this fall, including football. It's the first shoe to drop. Beware of dropping shoes. A lot more are coming.

In local news, Governor Sisolak closed all bars in the state. In casinos, people can get a drink at the bar, but can't remain there. I'm sure there will be lots of squawking.

We're now banned from traveling to Europe, Canada, and Mexico. Sports is a big indicator for society. Other countries have been playing ball for weeks and we're canceling seasons.

Saturday July 11, 2020

Good news and bad news. The good news: We took in the biggest handle since the world went to hell, writing nearly 300% more business than on any other day. The UFC drove the bulk of it, but all the other sports that no one gave a shit about six months ago also saw lots of action.

The bad news: We lost on every single sport. Every breakdown, which we do pretty thoroughly, lost. All five soccer leagues, Australian football and rugby, truck races, bull riding, golf, Korean and Japanese baseball—we lost on them all. That's pretty hard to do. Usually, we win here, lose there, and hopefully wind up with a few bucks on our side of the ledger. Not today.

When we came down to the last couple UFC fights, I could see we had a load of parlays running on both sides. We had a cushion, but not nearly big enough. That's just the way the accounting works. I explained that earlier. It wasn't unexpected on my part. I stayed to the bitter end, but it didn't do a bit of good. I could see we were going to lose no matter who won those last couple matches.

Sunday July 12, 2020

It's a special day for me. I had my bone-marrow transplant one year ago today. According to the bone-marrow community, it's supposed to be "your new birthday!" It sounds like a bunch of new-age bullshit to me. I'm not going for it. At least not in that sense. But I'll be happy to celebrate it every year. It's nice to be alive.

Monday July 13, 2020

Dan Snyder finally capitulated to the pressure and announced this morning that the Washington NFL team will no longer be known as the Redskins. The new name has yet to be announced, if indeed there is one. Snyder indicated they have to jump through some legal hoops before they can officially rename their franchise.

Don't start any movement to get Snyder some kind of humanitarian award. In his statement, he talked about pleasing his sponsors. In other words, he did it for the money.

Ready for another shoe that dropped? The Patriot League, a pretty decent college FCS league, postponed football until spring at the earliest. You won't see many of their games on television, but they manage to put a few players in the NFL at times. Plus, it's a group of highly regarded academic institutions: Holy Cross, Lafayette, Bucknell, Lehigh, Colgate, Fordham, and Georgetown. This is not insignificant.

In other shoe-dropping news, the National Junior College Athletic Association announced it's moving football season to the spring. This is also significant. Many teams complete their roster with junior-college players. It would have been even more important this year with players sitting out because of the virus and the liberal transfer-portal rules. These aren't a bunch of stiffs, either. Aaron Rodgers and Cam Newton both came via the JUCO route.

The NHL opened training camp today. Reports of multiple players testing positive abound, 43 in all, but the league isn't issuing any names. I do know Patric Hornqvist, one of the Penguins' top forwards, sat out today's practice, but no one is saying why. Rumors are out about other teams, but only Auston Matthews of the Toronto Maple Leafs has been confirmed.

In the NBA, Russell Westbrook of the Houston Rockets, one of the Association's top players, tested positive. He's gone into quarantine, which usually means two weeks, but that hasn't been confirmed yet, either.

Knowing the attitude of invincibility of many young people, especially athletes, this thing figures to get worse instead of better.

July 14, 2020

Late yesterday, James Harden of the Houston Rockets was diagnosed with the coronavirus. That makes the two top players for one of the Association's top teams. There's still time for them to recover and play the bulk of the season. They've traveled with the team to Orlando, so we'll have to see what happens with their health and its effect on the team. But it's certainly not a good thing for the team or the NBA.

Wednesday July 15, 2020

For years I've hated the baseball rule that totals and run-line bets are required to have listed pitchers. I've had so many beefs with guys who thought they had a winner, but got no action because there was an off pitcher.[5] I've looked into it intermittently, but because of our computer system, it's been impossible to change. Now that we have a new system, it's entirely possible.

There was some talk among some major bookmakers to shitcan listed pitchers. The game has changed in the past few years. Instead of "starting" pitchers in a regular four- or five-man rotation like baseball had done since its inception, many managers have gone to "opening" pitchers, who pitch for only an inning or two. Last year, managers changed their minds numerous times on the opening pitcher, shuffling their opener to the second or third man out of the bullpen. From a baseball standpoint, it doesn't make much difference, but for betting purposes, it voided any listed-pitcher bets, which covered all run lines, totals, and first-five-inning bets. Often, the customer had no idea and really didn't give a shit. He naturally pissed and moaned when he had a winner and didn't get paid. If he had what he thought was a loser, he often never even knew it was no action and never bothered to come in to get his money back.

This year with the late start, pitchers won't have their arm strength up. Pitchers and catchers always show up first at spring training; they need extra time to get their arm strength to where it should be. This year, they won't have the opportunity to do so. Whatever we saw last year with opening pitchers will be exacerbated this year. Plus, if we don't change it this year, with a 60-game season on tap, when would we try it? If there's resistance, we can always go back to the old rule.

This new rule will work out better for everyone, but change always creates problems. Michael and Frank put me through the ringer to convince them that this was the right way to go, but I did finally get my way. Those guys are tough, but you can talk to them.

Tomorrow, I want to make some parlay-card changes. The bosses will put me through the ringer again, but I actually en-

---

[5] Run lines and totals were automatically listed pitchers. It's just the way it always was and accepted throughout the industry. I've been trying to get it changed for at least 25 years, but all the computer systems had default protocols for run lines and totals to list pitchers and no option to do otherwise. Any change in starters was referred to as an "off pitcher."

joy presenting and debating with them. And if I can't convince them, I'll take my whupping like a man.

When you list pitchers and either of the designated pitchers doesn't start, the bet is no action. If you don't list pitchers on the bets on the side and one pitcher doesn't go, you get the adjusted price. Most casual bettors don't care; they just want the action. Some bettors, the professionals and wise guys, like it that way, because they know exactly what price they'll get. If the bet gets canceled, so be it; they just want to be locked in on the price.

Thursday July 16, 2020

COVID hit close to home today when it was announced Brendan Gaughan, Michael's son, was diagnosed positive. I talked to his sister-in-law, Sally, who told me Brendan has it, but is feeling all right. This is a strange disease that affects different people differently. Centenarians recover and 30-year-olds die. An awful lot about this disease is still unknown. I hope Brendan gets through it okay. I've gotten to know him fairly well in the last couple years. He's a good guy.

Del Mar Racetrack closed until at least next Friday after 16 jockeys tested positive. Del Mar has a short meeting. Closing for any period of time will cost them a big chunk of their revenue stream. Besides, it's one of the great horse racing venues in the world. If you ever get the chance to go, do it. You won't regret it.

The bigger picture is this: If what happened at Del Mar happened to a sports team, what would be the ramifications? Would teams have to forfeit? Would they play with a short squad? And more important for me (yes, it's cold-hearted, but it's my business), what do I do as a bookmaker?

This is part of what I'm looking at with parlay cards. If I put out a number on Wednesday, I'm stuck with it. If a game's number goes off the rails, what do I do? I hate to scratch games.

A lot of my customers won't understand. However, if I don't scratch such a game, I'm open for some huge losses.

I didn't make my presentation to Michael today. I needed to do some more research and get more facts straight before I see him. I talked to my cousin Art Manteris, who runs the sports books at Station Casinos, and Nick Bogdanovich at William Hill. Neither one knows what they'll do with their parlay cards this season.

The world has much bigger issues than what I have to deal with. Health-care workers, teachers, food-service employees, and anyone with an essential job has it 100 times worse than I do. Still, this is my little domain and I have to take care of it.

But man, this really sucks.

Friday July 17, 2020

I had lunch with Michael and laid out my concerns with the parlay cards. I had two years' worth of figures, but he wants one more year. He also wants Frank Toti to be there and Frank isn't coming in until later. We'll meet again on Monday.

In coronavirus news, America had the highest positive rate ever today.

Saturday July 18, 2020

Brutal day. We started out in the hole with early-morning Japanese and Korean baseball. European soccer wasn't much better. Golf third-round matchups were even worse. UFC had an unexciting card today, but we were grinding out a slight profit and finally went ahead for the day, when the only underdog bet up by the public came away with a big win. We went from slightly ahead to a five-figure loser.

Then we got the results from the Xfinity NASCAR race. Kurt Bush was the winner. Nice. We got close to even. Oh wait. An hour later he was disqualified and Austin Cindric got put up.

A five-figure swing. Fuck!

We started booking exhibition baseball and even though there were only two games, those kicked our ass, too.

Man, these days are so frustrating.

On the plus side, Jimmy Vaccaro is back in town after his unfruitful sojourn to Pittsburgh. He called me when he hit town just as I was leaving work for the day. He'll be back in the lineup tomorrow. It's so nice to have him back. He helps keep my head straight. We're both getting a little long in the tooth. It would be great to finish our careers together. If so, I'll feel profoundly blessed.

But let's face it. I already am.

Sunday July 19, 2020

All day: up, down, up, down, up, down, up, and …. we ended down.

We're on a bad run right now and we can't get out of it.

Monday July 20, 2020

I finally got to sit down with Michael about the changes I want to make on the parlay cards. I got four of the five I lobbied for, but he wouldn't budge on my main one. The ties-win parlay card pays 600-for-1 on the 10-teamer. It's just too much. I wanted to make it 500-1, but he wouldn't go for it.

I understand his point. We've made a couple million bucks on the card the past couple years and he doesn't want to screw that up. I don't either, but I wouldn't mind padding those numbers a little. Oh well. I'll deal with it. Now I just hope we have a football season.

On the plus side, it's bedtime and we're actually winning for the day. Yay.

Tuesday July 21, 2020

Gaming ruled in favor of Bellagio today and against the guy who had a theoretical $200K coming to him. He definitely past-posted them. I know that the ruling was correct. I just wish they'd have applied the same logic when they ruled against me on the David Toms bet.

Wednesday July 22, 2020

I had my bone biopsy today at USC. They do it a year after the transplant. They have to run some studies to make sure everything is proceeding as it should. Knowing how I feel, I'd be shocked if it weren't. Because of the coronavirus and the restrictions around it, I couldn't go in the night before like I would have ordinarily. So I had to wake up early, go to L.A., and come back afterward. And since I was getting morphine for the procedure, someone else had to drive. I recruited my cousin Zach for the detail. It was nice spending the day with him. What made it even better was going to Phillipe's for a lamb-dip sandwich for lunch, followed by a trip to Langer's for a #19 (pastrami and cole slaw on rye) to eat on the ride home.

The procedure itself hurt like hell. The morphine didn't do anything for me. For whatever reason, it's difficult to get a good bone-marrow sample from me, so they have to drill extra hard to get it. They finally got enough, though it took them an hour of pretty intense drilling. And make no bones (ahem) about it, it is drilling, the old-fashioned way—by hand, with one of those crank drills you see in an old movie. The poor woman doing it was working like a construction worker making a hole big enough to slide in a stick of dynamite.

I'm home now and ready to get in bed. In the scheme of things, what I went through was like a hangnail compared to some of the other stuff people are going through right now.

On to tomorrow, opening day of baseball.

Chapter Six
July 23-August 31, 2020

"A little bit of this town goes a very long way. After five days in Vegas, you feel like you've been here for five years."
—*Hunter S. Thompson*

Thursday July 23, 2020

We were jamming all day. The appetite for betting real American sports is insatiable. We had lines at the windows all day with virtually no let up.

So far so good on my "no-listed-pitchers" strategy. The Dodgers' Clayton Kershaw, arguably the best pitcher in the game, was scratched midafternoon, put on the disabled list with a back problem. He'll be out at least a couple of weeks. One guy bet $43,500 to win $15,000 (-290) on the Dodgers, assuming Kershaw was starting. Dustin May will start instead. May is pretty well regarded and it's still the Dodgers. The price dropped to -240, still a pretty significant favorite. Nonetheless, the Kershaw bettor doesn't have much of a bargain, though he's still a favorite to win his bet.

In other baseball news, Juan Soto, the defending World Series champion Washington Nationals' best player, tested positive today, putting him out of action for the near future. He needs two negative tests before he can return.

That's two extremely significant players going on the injured list before the first game. Not a good omen for what's to come.

Then the results came in. Yankees win, Dodgers win, South Point loses. When it's all chalk, we get murdered. Tonight, there were only two games, both big favorites. Both won. That spells disaster and that's what happened.

It's one day. We'll get 'em tomorrow.

Friday July 24, 2020

Well, we didn't get 'em today. In fact, they got us. Again. Thirteen of 16 favorites have won so far. That's bad bookmaking news in any sport, but especially in baseball.

Two days of baseball and we blew our entire fucking month. Tomorrow is a loaded baseball schedule and the biggest UFC card I've ever seen. We'd better get 'em tomorrow or I'm gonna jump off the top of South Point. With my luck, I'll probably just break my ankles.

Saturday July 25, 2020

I woke up in the middle of the night to find out we lost almost double the last figure I got before I went to bed. I know it will turn around, but damn, I hate this continuous losing.

Today, we wound up winning a decent amount. It didn't make up for the last two days, but that's not how bookmaking works. All we can do is continue putting out the right numbers, move them properly when we get bet, allow the results to come in, and let the chips fall where they may. Bettors chase and try to win back what they lost yesterday or last week or month or year. That's to their demise. A good bookmaker has to keep his shit together and let the grind work in his favor.

Sunday July 26, 2020

I was awakened early this morning with the devastating news that my 21-year-old godson passed away from an accidental prescription-drug overdose during the night.

I don't know what his demons were, but I do know he had a big kind heart. He became a bone-marrow donor long before I was diagnosed with my condition. So our relationship had nothing to do him stepping up to do what he could to help a fellow human being. That's the kid I'll remember.

The last time I saw him was at Uncle Jack's funeral about a year ago. He was his usual joyous loving self. He always called me Nouno, Greek for Godfather. I really loved him, but it's not like we hung out together. What 21-year-old kid wants to pal around with a 60-something-year-old? I had no idea he had any kind of problem.

I don't know how funeral homes and funerals work in this time of COVID, but I'm sure I'll find out shortly. All of us in the family can use the support of one another. I hope we can do that.

Hug and kiss your kids. Tell them you love them. Try to be aware of any danger signs. I realize those are all a bunch of clichés you hear at a time like this, but they're all true. Don't take life for granted. You never know.

Every family has its share of tragedies, but it sure seems like ours has had extra dose of it. I've only touched on a few in this book and this most recent one. There are plenty more.

I'll miss you, Danny, my beloved godson. May your memory be eternal.

Monday July 27, 2020

Sunday was another fine result for the sports book, though my mind was certainly elsewhere.

As soon as the worm turned, we got hit in the face with another baseball catastrophe. Twelve players and two coaches for the Miami Marlins tested positive. They played yesterday even though before the game there were four positives. At least one player was in the game knowing he'd tested positive.

Today, the Marlins canceled their scheduled game with the

Orioles. They were to travel from Philadelphia, where they played the last four days, to Miami. The last I heard they still haven't left Philadelphia. I'm not sure how they'll travel. An airplane is a germ-filled petri dish in a flying metal tube in the best of times.

Meanwhile, the Phillies were supposed to host the Yankees today, but there was no way the Yankees wanted any part of a visitor's locker room that had been home to the Marlins for four days. So that game got canceled.

No one is really sure how this will affect baseball's big picture, but I sure hope the other sports are taking notice. The NBA is playing in a bubble in Orlando, with frequent testing and a complete lockdown for the players. At last report, they're 100% clear of the virus. They're being extra careful, but I don't know how restrictive they can be with maintenance workers, security guards, and any other auxiliary personnel. It's a virus. If it gets a foothold, it will run rampant. It doesn't care who you are or what you do.

Tuesday July 29, 2020

Four more members of the Marlins tested positive. Their games have been canceled through Sunday. The schedule involving the Yankees, Phillies, and Nationals have been adjusted to compensate for the games lost to the absence of the Marlins.

A total of 25 NFL veterans have opted out of playing this season. Most are married with young children. Interestingly, six of them are Patriots. NFL camps open tomorrow, so we might see a few more opt-outs in the coming days.

The NHL has a few preseason games today. Their regular season starts in a few days. They tested every player and there are zero positives. Kudos to them.

Wednesday July 29, 2020

We had the memorial service for my godson today.

I loved him. I thought he was a terrific kid. Funny, personable, caring. But I was his godfather. Of course, I would think that. Our whole family did, but that was just natural.

I had no idea he had so many friends throughout the city.

It was an outdoor ceremony. There must have been at least 200 people there. I don't see how Danny could have connected with each and every one of them, but evidently, he did.

I'm going to miss this very special kid.

Thursday July 30, 2020

In college football, Notre Dame joined the ACC for football. They'd already been a part of the conference for basketball and other sports. With the scheduling challenges that face college football, they believed that this was the only way to have a representative schedule, rather than be an independent. The Big 10 and Pac 12 provided three scheduled opponents, but they'd already announced their teams would play only conference games—thus eliminating Notre Dame. If the ACC went the same way, there goes their season. And a shitload of money.

Whether this means Notre Dame will now be a permanent member of the conference isn't clear. Don't underestimate Notre Dame's arrogance or the size of its bank account. That will play a huge role in whatever they decide.

The NBA starts today with two terrific games. The underrated Utah Jazz take on the New Orleans Pelicans, in the midst of a fight to make the playoffs. And in the feature, the two favorites in the Western Conference, the Lakers take on the Clippers. Should be a big night.

Top-host Dave Jensen came by the office late in the day. Besides all his other duties, Dave has the ear of Frank and Michael. If you want to get a message to those two, tell Dave. And if you want to get it to them quickly, tell him not to tell Frank or Michael.

I pointed out to Dave that Nevada Gaming reported results for June. Sports books lost money for the first time since July

2013. Not South Point. We made money. Not much, but we were in the black. I know Dave will pass it on to Frank and Michael.

I also let Dave know that the handle for the first four days of baseball this year was up in excess of 20% over the first four days of baseball last year. That includes the very first day this year when only two games were played. Last year, they opened with a full schedule on Day 1. I got some grief from Frank and Michael about the no-listed-pitchers rule this year, but it obviously hasn't hurt our handle. So there.

Friday July 31, 2020

Some movement in college football today. Well, the plans for college football, anyway.

The SEC announced its conference will play only intra-conference games starting on September 26. The bad part is some SEC teams have rivalry games outside the conference: Georgia-Georgia Tech, South Carolina-Clemson, Florida-Florida State, Kentucky-Louisville. Some other teams like Alabama, LSU, and Auburn will play whoever has the balls to line up against them. The other SEC teams don't usually have too tough a time finding worthy opponents. Then there are the late-season cakewalk opponents they schedule every year, like Charleston Southern, Chattanooga, Mercer, The Citadel, and West Carolina. By the way, those are Alabama's blowout victims for the past five years. But every SEC team does the same thing late in the year just to get an exhibition win before playing a big opponent. It's smart on their part. Once they figured out how to manipulate the ratings process, their scheduling strategy has helped their national rankings. But honestly, it sucks. Play a real game, for God's sake.

The other Power 5 conferences are putting their schedules together now. Most are going to start earlier than the SEC, but all this is up in the air right now.

The St. Louis Cardinals announced a positive test. Their game was canceled today, but that's all for the time being. Two other games were canceled today, as well as two tomorrow. MLB Commissioner Rob Manfred made an impassioned plea to all the players and personnel to stay within the protocols or the season is in danger of being canceled. Some of the talking heads in sports media and even some national newscasters are saying the same: Get your act together or the sport will be shut down.

The other sports are taking notice. I honestly don't know how football, pro and college, can pull off their plans. Baseball is a relatively contactless sport. Football, not even close. And as I've said, there is no way for football to play in a bubble.

In baseball, the leagues don't matter as much as the divisions this year. All games, in league and interleague, are played within divisions. They could have put all the Western teams in Los Angeles, all the Central teams in Chicago, and the Eastern teams in New York. Each city has two major-league ballparks, at least one minor-league park (no fans, so why not?), and plenty of hotel rooms. They could play two games a day in each major-league stadium and one in the minor-league stadium.

But no one wanted that. Not the players, the union, the owners, the general managers, no one. So that idea never floated downstream for a minute. Oh well, it could have worked. Too bad no one asked me.

About 75 years ago, guys this age were going to fight a world war. Those young men were going to be gone for months or even years, if they ever made it home at all. A three-month bubble to play baseball is a sacrifice, but come on. In the scheme of things, it's not nearly that bad. I think I would have done it. In fact, I know I would have.

Saturday August 1, 2020

The plans for a college football season continue. The PAC-12 will begin its season on September 26, just like the SEC. It doesn't hurt to plan. At this point, you have to. I know I need college football. I just hope it all happens according to these newly revised plans.

Today was a huge day in the sports book. For the first time we had the NHL, the NBA, the WNBA, MLB, and UFC. Great action.

Sunday August 2, 2020

Another busy day with full-scale hoops, hockey, and baseball.

Baseball continues to change on the fly. We had one double-header, with double-header games now scheduled for seven innings. I'm not posting totals and run lines on those games, which have to go nine innings for action. To adjust our rules would just be too much of a hassle. I have enough shit to deal with right now.

A group of PAC-12 football players have come together in an informal alliance. They've put forward numerous protocols for the upcoming season. They're putting their health and possibly their lives on the line for … what? They get a free education and a chance to display their talents to the NFL for a potential pro career. Is that enough? They're starting to think it isn't. This movement has been gaining steam; with the virus gaining new momentum daily, it has come to the front. They're the talent that provides these schools with the money to pay coaches millions and employ hundreds of people, many with huge salaries.

Each year the NFL drafts 224 players. Let's say 20 players from each Division I team would be eligible for the draft and would like the chance to play in the NFL. That's 2,600 players. Most won't get drafted, a large number of those that do won't make a team, those that do will have a career that probably ends before they're 30 years old. The risk/reward is questionable in the best of times. With COVID, it's off the charts. I hope they take advantage of a free education. Many of them don't.

They have many "concerns" that have the potential to turn into "demands." The media is concentrating on the financial compensation they want, but it's much deeper than that. They want health care beyond their playing careers, an assurance they won't lose their scholarships or place on the team when the virus does subside, and a scholarship allocation for minority students.

More than 400 student-athletes have lent their voices to this, which is impressive. I don't disagree with any of their demands, but my question is, what can and will they do next? They don't have a union, so it will be very difficult to speak with one voice. The powers that be—the NCAA, school presidents, athletic directors, and coaches—will try to fight it. Their strategy will be to divide and conquer.

As the father of a college student, though not an athlete, I feel for their position. If I had a kid playing, I'd want him to sit out until this gets under control, which doesn't seem like it will in the near future. Your athletic career is fleeting, but so is life. Take it from an old guy, it goes by fast. Another cliché that happens to be 100% true.

Monday August 3, 2020

The website everydayshouldbesaturday.com is a college football site. Well, guess what? Right now, every day is Saturday in sports. We have baseball, basketball, and football starting early in the morning and going until late at night. Every day this month. The betting action has been monstrous.

I talked to my crew today. We need more people. A lot of people out there are looking for jobs and I could use a few of them. It won't make a dent in the national, statewide, or even local unemployment figures, but it sure will help the ones I hire.

In the NFL, 43 players have opted out for the season. We all know they're leaving a lot of money on the table. Another aspect of opting out is if they leave, they won't have access to the team health care. They'll have to be like the rest of us, where sometimes a test takes up to two weeks to get results. Living like the rest of us might be a very rude awakening for some of them.

Doug Pederson, the Philadelphia Eagles head coach, tested positive. He's asymptomatic, but he still has to wait until he tests negative before he can rejoin the team.

What a nightmare.

Wednesday August 5, 2020

This morning, the University of Connecticut announced the cancellation of its football season. It means something, but it's not a huge indicator for the rest of college football. UConn was going to play as an independent this year. It was difficult to find games at this point, because so many conferences were planning to play intra-conference games only.

Within a few minutes of the UConn announcement, the Big 10 announced its schedule for every team. I'll start working on some games of the year and conference-championship odds.

On Monday, the Detroit Lions quarterback Matthew Stafford tested positive. Less than 24 hours later, it was found to be a false positive. This is going to be one crazy season.

I shut down betting on the whole first week of the NFL season. South Point sports book customers had months to bet if they were looking for a good number. Now it'll just be a race between them and us to see who gets the information first. I don't want to play that game, especially with all this COVID stuff happening. I have to live with customers who aren't handicapping and are playing nothing but the information game, but only if they're part of the mix. I don't want to cater to them.

Late yesterday, I got a call from Michael. Our parlay-card supplier shut down her business. She was upset, because no one would commit to any kind of an order. Michael asked me if I'd put in an order, which I did. I had to cut it 25% on some cards and 33% on others. I was her only customer who committed to an order. Michael was glad I did; he's always tried to take care of that company (no surprise, he tries to take care of everyone). I have some alternative plans, so I at least have an idea of what to do.

Thursday August 6, 2020

The NFL Hall of Fame Game was supposed to be tonight. It got canceled a while ago. Now it looks like no preseason games will be played. Personally, I hope they permanently get rid of preseason games.

A story came out that last week about FanDuel, the fantasy sports site that continuously and ridiculously claimed that fantasy wasn't gambling. It's now operating sports books in numerous states. They had the odds of Major League Soccer's Atlanta team as a 5-goal favorite over Cincinnati. The rumor is that winning bets on Cincinnati, which won the game 1-0, total more than $200,000. The line was up for days and two fairly large bets were approved by a supervisor. Now FanDuel is trying not to pay, claiming it was a mistake on the betting line.

What a bunch of horseshit. But what else would you expect from an outfit that took money for a game, paid the winners, kept the money from the losers, and somehow with a straight face (and a bunch of lawyers) claimed it had nothing to do with gambling?

I got to my office right around lunchtime. Who was waiting for me but Michael? He wanted to know my plan for those parlay cards. Fortunately, I got in touch with my old parlay-card printer in Reno, which still supplies William Hill with their cards, both in northern Nevada and Las Vegas. They assured me they could take care of us, as well.

Today was the cutoff for NFL players to declare whether they'll sit out the year or not. A total of 69 players are. The

Patriots had nine, the most. The Steelers, Falcons, Rams, and Chargers had none. They each get $150,000 regardless. I guess we'll find out if they were the smart ones.

Friday August 7, 2020

Today we buried my godson.

The natural order of things is for children to bury their parents. Of course, it's hard for the children, but it's best that way. By a mile.

Unfortunately, life doesn't always work like that.

I know somewhere, sometime, someone will read this who has either gone through the tragedy of burying his or her child or will have to do so in the future. I won't pretend to know your pain. No one can know your feelings. They belong to you and no one else. Nonetheless, my heart goes out to you, my unknown friend.

Life will go on, but for you it will never be the same. Don't try to forget, because you can't. You're not supposed to. Do your best for those who are still here, those you love.

That will be your legacy.

Saturday August 8, 2020

I had other matters to attend to yesterday, but the Penguins got bounced out of the Stanley Cup playoffs. Just a personal note for me. I was hoping for a real run to the Cup for my old hometown team. Time is running out for Sidney Crosby, Evgeni Malkin, and Kris Letang, three Hall of Famers. Maybe next year. Hope springs eternal.

Early this morning, the MAC announced they were fore-going the fall football season. The MAC is a mediocre Group of 5 conference, but they make it a point for all their teams to play games with the Power 5. They've put a lot of players into the NFL as well. This is bad news, but the rumor had been out there for a while. I'm surprised it took this long.

The Big 10 presidents met today. The rumor was they'd pull the plug on the football season. Nothing happened. But the possibility is hanging out there. Pat Forde, a well-connected college-sports journalist, thinks we might lose college football completely by the end of the week.

Travers was run at Saratoga today. Tiz The Law coasted home. He was hardly breathing heavily. He totally dominated the field. I think he has a great chance to win the Triple Crown. He would be a well-deserving winner, but I hope he doesn't do it. It's just too different from the traditional Triple Crown.

Meanwhile, I tried to beat him again. All I got for my hard-earned cash was a few scraps of paper.

The Mountain West Conference canceled football. That hurts. I'm assuming the PAC-12 will cancel; all indications are that it will. At least if we had the MWC, we'd have a west coast team playing in the latest time slot on Saturday nights this year. Timing is more important than people realize. Sports books need a few good morning games (9 a.m.), afternoon games (12:30 p.m.), the best games in the evening (5 p.m.), and some decent late games (7:30 p.m.). That leaves the players to bet, cash, double up, get even, or get even worse. It looks like we'll lose that late spot. Damn.

Baseball still hasn't solved its COVID problem. The Pirates-Cardinals series has been canceled. The Cardinals have the most cases in baseball; they've played only five games so far. Some other teams have played as many as 18. I have no idea what baseball can do to rectify this thing. I don't think baseball does either.

Tuesday August 11, 2020

It's almost lunchtime and we're still waiting to hear something from the Big 10. The whole season might turn on this decision.

I've said from the beginning that if most college conferences canceled and the SEC plays, we'll be all right. This morning SEC commissioner Greg Sankey said he doesn't see how the SEC could play their schedule as the lone conference. One more strike against us.

Well, the Big 10 caved. No football for them this fall. Now we await the PAC-12, but no one I know is optimistic they'll play.

It didn't take long. The PAC-12 joined the Big 10 in postponing the fall football season. They say they will try to play in the spring, but I'm doubtful.

I'm also disappointed. But I get it.

Meanwhile, where is the NCAA leadership? Nowhere to be found—amidst the biggest crisis in its history. But if a kid gets free cream cheese on his bagel, they'll be right there to serve notice of an infraction. Whenever you see a failing institution, the petty rule enforcers are the last to crumble.

Reno people will appreciate this. I went to the movies at the Park Lane Mall multiplex. I was late (big surprise) and parked in an illegal spot. OK, I was wrong. But I came out to find one of those stickers that are impossible to remove, right on my windshield, warning me of something or other. It took me about a half-hour to get enough of the sticker off the windshield just so I could drive home. My car was only a few days old, and I never got all the junk from that sticker off my windshield the whole time I owned that car. Meanwhile, and I swear this is true, the whole mall was imploded days later. Nice outfit. They couldn't run a mall, but they sure as hell were right on top of parking enforcement.

This is my image of the NCAA. They bring in millions, have zero respect from essentially anyone, and are big swinging dicks on every meaningless little thing. When we could really use a strong hand to guide us through these troubles, their heads are firmly up their asses. I'm not sure what their plan could or would have been, but should they have at least something in mind? Don't be surprised if this is the death knell for that organization. They run a hell of a basketball tournament, but tell me one other thing they do to make college sports more enjoyable? I hope they sink like a Mafia rat wearing cement boots dumped into the East River.

Wednesday August 12, 2020

The SEC, ACC, and Big 12 have every intention of playing football this fall. So far. Flying under the radar are the smaller conferences: Sun Belt, Conference USA, and AAC. I haven't heard anything official, but I'm assuming they still intend to field teams and play this fall.

Business-wise, if that happens, I think we'll be fine. I just hope they can do it safely. The U.S. set the dubious record for the most COVID-19 deaths two days ago. People are scared. I'm scared.

In baseball, the Cardinals have still played a total of five games. The Braves are up to 20. I have no idea how MLB fixes this.

Friday August 14, 2020

Some TV talking heads are calling this week's decisions "the most significant moment in the history of college football."

Not so fast. If they want to play, if they're going to play, let them play. I hope they can pull it off. If not and something happens to abort the season, that will be the most significant moment in college football history. If they can pull this off without a hitch, that will be the most significant moment.

The Cardinals are still stuck on five games played. MLB came up with a plan today for them to play 11 doubleheaders from now to the end of the season. That's assuming no rainouts or any more COVID-19 cases that will directly affect them.

Saturday August 15, 2020

Busy day. We had a huge schedule, but we've been getting waxed the last few days, so the players have a lot of money right now.

The Vegas Golden Knights were in a late game, which always promotes a ton of business. Typically, today we had action from the public on the Knights, while the wise guys bet against them, putting their money on the Blackhawks.

Sunday August 16, 2020

Another massacre. I'm starting to think we'll never win again.

Monday August 17, 2020

Big 10 players, led by Ohio State quarterback Justin Fields, want to play this fall. Big 10 parents are requesting answers as to why their kids aren't playing. There's a lot of noise trying to reinstate the season. Will it work? Who knows? I don't even know exactly how I feel about it.

One of the consequences of canceling the season will mean a big added recruiting advantage for the schools in the conferences that do play. That might have ramifications for generations to come. That's mere speculation, but it's how these guys think. And that will be the result. Bank on it.

A lot of early action today. We have a huge schedule. I hope we can get a few wins in some of the bigger games.

The day didn't start out too promising. We had some big play early on the Denver Nuggets in the first game of the NBA playoffs, which started today. The Jazz had a double-digit lead in the fourth quarter, but allowed the Nuggets to tie the game at the end of regulation. Do I even have to tell you the Nuggets won and covered in overtime? Not a good omen for the rest of the day.

True to form, things did get worse.

Tuesday August 18, 2020

I get the day's figures texted to me every night. Sometimes I'm asleep when they arrive. Some nights, I don't see results until my middle-of-the-night visit to the toilet. (Go ahead, laugh, kids. You'll get there someday.) Yesterday, I knew it was going to be bad, so I called in to tell them not to send them. If I saw them, I knew I'd never get back to sleep.

I'm glad I called. Out of yesterday's 21 events across all sports, the favorites went 20-1. I'm still not sure what the one winner was. It was the worst one-day non-football loss of my career.

I need to tap into my inner Jimmy Vaccaro.

When I got into the office this morning, I had an early meeting with Ryan Growney. We needed to make a decision on which company to use for our parlay cards. Reno Printing convinced Ryan and me they could furnish all our needs and do it in a timely manner. Fine. Now we had to go meet with Michael.

I was a bit tense, to say the least. The loss the night before was weighing heavily. I thought I could be in some serious hot water.

Wrong. In Michael's office, he immediately started busting my balls. When Michael is busting your balls, all is well. When he's serious, you might be in some trouble. I know how to take him. He was pretty much making fun of me for losing so much. Once he started in on me, I knew I was in good shape. We figured out the parlay-card supplier issue and off to work we went. I gotta tell ya, it's nice to work for a guy like that. He knows if 20 out of 21 favorites win, you better get your ass kicked or you're not taking care of business like you're supposed to.

Two first-round number-one seeds were upset in the NBA tonight. The Lakers and Bucks lost outright. Even though the Knights won and took some money out of our pockets, we finished with a real nice day. Not enough to make up for yesterday, but again, that's not how bookmaking works. The grind is on our side and that's the way we have to play it. The players go for the big scores. And they get them once in a while. But as Warren Nelson said, always bet on the butcher. The lamb might get away once in a while, but the butcher is going to get him eventually.

Well, the butcher got them today.

Honest to God, I barbecued lamb steaks for dinner tonight on my new grill. And they tasted damn good.

Thursday August 20, 2020

Another huge handle today. We had two particularly big plays, both from regular customers who play pretty high.

The first, on the Indians, who have just been roasting the Pirates in the first two games of the series, was $65,000 to win $25,000. Naturally, the Indians won, so we bore most of the loss without getting much back on the Pirates.

The second was on the Blazers, who beat the Lakers in the first game of the series as a very popular underdog. Our big player bet the Blazers +245, $30,000 to win $73,500. It wasn't hard to get plenty back on the Lakers, who blew out the Blazers.

It's definitely the way you're supposed to book action like that, but it always seems to work out that way. Win less than you should on one game and lose more than you should on the other.

Unfortunately, it was one of those days with a shitload of action and not a goddamn thing to show for it.

Saturday August 22, 2020

Huge handle today and what I thought would be a huge win. No such luck.

I left a little after 6 p.m. and we were way ahead. I don't watch much sports at home, but I check the scores on my app. We had a lot of action on the Lakers/Blazers game. We moved the line back and forth all day from Lakers -7.5 to -8. The total got jockeyed around from 223 to 225 with terrific action both ways. The Lakers were ahead throughout, but could never put the Blazers away. I turned the game on to watch the final four minutes and not much changed. Back-forth, back-forth, with the winner never in doubt. With the score Lakers 116-106, the Blazers got the ball with nine seconds left. The Lakers put forth no defensive effort whatsoever and one of the Blazers went straight for the bucket and laid it in as the clock wound down to 0:00. The final: 116-108. We got middled on the side and the total.

Twitter lit up. Half the twittiots said, "The fix was in! Vegas made a phone call!" (I'm still waiting to meet this "Vegas" guy.) A bunch of others said, "These Vegas guys are so sharp, they know exactly what's going to happen!" The second guy has a slight point, but not really. Sometimes, the math just works perfectly. And when it does, it's the worst thing that can happen to the bookmaker. I had a bunch of messages telling me how smart we are, as if predicting the score with our betting line was a good thing. It wasn't. It killed us.

Then the parlays kicked in. The Dodgers, as usual, were big culprits. But the UFC, which has been largely forgotten except for their most diehard fans, really hurt us. Big action on mostly favorites from players who actually know what's going on. That was a bad combination.

We actually won a little, slightly less than 1%. I'm glad the handle was there.

Sunday August 23, 2020

Two really big games for us: In baseball, the Tigers beat the Indians as a +240 underdog and in the NBA, the Mavericks beat the Clippers as a +275 dog.

The Tigers took an early lead, tried to give it away in the 9th by surrendering three runs, but held on to win 7-4. The game didn't make any highlight reels and in a day or two will be completely forgotten.

Not so the Mavs win. You might be seeing this on NBA

promo videos for years to come. The Clippers were up 21 points early and double digits in the second half, when suddenly the Mavs got hot. Mostly it was Luka Dončić who got hot. The twenty-one-year-old from Slovenia turned in one of the best playoff performances of all time: 43 points, 17 rebounds, and 13 assists—all on a bad ankle.

Late in overtime, the Clippers took a one-point lead. The Mavs got the ball with nine seconds to play. Everyone knew who they were going to. Luka went around two screens to get open and for some reason, Kawai Leonard, one of the best defenders in the league, switched off him. Reggie Jackson did his best, forcing Luka to shoot a step-back three, but in it went. The Mavs won the game and tied their series at 2-2.

Those two games set the table, but we won money on just about every other category. We needed a day like this. We're still having a tough month.

In other NBA news, the Celtics swept the 76ers and the Raptors swept the Nets. They play each other in the next round. Should be a couple of good series.

In the NFL, 77 players tested positive for COVID. All the positive tests came from the same lab. Practices were canceled throughout the league. The players were re-tested. Every single test came back negative. This is a huge issue. The NFL is painting this as "a good thing." As in, "We're glad it happened now, so we know how to deal with it." It sounds like they're pissing down our backs and telling us it's raining. They should all find employment in politics.

The only good thing is they're dumping this lab from their testing protocols. For this to happen during the season would be a nightmare.

Tuesday August 25, 2020

I'm still trying to keep politics out of this book as much as possible, but videos are now showing Jacob Blake, an unarmed black man, getting shot by the Kenosha, Wisconsin police. You can clearly hear seven shots fired, though his father claims there were eight. Potato, potahto.

Blake survived, but he's paralyzed from the waist down. The cops said they thought he was reaching for a gun, which he wasn't. Even so, one shot in the leg wouldn't do the trick?

Wednesday August 26, 2020

It's 1:45 p.m. The Milwaukee Bucks were scheduled to play at 1:05, but they refuse to take the court in protest of the Jacob Blake shooting, which happened in their home state. Houston-OKC canceled. Lakers-Blazers gone, too. The Milwaukee Brewers have canceled tonight's baseball game and \the WNBA's three games all canceled.

Let's see, we have the largest fires in our nation's history going on in California, a Category 4 hurricane hitting the Gulf Coast with another one right behind it, racial unrest in Wisconsin that has spread throughout the country and into the sports world, and COVID has killed 179,000 Americans with over 1,000 deaths a day. I don't know if an alien invasion or an asteroid hitting us is next up, but c'mon, would either surprise you at this point?

I took all the games off the board and closed the futures. I have no idea what will happen and I'm not sure even the players do. I don't want to jump the gun and I'm waiting until I hear something official.

Who would've thought COVID would get trumped by racism? Welcome to 2020.

Thursday August 27, 2020

The NBA will resume play. Today's games are canceled, but they will supposedly restart play on Saturday.

Saturday August 29, 2020

College football was supposed to start today and in a way it did. Central Arkansas played Austin Peay. Okay, not the kind of teams that we usually book, but we did book this game and took some pretty decent action on it. Next week we'll have some of the regulars we always book.

I'm pretty sure this is the first day in gambling history we have college football, NBA, NHL, MLB, NASCAR, and the fights (UFC) all on the same day.

We were busy, but I thought our handle would be a lot higher. I wonder if the two-day pause by the NBA and NHL stymied some of the enthusiasm we've been building. I hope it's only a temporary lull in the action.

Monday August 31, 2020

I was off yesterday and I'm off today as well. I'm trying to relax as much as possible. This will be my last Monday off for a few months as long as we have a semi-normal football season.

We woke up this morning to the news that former Georgetown basketball coach John Thompson passed away.

Thompson made Georgetown a national power in college basketball. He was a Hall of Fame coach who won a national championship and took three teams to the Final Four.

He was the first black coach to win a national championship and as much as he was as a coach, he meant more as a cultural icon. His teams were mostly black, which was very odd for the time at a prestigious, iconic, private university. Only two players who spent four years as Georgetown Hoyas failed to get their degrees. Those kids were in school to play basketball and get their degrees. I'll let others explain his importance to the black community. If you don't know much about him, you should explore his legacy. It's quite significant.

Leonard Fournette, the number-four draft choice in 2017

who spent three productive years with the Jaguars, was cut today. The team said they tried to trade him, but could get nothing in return. Nothing. Not a sixth-round draft choice, not cash, not a cold six pack of beer. Draft a running back at your peril.

Personally, I miss the days of the great running backs that teams were built around. Sometimes things come back. Maybe running backs will. I have a huge collection of LPs on vinyl, which makes me super cool in some eyes. Take that, hipsters.

The Padres made the biggest trade at yesterday's deadline, picking up Mike Clevinger from the Indians. No doubt Clevinger is a top pitcher, but he wore out his welcome in Cleveland for not following the bubble protocols this season.

Betting-wise, we already lose money on the Padres if they win the division or the World Series. They already had a decent shot. Now they're certainly a major player.

Nice action today, particularly on the NBA. Both underdogs won, which gave us some plus figures. Then we won a little on hockey and baseball. It's nice to finish the month on a high note. We had a couple days that really hurt, so our hold percentage wasn't great, but the handle was terrific. We were on pace to double last August's handle until the Jacob Blake protests stopped some of the play. All in all, I'll take it.

Chapter Seven
September 1-23, 2020

"A cynic is a man who, when he smells flowers,
looks around for a coffin."
—H.L. Mencken

Tuesday September 1, 2020

We're opening the first two weeks of college football this morning. The big question is, what do I give teams for home-field advantage? I'm thinking about half of what I would ordinarily. We'll see what the bettors think.

Very little action in college football today. I must say, I was quite surprised. Only a few other lines are out there, so very few arbitrage opportunities exist. Nonetheless, I thought we'd do some brisk business. It wasn't to be. A lot of time is left and I'm sure it will be fine in the end.

Thursday September 3, 2020

Today was the first day of college football with two teams regularly on the board. No, not a classic rivalry. It was Southern Miss vs. South Alabama. South Alabama won outright as a double-digit dog, which is usually good, but not in this case. We had a lot of money on the dog, with both the points and on the money line. There was another game with UAB, a board team, and Central Arkansas, an FCS team. We split the action on that one, but it wasn't a big deal either way.

The Vegas Golden Knights had a chance to close out their series with the Vancouver Canucks, but lost 4-0. That's big news here in Las Vegas. The expectations have been high for the Knights and the consensus was they would take care of the Canucks easily. It looked like that was true when they took a 3-1 series lead. But Vancouver won two straight to force a Game 7 tomorrow. The Avalanche and Stars also are involved in a Game 7 tomorrow. So two Game 7s in hockey in one day. Gotta love it.

In a play you will probably see on highlight shows for years, the Toronto Raptors beat the Celtics on a last-second shot that looked nearly impossible. First, Daniel Theis scored on a beautifully set-up dunk to give the Celtics a 103-101 lead with 0.5 seconds to play. After a time out, the Raptors inbounded the ball from half court—no time for anything but a catch and shoot. The diminutive (by NBA standards), 6'0" Kyle Lowery was the inbounder. The Celtics countered by putting 7'6" Tako Fall in to pressure the inbounds pass. I don't use the word "miraculous" very often, but for Lowery to find OG Anuoby deep in the opposite corner and for Anuoby to catch the ball and get it up in time to swish a three-pointer to win the game, well, my friends, that was as close to a miracle as you will ever see. Raptors 104-103.

The score was especially nice from my point of view. First of all, we want as many games played as possible. If the Celtics won, they would have gone up 3-0 in the series, making it nearly impossible for the Raptors to come back and win. Now at 2-1 Celtics, it's a competitive series.

But even better was the way the betting pattern worked. We opened the Raptors at -1.5. Bettors laid the -1.5, then -2, and even -2.5. No one was interested in the Celtics with the points, but I did manage to get back a pretty good whack on the Celtics money line. A win and cover by either team didn't mean much for the day's bottom line, but an exact one-point Raptors win meant all the folks laying the points lost and all the folks with the Celtics on the money line also lost—an absolutely perfect outcome for the sports book. I set us up for this sort of thing all the time, but it seems like it never comes in. This time it did. Hallelujah!

Friday September 4, 2020

I got in this morning with a message to call Michael. He wanted me to look at some chairs we had to rearrange to comply with the governor's COVID mandate. He loved it when I told him about the lucky outcome we had in the Celtics-Raptors game. I love making him laugh and I got a good one out of him today.

The first Stanley Cup playoff Game 7 went into overtime. How appropriate. The Stars won 5-4. I spent a lot of time in Colorado, so I always sort of rooted for the Avalanche, but today wasn't their day. Now Dallas plays the winner of the Knights-Canucks series.

The second game didn't go into overtime, but was tied 0-0 late in the game when the Knights scored with 13:52 gone in the third period. They then added 2 empty net goals to cap a 3-0 win.

We were pretty balanced on tonight's game, but I did want the Knights to win. It's good for the town and good for our action to keep them going. All the way to the Cup, if possible.

The Bucks, with the best record in the NBA, went down 0-3 to the Heat. That game didn't mean much either way financially. In the later game, the Lakers fell to the Rockets, 112-97. That one did mean a lot. People couldn't get enough of the Lakers, on the money line and ATS. I'll probably be in bed by the time they text me the results, but I'll bet they're pretty damn good.

Saturday September 5, 2020

It's the first Saturday in September, the traditional Kentucky Derby Day. Okay, not even close, but here we are. This country is still on COVID tilt and that includes horse-racing's biggest single event. I bet Tiz The Law, an odds-on favorite. I honestly don't think I've ever bet a Derby favorite before today, but this one looks unbeatable. I bet him in a bunch of exactas and trifectas to see if I can get lucky with a decent payout.

Because of a dispute with Churchill Downs, Nevada isn't allowed to book the race as a part of the pari-mutuel pool. If you book as a part of the pari-mutuel pool, you can take any bet someone wants to make; there's no risk whatsoever. You take out your percentage and pay out the rest. It's the one area of the casino where you're rooting for the customers to win—the more they win, the more they can put back through the windows, known as the "churn." The higher the churn, the more the race book makes. This year, we need to book the race and make money. The churn doesn't mean anything. We have to beat the players. Why?

I was on a couple Derby podcasts and radio shows this week and I echoed the same story on each: The Derby is great. I love it. And it's a great day for the casino, particularly the race book. But it's one day out of 365. You don't pay your bills with one event a year. A lot of meets in their entirety are better: Saratoga, Del Mar, Belmont, Santa Anita, and anywhere they hold the Breeders Cup. I said that Churchill has been screwing Nevada for 30 years with what they want in participation fees. They perpetually overplay their hand. We finally drew a line in the sand. If we weren't going to do it this year, when would we ever? So the hell with them. We'll book it ourselves. They're not bigger than Las Vegas. I hope their handle takes a hit.

I'm not involved in the horse-racing side of the book. That's all Mary Jungers. But I'm the last Nevada bookmaker who was booking horse racing on a daily basis. When I was at Cal Neva, we booked horses non-parimutuel longer than anywhere in the state. I offered my services to Michael for the Derby, but he was sure Mary could handle it. I am, too. Mary has been booking it almost as long as I did, so she should be fine. I was just offering.

Meanwhile, someone whose name I won't mention got to Michael and convinced him to book Kentucky Derby matchups. This, of course, falls on me. I was already busy today, but now I've got a homework assignment. I don't want to book these things. They usually cost us money. It always aggravates the hell out of me when guys make these suggestions. It takes them seconds to call someone and tell them what they should do, then they're done with it. I'm the one who has to set it up in the computer, make betting sheets, put up the prices, book the action, get the right results, not fuck anything up along the way, then hopefully make a little money in the end. Meanwhile, if all goes well, the guy who made the original phone call tells Michael how smart he is for making the suggestion. If something goes wrong, that fucking Chris Andrews must have dropped the ball.

Tiz The Law ran his heart out, but couldn't overcome Authentic, who took the lead into the first turn and never relinquished it. Bob Baffert trained. Again.

The race book had a great day, holding over 32%. Good. Fuck Churchill. Meanwhile, I heard Churchill wrote a scathing letter to each of the Nevada Gaming Commissioners. For once, I will greatly appreciate the arrogance of the commissioners. I don't see how this can work in Churchill's favor. Someday, they might want a Nevada gaming license. This will be remembered.

Our matchups made a little over $800 on a $5,800 handle. I'm sure that other guy will take all the credit. And so it goes.

Sunday September 6, 2020

If all goes well, this will be my last Sunday off until February.

We had a huge day yesterday, both in sports and the race book. I'm glad Mary did so well booking the race. First of all, it means she won't need my help if this fiasco happens again. Second, it's nice to show Churchill we don't need them. Churchill's Derby Day handle was down about 50%. I know it's a lot more than just losing the action out of Nevada, but I was happy to see it drop like a rock.

Gigantic win in sports yesterday, too. Yesterday was one of those days where everything fell just right. I've got to enjoy these when they occur. They don't happen very often.

Monday September 8, 2020

Terrific handle on both Sunday and Monday over the Labor Day weekend. We had a solid winning percentage, though nothing outrageous. Monday we had football, basketball, hockey, and baseball. A rare confluence, indeed. I rested Sunday, but busted my ass today. Tip of the iceberg. The NFL starts Thursday.

I stayed up too late tonight to watch *A Hard Day's Night* for the 20th time. I laugh and enjoy the music every single time I see it. George Harrison said it best: "The Beatles saved the world from boredom." I've been listening to them for 57 years now and I've yet to get tired of them.

We start working on parlay cards tomorrow.

Tuesday September 8, 2020

We sent the first few parlay cards to the printer. On Tuesdays we'll start with the Sunday-Monday prop card. It's a ties-lose card that holds a huge percentage for the house. It's pretty formulaic. Only a little decision-making goes into the card; in fact, I provide only the pointspreads and totals and my crew does all the props.

Next up, I made the Big Teaser, another card that holds a sizable percentage. This card gives each team and total an extra 8 or 9 points the best of the number. Of course, they pay a steep price for those extra points. It looks a lot better to the player than it really is.

After that is the Super Teaser, which gives the player an extra 5 or 6 points. Players pay a smaller penalty for those few less points. I wait a little longer in the day to put this one out, anticipating moves that ordinarily come later on Tuesday. This card has a smaller hold for the house than the Big Teaser, so I have to be a little more careful putting out the numbers on this card.

Later, I got a call. A guy was betting against the Broncos in this week's game and the season-win totals. I had them give those lines a stiff move. I was still out, so I didn't realize until I got home that Von Miller, one of the best defensive players in the NFL, got hurt and is likely out for the season. I made some further adjustments. We had individual teams matched up against one another in props and odds on each team to make or miss the playoffs, so I had to adjust those, too.

The sports world never stops.

We lost two games this week to COVID. That's besides all the games that have been postponed and rescheduled.

Oklahoma State/Tulsa was postponed early in the week and late yesterday, the Baylor/Louisiana Tech game was postponed. Both Tulsa and Tech had COVID cases. I'm hoping these events are few and far between.

Thursday September 10, 2020

Finished the first week of parlay cards this morning. It went a lot more smoothly than last night. I'm sure it will get easier as the season goes on.

We won money tonight. I have no idea how, but we did. I thought they were going to text me a six-figure loss, but instead it was a plus. Not much of one, but a plus nonetheless.

It was opening night of the NFL and as tradition has it, the defending Super Bowl champion kicks things off. We opened Chiefs -10, soon went to -10.5, then all the way down to -9, and back up a notch to -9.5. If you look at those numbers cold, it looks like we needed the Chiefs. We didn't. The early moves are made without much money behind them. Opening numbers, particularly those opened months in advance, move quickly. On the day of the game, it takes exponentially more to move that same number. Don't be deceived, though; we needed the Texans to cover the pointspread and an outright win would have been a thing of beauty.

The Chiefs won 34-20. The game also went over the total. When televised games come favorite and over, exactly what this one did, kills a sports book.

But wait, that's not all. One customer bet the over 53 for $25,000. To balance his action, I took a bunch back under 54. If you don't know, that means we got "sided" on the game—one side won and the other pushed. All the over bettors won, while the under bettors got their money back. Bad for the bookmaker. The guy who bet the $25K made one big bet, but a host of others also had the over. Landing exactly on 54 for a final score hurt.

Another guy bet $100,000 on the Chiefs money line at -450, so it won $22,222. We used to see bets like this occasionally, but now we see them all the time. That was the biggest money play on the Chiefs, but not the only one. The business has really grown in the last few years. No signs of it slowing, either.

We lost those big plays. We also had a college football game, Miami-Fla played UAB. Miami won and covered as a -15.5-point favorite. That hurt, too.

The Lakers beat the Rockets as a -5-point favorite, 110-100. We lost on that one, as well.

The Knights lost to the Stars in overtime 2-1. That helped. The parlays were all on the Knights, but we had some wise-guy play on the Stars and lots on under the 5.5 total, so the VGK loss didn't help as much as it might have.

So the only thing that could save us was a big night in base-ball—and we got it. Thank goodness. Otherwise, we were in deep shit for the day. Tomorrow, when the figures go to Michael, I'll give him my standard answer: superior bookmaking.

Ken Barlor, general manager of my old casino, the Cal

Neva, was in town tonight. We usually try to get a poker game together when Kenny is in Las Vegas. Tonight, we played at Richie Baccellieri's house: Kenny, Richie, Vinny Magliulo, Nick Bogdanovich, Barry Phillips, Jeff Whitelaw, Jimmy Vaccaro, and of course yours truly. There were stories, ball busting, food, beer, booze, even a little poker. More important, we pooled our money to play in the Circa football contests. They have two, each worth over a million bucks. It would take a miracle, but we're looking to take them both down.

Friday September 11, 2020

This morning I got a message that 17 players from Arkansas State, including seven starters, tested positive. They play Kansas State this week. Later, we got word that the Texas State quarterback, who missed last week because of COVID, might be scratched for the same reason this week. He's questionable right now, but we scratched that game, as well as the Ark State/Kansas State game. A little later, we adjusted the numbers and put the games back up. I hate leaving games off for long.

Huge action today. Some big plays in baseball, mostly on the big favorites. We couldn't knock down any of them. Last night baseball saved us; tonight it buried us.

Hockey contributed to our win last night, but to our loss tonight. That's the way it goes sometimes.

On the Game 7 in the NBA, Celtics vs. Raptors, we had some huge action and it was two-way, which was fantastic. We split it out pretty well and made some decent money. The Celtics won. Now they go on to play the Miami Heat for the Eastern Conference championship. The series will feature two of the best coaches in the NBA, Brad Stevens of the Celtics and Erik Spoelstra of the Heat. The Celtics have to be a very slight favorite. They played better all season, but the Heat have been terrific throughout the bubble, losing only one game. Should be a hell of a series.

Already some big play for tomorrow's football action. Even

119

more for Sunday's. I'd better get some sleep.

Saturday September 12, 2020

Pretty good action this morning off a pretty lousy schedule.

The most interesting news of the morning was Georgia Southern announcing a whopping 33 players will miss today's game against Campbell. We scratched the game, but not before taking a few bets on Campbell. If the missing players are COVID-related, we better get used to it. With fall weather coming, it figures to get worse.

All morning, I was kicking myself for letting one of our regular customers bet us $50,000 to win $10,000 on the Kansas State money line. That's the game where 17 players, including seven starters, were missing for the other side, Arkansas State. Despite a few turnovers and some stupid penalties, Ark State pulled out a late 35-31 win. I still believe I made a mistake putting him on for that much, but I'll take the win and the $50,000 in our pocket.

Overall, the Big 12 had a pretty rough day. Besides Kansas State losing, Iowa State lost to Louisiana, Kansas lost to Coastal Carolina, and Texas Tech struggled to beat Houston Baptist. On the plus side, West Virginia beat Eastern Kentucky, Oklahoma beat Missouri State, and Texas beat UTEP.

The Texas win deserves a special note: A guy bet $1,000 to win $1 on the Texas money line. I tweeted that out and as of this morning, it has gotten over 300,000 views. I thought it was kind of interesting, but I can't believe the attention it garnered.

In the NBA, the Lakers put the Rockets out of their misery. It's strictly personal, but that makes me exceedingly happy. If you don't know why I hate the Rockets, well, I'm not allowed to tell you. But you can figure it out if you try.

Bottom line is we had a great day on a surprisingly good handle with such a terrible array of games.

On to Sunday and the NFL.

Sunday September 13, 2020

We were super busy, which is no surprise at all. This year we added seven kiosks, which really helped getting everyone in for the 10 a.m. posts.

As it was, we didn't win many games. Wise guys were on the Bills, Bears, Jaguars, Packers, Patriots, Washington, Cardinals, and Rams. All winners. They lost with the Falcons, Browns, Panthers, and Bengals. Fortunately, we split out the public pretty well and somehow made a bit of money. Not a whole bunch, but reports in the media are a lot of places lost money or broke even for the day. All things considered, I'll take the meager win off the huge handle.

We're still under strict COVID limits. Everyone has to wear a mask at all times unless they're eating, drinking or smoking. (Like smoking isn't stupid enough, with the whole west on fire. The air quality is worse than Beijing in Portland and Seattle and Nevada isn't much better.) People are supposed to social distance, which is a phrase that didn't exist six months ago, but now it's something we hear and talk about every day. Security is enforcing the rules. It was a never-ending battle, but they did the best they could. From media reports, we did fairly well in that department, compared to the other sports books in town. Hopefully, it's enough to spare us the wrath of the governor.

Besides football, the Cubs' Alec Mills pitched a no-hitter, , a five-set marathon in the U.S. Open tennis was won by Dominic Theim after being down 0-2, the Nuggets overcame a 16-point deficit in an NBA playoff to beat the Clippers and force a Game 7, and the Tampa Bay Lightning won a Stanley Cup playoff game. It was one hell of a day.

In our Circa contest plays, we had winners with the Bills and Rams on every entry, then added winners with the Jaguars and

Washington on one entry each. We lost with the Vikings and Browns on all three of our entries. So on two entries we're 3-2 and on the third, we're 2-2 with the Giants going for us tonight. It's not great, but not terrible either. We just have to avoid the 0-5 and 1-4 weeks this early in the season. For our Survivor contest, we had the Bills on three entries and the Patriots on the other two. One week in and 42% of the Survivor contest has been eliminated courtesy of the Colts, Eagles, and 49ers. I'm happy to have dodged all those bullets.

Monday September 14, 2020

I love these opening-weekend Monday-night NFL double-headers. I wish they'd shitcan the Thursday night games and give us the doubleheaders every week. I really hate the Thursday night games. The performances are horrible, ordinarily for one team, but often for both.

Tonight, we have the Steelers at the Giants in the first game, then the Titans at the Broncos in the late game. We opened the Steelers -3.5, but closed them -6. I'm writing this just as the game is kicking off, but let me tell any would-be-serious bettors out there, you don't lay 2.5 points the worst of it and have any kind of value. You'd have to either take the points with the Giants or pass. I'm not saying who the winner is; my power ratings have the Steelers a 6-point favorite. You just don't get value. And in the long run, if you don't get value, you'll lose. In betting the NFL, you have to buy low and sell high. Pick your spots; being straight contrarian will get you killed. But look for an overpriced favorite, usually a team coming off a big win or in a must-win situation. Those are the best spots to play the dog.

The second game is even worse. We opened the Broncos at -3 and now we have the Titans -3. That's a 6-point swing. Maybe that opening line was off; I personally believe that was the case. But again, you have to go against the move or pass.

There's nothing wrong with passing on a bet. That's a bettor's best friend. A bookmaker has to dance every dance, while bettors dance only when they like the music and have the right partner.

The Knights are playing for their Stanley Cup lives tonight. They're down 3-1 to the Stars. We've had money on the Knights all day. I understand the mentality of it; the VGK has the talent to do it, now they have to execute. So far, they haven't.

The Giants were totally outclassed by the Steelers, who won 26-16. Even so, the Giants could have had a miracle and pulled out the cover with another touchdown. That's life in the NFL. You can be completely out of the game and still get the backdoor cover. Unfortunately, it wasn't to be tonight.

By losing that first game, we were on the hook for the second game of the night. The first final not only handed us a loser, but every single teaser combination was alive going into the late game. We needed a Broncos win for a couple hundred thousand. The first half ended 7-7. Steven Gostkowski, one of the most accurate kickers in NFL history, missed a relatively easy field goal for the Titans, which was a huge help. The third quarter started and the Titans held the ball nearly the whole time; the Broncos had all of three offensive plays the entire quarter. Gostkowski's woes continued as he missed two more easy field goals. Finally, in the fourth quarter, the Titans got in the end zone, and don't you know, Gostkowski missed the extra point. Denver marched down the field, scored its own touchdown, and made the extra point to take the lead. After holding the Titans to a three and out, they got the ball back with a little over four minutes to play and instead of milking the clock, they had their own three and out, which took about 30 seconds off the clock. That was really really stupid. You've got to run time off the clock when you have the lead that late in the game.

The Titans got the ball back and drove inside Broncos territory. Even though he'd missed three field goals and an extra point, a Hall of Fame kicker could make an easy field goal and be the hero. The Broncos should have been calling time outs to leave themselves time, were he to do exactly that. Well, he did do exactly that. The Broncos, thanks to their clock mismanagement, got the ball back with 17 seconds left. Not enough time to get into field goal position to give themselves a chance to escape with a win. It was one of the worst time-management performances by an NFL team that I could possibly imagine.

We wound up with a slight loser for the day. We averted the disaster a Titan win and cover would have brought, but we could have had a big winner if the Broncos had won outright, rather than lose by two. Just before game time, we went as high as -3.5 on the Titans. So all the latecomers on the Titans lost, even though the first guys in got the win. If you don't get a decent number on your bet, you're begging the gambling gods to punish you.

The Knights blew a 2-0 lead and lost to the Stars in overtime, 3-2. So once more, no Cup for Las Vegas. Superstar goaltender Marc-André Fleury got benched for the payoffs. Robin Lehner outplayed Fleury during the second half of the year, but I thought they might go back to the veteran in the clutch. His name is already on the Cup three times. That doesn't happen by mistake. It's Monday morning quarterbacking on my part, but I would have loved to see the Knights return to the veteran goaltender, who has been the face of the franchise since his arrival in Las Vegas.

Tuesday September 15, 2020

I started at South Point in 2016, so I'm in my fifth year here. I got upset at Michael Gaughan today for the first time.

I stayed home today, as I always do on Tuesdays. I do some catching up and parlay-card setups, nothing I have to go into the office to get done. While I was home, I got a call from Tom Blazek. Michael said the line on the Chiefs-Chargers was too low. We had the Chiefs -8.5, like virtually everyone else in the world. Michael wanted to make it -9. I shrugged my shoulders, told Tom, what the hell, he owns the joint. We have to do what he says. A short time later, I got another call, this time from Jimmy Vaccaro. Michael wanted to make the Chiefs -10 and take $30,000 on the Chargers before we moved it back.

Well, it didn't take long. We got $30K pretty quick and I told my staff to go back to Chiefs -9, still the highest price around. I know the wise guys are usually looking to bet underdogs, especially home dogs. One of my mantras is, "Never say always, never say never." Well, whenever you get someone who likes sports and bets on them occasionally, and they look at a game they think is off, it's always always ALWAYS the same thing: The favorite isn't high enough. And about 90% of the time, it's a road favorite that really gets them going. Most guys bet the favorite and when it loses, they say, "That was the bookies' trap game."

News flash: Bookies don't set traps. Traps are when a guy bets a favorite that loses. They think the bookie must have known something. Yeah, we know the value of an underdog and try to put up the right number. But I gotta do what the boss says. Even though I know he's making a mistake.

The Clippers blew a double-digit lead in the NBA playoffs. That's three times. They were up 3-1 in the series when they wasted those big leads. Hold on to any one of them and they advance to the Conference Finals. I've really liked this Denver team all year, but I didn't think they had the talent to beat the Clippers. Man, was I wrong. First of all, they did have the talent. Second, they had the guts to overcome.

Jamal Murray and Nikola Jokic led the Nuggets. I'm not the biggest NBA fan. So seeing just how good these two were was a revelation to me. It was fun to watch. Murray I knew a little about and he's terrific. But Jokic is a unique player. He's listed as a center, but even at seven feet tall, he's like a point guard offensively. He's one of the best passing big men I've ever seen. People are comparing him to Bill Walton, which is about the highest praise you can give a player.

Now the Nuggets advance to the Western Conference Finals. I don't know who we'll need, but at least a part of me will be rooting for this team against the Lakers, no matter what.

Wednesday September 16, 2020

The Big 10 announced that it starts football October 24. They will play an eight-game intra-conference schedule in eight weeks and conclude on the day before the playoffs are announced. Obviously, they hope to get at least one team in the playoffs. All the other bowl games will fill out their schedule in the aftermath of CFP's announcement.

It's great news for me personally. But I've said it before and I'll say it again, I hope they can do it safely. The players will get continuously tested, but the rest of the student body won't. Neither will the tailgaters. Or bartenders, waiters, cleanup crew, ushers, ticket takers, and a whole bunch of others I'm not thinking about. And evidently, neither is anyone else.

Yesterday LSU coach Ed Orgeron said most of his team had already contracted COVID. What? CNN reported it and I saw the film clip myself, but there is virtually nothing else being said about it.

It was also reported that 27 players from Texas Tech had contracted the virus. They were life and death to beat Houston Baptist on Saturday as a 40-point favorite.

We've been hearing how there are some long-term effects of this virus. I realize that isn't conclusive science, but it sure looks like it to me.

Thursday September 17, 2020

This morning, Greg Doyle, a highly respected writer for the Indianapolis Star, wrote a story on how the various campuses are facing a slew of COVID cases. According to Doyle, the Big 10 presidents caved in to pressure. They saw three other conferences playing, all the NFL teams opening their season, and most high schools planning on playing. It's hard to stand alone.

The Big 10 tried to, but couldn't hold the fort against the tide of criticism it faced.

Now the Mountain West Conference is looking to join the party, trying to come up with a plan to put together an eight-game schedule to be done by December 19.

The battle of Ohio, Browns vs. Bengals, was the featured event of the day. The Browns really needed the win after a dismal performance in Week 1. There were a lot of rumors about a rift between their two highest paid and biggest offensive stars, Baker Mayfield and Odell Beckham, Jr. Well, they quieted the critics for at least another week with two strong performances. Meanwhile, the Browns opened as a 5.5-point favorite, quickly went to -6, then closed -5.5. We needed the Browns to cover. In spite of Mayfield and Beckham, they won 35-30, failing to get the dough.

The Tampa Bay Lightning beat the New York Islanders 2-1 in overtime to capture their series and head to the Stanley Cup Finals, where they face the Dallas Stars. I opened the Lightning -200 over the Stars in the series.

The Miami Heat fell behind the Boston Celtics by 17 points in the second game of their series. It looked like the Celtics would tie the series at one game apiece. Then the Heat outscored the Celtics by 20 points in the third quarter. After that, the lead changed hands throughout the fourth quarter until the Heat pulled ahead late for a 106-101 victory.

Even though it was a great day of sports with a slew of action, we eked out only a tiny profit. I thought it would be a lot better. But that's the way it goes sometimes. Last night we had this monster win with nothing but baseball going. I even had to call the book after they texted me the figure just to make sure I saw it right. This is one crazy business.

Friday September 18, 2020

Right at post time, a well-known local athlete came in to bet the Campbell-Coastal Carolina game. Right away, I had to tell him that we couldn't accommodate him. I know he plays real high. He told me he didn't want anything crazy, just $15K on the first half. I could handle that, but we don't book the first half on the added games. So he bet the full game for the same amount instead. Only then did he ask the price. Of course, he bet the favorite.

Another guy, fairly young, is betting huge parlays, 3- and 4-teamers, for anywhere from $15K to $30K. I don't know where these people get that kind of money. It's definitely not from betting sports. We've beaten him so far, but if he hits one, it will put a pretty big dent in our figure.

We beat the Coastal Carolina game, which was a nice unexpected pickup. Then we beat the parlay guy on both his bets for another $60k. We lost $20K on the Indians, a huge chalk at -220. They won 1-0. The Tigers couldn't even muster a run. The Lakers won and covered and the game went over, which is never a good outcome. Otherwise, it was a typical night of zigging and zagging. A bookmaker's life. Every night.

Saturday September 19, 2020

I'm hoping this is the last lousy weekend of college football this year. Next week, the SEC should be starting. The ACC and Big 12 will be playing more conference games, which should also provide us with some decent matchups.

The Dallas Stars won the first game of the Stanley Cup Finals. Their goaltending was superb tonight. Sometimes a hot goaltender can carry a team, especially in a short series. I believe Tampa Bay is better, but they might be up against it with Khudobin in the net for the Stars.

The Celtics won Game 3 of their series, a true must-win or else they would have faced the near-impossible task of beating the Heat in four straight. Instead, they're down 2-1, but the truth is, they've carried the play for most of the series; they've just wound up on the wrong end of the final with a late collapse.

They still have a big shot to advance.

Sunday September 20, 2020

Today was a bloodbath.

About halfway through the morning, my cousin Art Manteris from Station Casinos texted me. "We're in trouble." I don't like to hit the panic button too early, but I knew he was right. We could have still pulled out of it, but we needed to catch a break. Or two.

Of the 16 NFL games, we went 2-14. Some were double losers, where the favorite won and didn't cover, while the wise guys took the underdog with the points.

After the 10 early games, we were up a couple hundred thousand. You have to understand how the system works. Before all the scores come in final, all you do is punch out the losers. The winners haven't been counted yet. I showed Jimmy that even though we were up pretty big, the parlay cards weren't doing so well. That's a really bad sign.

Nonetheless, we still had a chance to pull out of it. In the Chiefs-Chargers game, we needed the Chiefs to cover the -10 or the Chargers to win outright. You could see early on the Chiefs weren't going to cover (a "trap" game!), so what we really needed was a Charger win. A couple of our big players like to bet money-line parlays, mostly with the day's biggest favorites. We had a few of those parlays going to the Chiefs. The Chargers started rookie Justin Herbert, who got the call minutes before the game. He played impressively, but the Chiefs are Super Bowl Champions for a reason. They tied the game on a late field goal and won it in overtime. Turn the result around, which would have been very easy to do, and we would have probably won for the day or at least been well ahead going into the Sunday Night game.

Instead, we were stuck big and needed a New England upset over the Seattle Seahawks in the finale. We opened the Seahawks

-4 and closed -5. The game went back and forth, mostly with us trailing. The Pats got the ball back with their new quarterback, former number-one-draft-choice and MVP, Cam Newton, at the helm. Newton looked great as he led the team down to the Seattle one-yard line with a second to play. With the Seahawks ahead 35-30, the Pats lined up in shotgun formation, heavy to the left side, prime to run Newton's left. It's a simple strategy: Put more of your men than they have at the point of attack and bulldoze them for the one yard you need. Like any strategy, it isn't foolproof. Seattle stopped Newton at the one-yard line. That one freaking yard cost us hundreds of thousands. It was the most expensive yard since Mike Jones stopped Kevin Dyson at the one-yard line in Super Bowl XXXIV. That one cost me a fortune personally; this one cost the company. But the South Point losing that much doesn't do me any favors.

Monday September 21, 2020

Today was the opening of Allegiant Stadium, home of the Las Vegas Raiders. There's a lot to cut through here, but let's start with the football part of it.

The Saints opened as a 6-point favorite everywhere, but in my infinite wisdom, I opened at -6.5. Bad move. I thought the Saints had enough talent to carry an aged Drew Brees, but he looked like age hit him suddenly and hard. They do have talent and coaching, but Brees is no longer a championship-level quarterback. I guess it could turn around, but I wouldn't count on it.

The wise guys were all over the Raiders tonight, taking the number all the way down to Saints -4. We took a bit back at -4 to even us out a little, but we still got our asses kicked again. Actually, it was a drop in the bucket compared to what we lost yesterday.

The Raiders looked pretty good offensively with Derek Carr as good as I've seen him. They have some talent on offense, but the weak defense will hold them back.

South Point Casino & Hotel

The South Point sports book

Father and son, Jackie and Michael Gaughan

Long-time business partners, Frank Toti
and Michael Gaughan

Hanging out in the sports book (left to right): myself, Kam Irvine, Jimmy Vaccaro, Circa owner Derek Stevens, and Vinny Magliulo

Poker night. From left to right: Vinny Magliulo, Richie Baccellieri, Jimmy Vaccaro, Ken Barlor, me, Nick Bogdanovich, Barry Phillips

Gill Alexander, my dear friend. I still love doing his show every Monday during football season.

Chris "The Bear" Fallica, who has become a good friend and confidant

My bull-riding maven, Christian Cianci

During the pandemic, it seemed like everyone had a picture of themselves in front of their bookcases. Here's mine.

Once I was out of quarantine after my bone-marrow transplant, some friends had a dinner for me at the Italian American Club. We had no idea another quarantine was right around the corner. Left to right: Lee Magliulo, Vinny, Ashley Eck, Nick Se-mich, Jimmy, Pam, me, Tom and Lisa Blazek, Kam Irvine, Lou Vargin, Trevor Darnell

Four generations of our family: my Uncle Jack, my daughter, grand-son, and me

Just before the looming pandemic, Pam and I got away to Santa Barbara for a few days.

Another shot of us in Santa Barbara. You'll notice I have a pen clipped to my shirt. My Uncle Jack got me into the habit of carrying one. In his words, "You never know when someone might want to make a bet."

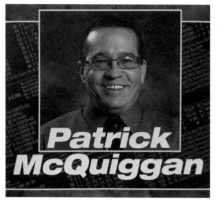

Patrick McQuiggan, my first personal loss of 2020.

With good friend Tony Stempeck. I wouldn't recognize him without a bottle of Jagermeister in his hands. COVID took him from us far too soon. RIP, my friend.

My godson Danny Larsen. May his memory be eternal.

On the NFL-Las Vegas scale, the story goes much deeper. The NFL has fought Las Vegas and gambling my entire life. I know they really didn't mean it. It was just posturing. They knew, like everyone with an ounce of common sense, that gambling made football number one in this country. They should have put away the bullshit cloak of puritanism a generation ago and partnered with us. Now they see the light. The word has leaked out that prominent owners like Jerry Jones and Robert Kraft have a substantial financial interest in DraftKings, vying to be the biggest bookmaker in the country. They're just the ones we know about. I bet a bunch of others have the same or similar investments.

Five years ago, Dallas Cowboys quarterback Tony Romo was threatened with a suspension for hosting a fantasy draft in a Las Vegas casino. A few years before that, Las Vegas was prohibited from advertising during the Super Bowl. Even now, Las Vegas is still not permitted to use the term "Super Bowl" when we advertise our parties. We have to say stupid shit like the "Big Game," or like most sports books use on their tickets, "The NFL Championship." Those are just the first things that come to mind. Their bullshit could fill a book. And it probably will.

Of course, the NFL owners never saw a dollar they couldn't take advantage of. Now that sports betting is legal in many states and probably will be in most states in the next five to 10 years, they've found another way to grab their piece of the pie. Las Vegas is the crown jewel in the gambling landscape, so now they've embraced the city with a billion-dollar stadium that has all the bells and whistles envied by everyone who cares more about marketing than fielding a great football team.

Despite my cynicism, this team in this town with this stadium will be a screaming success. The marketing is already off the charts. Someday the team might catch up to the hype. I know Coach Jon Gruden wants that. I hope he gets some support from the front office. It would be really good for the city. Plus, I'm married to a Raiders fan. As long as they don't beat the Steelers, her happiness makes me happy.

Personal note: In our contests, the fellas and I had the Raiders on all our entries tonight to cap off a good weekend. So, we went 4-1 on two entries and 5-0 on the other. So far so good, but not perfect. In our Survivor pool, we won on all 5 entries. Nothing to brag about there. Every favorite won, though a bunch didn't cover. Still perfect after two weeks. Can't be any better than that.

Tuesday September 22, 2020

The Nuggets beat the Lakers tonight in the only contest of significance. They came back strong after losing a heartbreaker on Sunday that almost no one saw. They're down 2-1 now and even though we lost on tonight's game, I need them to win the series or at least take it to seven games.

Wednesday September 23, 2020

The Celtics lost to the Heat to go down 3-1 in their Eastern Conference finals. It's hard to believe how the Heat came together this year. They're not devoid of talent, but they don't have a star-driven team like the others that have made any sort of noise in the playoffs.

The Tampa Bay Lightning also won to go up 2-1 over the Dallas Stars. Steve Stamkos, one of the NHL's best players who had been out since February, came back for the Lightning and scored a goal. It's not all good news for Stamkos, however. He played a few shifts in the first period and even though he was on the bench and skated to loosen up when there was a break in the action, he didn't get any more ice time. With or without Stamkos, the Lightning look like much the better team. But Lightning bettors shouldn't start counting their money yet. The best team doesn't always win.

Chapter Eight
September 24-October 22, 2020

"A wrong decision is better than indecision."
—*Tony Soprano*

Thursday September 24, 2020

The PAC-12 announced today the start of its football season in early November. A little later, the Mountain West Conference announced a schedule starting along with the PAC-12.

Mattress Mack's guy got hold of me today. Mac wants to bet on the Astros to win the World Series. We have it 30-1. We put Mac on for $10,000. So that's a $300,000 whack if the Astros win it. I don't think they can, but it's all in the price. I've seen a lot of crazier things.

Even a lousy game like tonight's Jaguars vs. Dolphins match-up out-handles anything else by so much, it's ridiculous. We did a ton of business on this game, while the Nuggets and Lakers are involved in a dramatic and consequential playoff series, but it's only about a quarter of the handle of the football. I can't tell you why, I can just tell you it is.

The Dolphins won and looked pretty good. Ryan Fitzpatrick, on the scrapheap more times than I can remember, had a big night. By the time you read this, he's most likely retired, but what a story he has to tell.

In the NBA, the Lakers could never quite get any distance between themselves and the Nuggets, but did manage to win the game and take a 3-1 lead in the series. It will take a miracle now for the Nuggets to pull this out. On my end, I'm still pissed at the Rampart, where we have a satellite book, for taking a big bet on the Lakers to win the series from one of its customers, knowing he was one of the sharpest guys in town. The sports book gets its allocation of the bottom line based on handle, not win. So it wants to take the biggest bets possible and leave it my lap to figure out a way to make it profitable.

Like I don't have enough problems.

Friday September 25, 2020

A couple of weeks ago, Alan Pecin showed me some of his ideas for South Point 400 props. South Point sponsors a NASCAR race every year and naturally, it's a huge event for us. This year, fans won't be allowed at the track, which really hurt us, like so many planned promotions that just were not able to come off because of COVID.

Alan handles a variety of things for South Point, including the movie theaters, outdoor billboards, and pretty much anything else Michael and Frank ask him to do. No doubt he has their ear and the 400 is of prime importance to Michael. Most of the things he wanted me to do, we were going to do anyway. Ohers are impossible; it's too much data for our computer system (win, place, show, exactas, daily doubles). One of his ideas was the winning-team owner, which I thought was a good one.

Until I fucked it up.

I don't know much about NASCAR and don't pretend to, but I did my homework and made those team-owner odds. Well, the customers made me aware all too soon that I had a bad number on Stewart-Hass Racing. I opened them at 20-1 and as I write this, I'm down to 3-1. If they race now, I'm on the line for a $23,000 hit. It's not much in the scheme of things, but I hate to be that far off on my oddsmaking. I know it happens, but damn, I'm pissed at myself.

Still, it's yet another example of someone tossing out an idea and then they're done with it. I've got to do all the grunt work to somehow turn it into revenue. Put out the wrong number and you're out $23,000.

It looks like the MAC is now joining the football party late in the fall, looking at a November start to the season with a 6-game schedule per team and a championship game.

Two playoff results tonight. The Celtics faced elimination, down 3-1 to the Heat. They were losing throughout the first half, but went on a 23-3 run to take control of the game and never relinquish it, winning 121-108. Game 6 is scheduled for Sunday.

In the NHL, the Tampa Bay Lightning won 5-4 in overtime to take a 3-1 lead in the Stanley Cup Final. Tampa was the beneficiary of a bad call in overtime that resulted in a game-winning power-play goal. I need Tampa, but it's a shame to see such key games end like that.

Meanwhile, worldwide COVID deaths passed one million. And to quote Ned Stark, "Winter is coming."

Saturday September 26, 2020

For years, I've joked about it being an annual rite of fall for me to overrate Oklahoma. Well, here we go again. I didn't particularly like Oklahoma -28 over Kansas State today, but I thought it was a good number. Oklahoma led 35-14 at one point and took a 14-point lead into the 4th quarter. They lost 38-35. There goes everyone's power ratings, including mine.

We have our first potential COVID-related situation in the NFL. A.J. Terrell of the Atlanta Falcons tested positive for the virus. Early money showed on the Falcons, taking them from -3 to -3.5. Today, money came back the other way, while the Bears +3.5 got gobbled up in the market. A lot of followers were just grabbing good numbers, but my hunch is the first wave taking the +3.5 was from people who knew something.

Besides Oklahoma losing, LSU also lost. Even though they were defending champs, their loss wasn't such a big upset. Mike Leach—a quirky character, but a hell of an NCAA coach—passed LSU silly with an offense not seen in the SEC. Just before game time, it was announced defensive back Derek Stingley, Jr., perhaps the number-one pass defender in the country, would miss the game for LSU. It certainly didn't help, but it also shouldn't have meant over 600 yards and 44 points.

Otherwise, most of the usual suspects won and lost, though Texas needed a late comeback and overtime to beat Texas Tech. We're just getting under way, but this year should be crazier than most. For example, Virginia Tech beat NC State 45-24 despite 23 players, including their starting quarterback, unavailable due to COVID issues.

In the playoffs, the Lakers beat the Nuggets to advance to the NBA Finals and the Stars went into a second overtime to beat the Lightning to stay alive in the Stanley Cup Finals.

Sunday September 27, 2020

Rough day. The NFL wasn't terrible, although we lost on it. We had so many games go over that we got beat on first- and second-half parlays. I'd just gotten done telling my crew to concentrate on the straight bets and that the parlays will take care of themselves over time. Well, not today. The totals parlayed to the sides killed us.

To add salt to our wounds, the Heat took the series, which wasn't good, and the final score, 125-113, flew over the total. Then the loss on the football total threatened to be twice as bad if the Packers-Saints game went over, which, naturally it did.

Big game tomorrow night and I'm sure we'll need the under again. That won't not be easy. Sheesh. What a month.

Monday September 28, 2020

We had a ton of live action going into tonight's game. As I suspected, the total was the biggest decision for us. When I talked about Super Bowl betting, I showed how we chart the possible outcomes throughout the last few days before the game. If you're booking right, those outcomes should improve over time. We do the same with big Monday-night games. And this was a big one. We didn't do anything drastic, just kept taking bets all day and adjusting the numbers accordingly. The result wasn't the greatest, Chiefs 34-Ravens 20. We opened the total 53.5, closed it 55, and took a lot of action under 55.5. So the total landing on the number hurt a little, but had it just gone over, like it looked like it would, it would have been much worse. Just call it the final notch on our record on a shitty weekend.

In hockey, the Tampa Bay Lightning won the Stanley Cup. A very good result for us in the end. For the season, which started way back in October, the NHL handle was a little over $10 million and we won over $400k. Not bad. If the Knights could have stayed in it a little longer, I'm sure our handle would have been higher. The win? You never know.

In our Circa contests, we were 3-2 on all three of our entries. Not bad if you're betting, but no bargain if you're looking to win one of these competitions. In the Survivor contest, we won on all five of our entries. I found out our group is in a DraftKings contest, too, and we're 10-5 through three weeks.

Tuesday September 29, 2020

We knew it was going to happen sooner or later. Today, three Tennessee Titans players tested positive for COVID, along with five staff members. They played the Minnesota Vikings last week, so although none of their players or staff has tested positive, both teams are under lockdown until at least Saturday. The NFL has said their games are intended to be played on time.

The Vikings play at the Houston Texans and the Titans host the Steelers. Both teams are being told to prepare for play and, at least publicly, that's the NFL's stance.

In college football, Notre Dame still has 20-some players who are under some type of COVID restrictions. It's just getting started.

The baseball playoffs got underway today with the early best-of-3 series to start. The White Sox beat the A's and the Astros beat the Twins. I was hoping to knock out Mattress Mack early with a Twins sweep, but it's not to be.

Wednesday September 30, 2020

This morning, they postponed the Steelers-Titans games when one more member of the Titans tested positive. Had they played under the current protocols, it would've been terribly unfair to the Titans, who couldn't even be in their facility until Saturday. It hasn't been determined when the game will be played, but it might be as early as Monday.

The schedule is full of baseball playoffs today, with games in all eight series.

The Astros advanced to the second round, meaning I still have to sweat Mattress Mack's bet. The Tampa Bay Rays, top seed in the AL, advanced by beating the Blue Jays. Then the Yankees pulled one out with two runs in the ninth to beat the Indians and advance.

In the NBA, the Lakers won the opening game of the Finals. Three key Heat players were hurt in today's game. Jimmy Butler returned. For Goren Dragic and Bam Adebayo, their returns are questionable. If they aren't 100%, the series could be ugly and over quickly.

Thursday October 1, 2020

The NFL looks like it has given up on playing the Titans-Steelers game. One more member of the Titans tested positive today. It sounds like they want to try to replay it at some future date, but logistics will be a challenge.

Tonight, we had a slew of baseball games, all significant in the outcome of the championship.   In baseball, the Braves eliminated the Reds, who were shut out in both games. The A's defeated the White Sox, which was very good for the futures book. The Padres beat the Cardinals to tie their series. The Dodgers eliminated the Brewers—and, of course, it cost us a shitload.

The football game was between two 0-3 football teams, the Jets and the Broncos. We did so much more business on the football, it's incredible. Two totally shitty teams playing a game that will more likely decide the number-one draft choice than have any bearing on the playoffs. We opened the Broncos -3, went to the Jets -1.5, and closed it pick 'em. Line movement always helps the action, but the action on this game was crazy. We really didn't need a result, but I'm glad the Broncos won, just because I hate the Jets.

The final figures for September weren't pretty. Handle was down 15%, the win down a whopping 70%. Yeesh. Those are some unsightly numbers. What can I do? I'll try to make it up.

Friday October 2, 2020

I returned a call from Mattress Mack this morning. He's looking to bet a ton on the Astros over the A's in the next round of the playoffs. We could handle only about $50K on a bet like that. He said he'd get back to me. I'm sure he will.

Meanwhile the Marlins beat the Cubs to advance to the next round. Great. Now I have a team on each side of the ledger that can cost me a couple hundred thousand. Most years, I wouldn't worry too much. But this is 2020, when it seems like a disaster awaits your every step.

The Padres also advanced, beating the Cardinals. Things get very interesting from here. I knock baseball plenty, but this playoff has been drama-filled so far.

The Lakers went up 2-0 on a depleted Heat team that still showed tremendous fortitude. It looked like they were going to lose by 30 early in the game, but they hung in there, losing 124-114, thus covering the number. The game flew over, unfortunately for bookmakers around the world, costing us like it usually does in these solitary events.

Bob Gibson, the great St. Louis Cardinals pitcher, passed away today. He was 84 years old and had been battling cancer. Gibson was the best right-handed pitcher of my lifetime and second overall only to lefthander Sandy Koufax. Look up his stats; they're amazing. In 1968, he was so dominant they had to lower the pitcher's mound. I was so fortunate to see many of the pitchers of that era, thanks to Uncle Jack. If a great pitcher was going against the Pirates that night, you can guarantee he was taking Zach and me to the game. And I got to see Gibson a few times, so I have some great memories.

One in particular that sticks out was Game 7 of the 1968 World Series. Gibson pitched against the Tigers and Mickey Lolich, a good pitcher in his own right, but never on the level of Gibson. Jack bet on Lolich. I thought he'd lost his mind. Of course, Lolich won and so did Jack. My God, Jack Franzi was amazing.

On a personal note, I had a doctor's appointment today after some blood tests yesterday. All my numbers have been improving since my transplant in July of 2019. Until today. It's only one number, but it's the main one. My doctor says it's too soon to worry. It could be an aberration. I think he means it, because he scheduled my next appointment for a month from now, like we always do. But I'm worried.

Saturday October 3, 2020

By the time I left the house and took the 15 minutes to get to work, I walked into the news that Cam Newton tested positive. Supposedly, all the other Patriots have tested negative. But one player alone getting COVID would be highly unlikely. Within a few hours, their game against the Chiefs scheduled for Sunday had been postponed.

Forty-five minutes before post time, it was announced that 21 players and two coaches will be unavailable for Virginia Tech today in its game against Duke. Well, at least we have a ton of money on Va Tech. We needed Duke pretty bad.

One customer beats the hell out of us. He plays 95% favorites and lays bad numbers. Jimmy and I talked about him earlier in the day. I said we just have to keep booking him. The numbers will catch up with him sooner or later. I pointed out another customer who'd been doing the same thing for a couple years. He was betting anywhere from $30K to $50K a game—until the numbers ground him down. Now $2K is a big bet for him.

So yesterday, this big player bet $20K on Oklahoma State -23 over Kansas. Minutes later, it came out that the Oklahoma quarterback was out and the number dropped to -21. Oklahoma State beat them 47-7. Then he bet Cincinnati -21.5 over South Florida for $10K. He could have laid -21 on Cincinnati anywhere else. We opened at Cincy -19.5 and he could have laid that if he'd had the foresight. Cincy won 28-7. That's why you have to keep booking these guys.

But he was still up $9K for the day. I've seen guys who bet favorites like this and expect to win every bet. He wanted to win back the $11K he blew on Cincy. He bet Oklahoma on the money line -300 over Iowa State, $60k to win $20k in what he expected to be an easy win. In a terrific game, Iowa State beat them 37-30. So he blew an extra $60K trying to chase an $11K loss he brought on himself by laying a terrible number. I expect to see him tomorrow.

147

A few other upsets on the day: TCU beat Texas, NC State beat Pitt, Tulsa beat UCF, and Arkansas beat Miss State. Some other big-name teams won and didn't cover, and of course some won and covered. Overall, it was a terrific day for us on a very good handle. The Saturday handle still isn't up to what it was last year, but with better games coming, we might get there yet.

Sunday October 4, 2020

The day started busy. I knew the guy from yesterday would be back with a vengeance. He bet us seven games, $30K each. He won 4, lost 3. He made a little, but with juice on our side, it wasn't so bad for us.

Weird game to close the night. All week, we took money on the 49ers over the Eagles. In the last hour, it was all Eagles. We got completely turned around and not from wise guys, but the general public. I can't recall seeing anything like it before. I don't think this was some wise-guy head fake to get a better number. It was just a strange occurrence. And, of course, it won.

Around the league the Panthers, Vikings, and Browns were the only upsets. Despite those, which were relatively mild, a bunch of teasers hit, along with most of the games going over.

We managed to squeeze out a slight profit for the day.

Just as I was leaving South Point, in an exchange of gunfire at valet parking, our security guards killed the gunman. I talked to a friend who witnessed the whole thing. He said security practically begged the man to drop his gun, but he refused. He made a move to aim at security and they had no choice but to shoot him. It's a shame. I don't know if the man had mental or personal issues, but when you threaten someone with a gun, something bad is going to happen. My heart goes out to his friends and family, but I'm glad it wasn't our guys getting carried by pallbearers this week.

Monday October 5, 2020

I did "Guessing the Lines" with Gill Alexander on "It's a Numbers Game" this morning like I do every Monday morning, then got busy finishing up my college power ratings and putting out the college numbers. All a typical Monday—very busy. I got into work just as the A's and Astros opened their playoff series. We don't need much in the game, but I'm still looking to knock out Mattress Mack on his Astros World Series bet.

A little after that, we had our first firing of the NFL season. Bill O'Brien, coach and general manager of the Houston Texans, was let go. It wasn't a surprise to anyone. I always rooted for O'Brien. He came in and rescued Penn State after the Jerry Sandusky debacle. He saved the school from being a MAC-level football program. I always thought he should have stayed at Penn State. He could easily have had a 20-year career with fields and buildings named after him. I'm very happy with James Franklin as Penn State's coach, but O'Brien made a mistake.

The Astros beat the A's (damn it) and the Yankees won big over the Rays. I didn't watch much of the Yankees' game, because of football, but I did get to see the Astros score eight runs and run all over the A's. They're going to be tough to beat.

You're always in the catbird seat as a bookmaker on Mondays. Today we had two games, the regularly scheduled Packers-Falcons and postponed Chiefs-Patriots. We did as well as we could to even up the action, but with both big favorites winning big, it was impossible to do anything but lose. And lose we did.

Wednesday October 7, 2020

Our handicapping-contest entries look like shit. We were 2-3, 2-3, 0-5 and 1-4. We might be eliminated already. We're still alive in our Survivor contests, where we've yet to lose a game. If we win one of those, that's still a ton of money, but there's still a long way to go.

In last night's action, the Lakers beat the Heat to take a 3-1 lead in their series. It was close throughout, but L.A. pulled away a little at the end. They went ahead 102-93 in the last minute, which was significant, because we closed the game Lakers -7.5. The Lakers let the 24-second clock expire in the last half-minute. Then the Heat took the ball and Tyler Herro hit a long 3-pointer as the buzzer sounded, changing the fates of countless bettors and millions of dollars. For once, I wound up on the right end of the miracle. I was nodding off during the whole fourth quarter, then went to bed with a smile on my face.

In baseball, the Astros went up 2-0 on the A's; the Rays tied up their series with the Yankees, 1-1. The Braves won their series opener over the Marlins and the Dodgers won their opener against the Padres. I wish I knew how much money the Dodgers have cost me this year. It has to be a fortune.

The Seattle Storm beat the Las Vegas Aces to win the WNBA—and I almost knew it was being played. I'm embarrassed to admit how little I follow the WNBA. I really only knew they were in the final game after the Storm won last night.

The NFL is talking about more stringent punishment for the Titans, with 22 team and staff testing positive. But no one is mentioning any details.

In baseball today, the Braves went up 2-0 on the Marlins, the A's stayed alive with a win over the Astros, and the Rays are on the doorstep of knocking off the Yankees, taking a 2-1 lead. The Dodgers held on to beat the Padres, going up 2-0 and looking unstoppable in the National League.

Thursday October 8, 2020

Yet another Titans player tested positive this morning. I don't know how long the NFL will let them get away with wreaking havoc on the rest of the league, but I think it's time to draw a line in the sand. They should have forfeited last week against the Steelers and if this week's game against the Bills can't be played, they should forfeit it, too. Still, one of the big problems in doing that was made public today. If games aren't played, including forfeited games, the players don't get paid. I don't know how that makes sense for the teams that did nothing wrong, but if I were a Steeler or Bill, I'd be pissed. Do nothing wrong and get docked a paycheck. We'll have to see. All this is uncharted territory.

Two games were moved today in the NFL. The Broncos-Patriots game was moved to Monday and the Bills-Titans game to Tuesday. We were fortunate that we never booked the games at all or put them on the parlay card, so that's one major headache alleviated.

Tonight in the NFL, the Bears hosted the Bucs. A Super Bowl rematch between Nick Foles, then of the Eagles, versus the great Tom Brady, then of the Patriots. It was the first time two Super Bowl quarterbacks faced each other later in their careers when both were with different teams. Foles, of course, won the original matchup. I knew we would need him to do it again.

We opened the Bucs -5.5 and the number sat there for a few days. Today, the floodgates opened on the Bears. Wise guys jumped all over the underdog, although the public was still firmly behind the Bucs. We went as low as Bucs -3 before the money started really flowing back in on the Bucs. We went to -3.5 and eventually up to -4 before we got some more money on the dog. I see it sometimes; the move will come on one side or another, but after the original rush, it kind of gets forgotten. I think that's largely what happened today. Sharp players were taking all the +3.5 they could get, but once they got down on that bet, they turned their attention elsewhere. Once we got up to +4, that retriggered their memories and back on the dog they came.

Early on, it looked like the Bucs would blow them out, but the Bears, behind Foles, scored two touchdowns in the last two minutes of the first half to take the lead.

The second half went back and forth with six lead changes

before the Bears hit a field goal with a little more than a minute to play to take a 20-19 lead.

Tom Brady had plenty of time to get the Bucs into position for a game-winning field goal. Then I saw a first. Brady lost track of the downs, thinking fourth down was actually third down, and made a much too risky pass down the field rather than get the first down they needed to continue the drive. Fortunately, it happened in my favor. It was one of our biggest Thursday night wins since I've been at South Point.

In baseball, the Astros beat the A's to make it to the ALCS, playing the winner of the Rays-Yankees series. The Braves, thankfully, put away the Marlins and will play the Dodgers, who swept the Padres, in the NLCS. I'll be rooting for the Braves and whoever wins the Yankees-Rays series.

Just as I was going to bed, one of our big players made a tennis parlay, Djokovic -330 and Nadal -750, $26,000 to win $12,300 in the French Open semi-finals. I expect to come to work in the morning stuck $12,300, but you never know. I have the Greek, Stefanos Tsitsipas, going for me, so I don't mind rooting for him. He plays Djokovic in the late match.

Friday October 9, 2020

I didn't wake up to a $12,000 loss, mostly because the tennis is still going on. Instead, the first thing I heard today that was a player for the Jets tested positive. The whole Jet facility was closed down and all personnel were sent home. We had to take the game off the board, although more thorough testing is underway for the Jets player. There have been false positives, and obviously the Jets, their scheduled opponent the Cardinals, and the entire NFL are hoping this is one more case. If it's a false positive, the Jets could be back in the facility today. As of now, the game is still scheduled for Sunday morning.

The rumors continued throughout the day that the Jets player wasn't actually positive, but we never got anything confirmed.

So we left the game off the board.

In baseball, we needed the Rays, who faced off with the Yankees. For both teams, it was win and advance or lose and go home. The game remained 1-1 until the bottom of the 8th, when Mike Brosseau homered off Aroldis Chapman.

Besides the fact that he hit a game-winning home run, some other drama surrounded the pitcher and batter. Earlier in the series, Chapman threw a 100-mile-an-hour fastball behind Brosseau's head. Brosseau wound up striking out, but then there was a shouting match before the two retreated to their dugouts. The next day, Brosseau hit two home runs for his revenge, though neither was against Chapman. Today, Brosseau hit the late game-winner after forcing Chapman into a 10-pitch at bat for the ultimate "fuck you." Let Chapman stew on that over the winter.

I don't particularly care for Chapman, in case you haven't picked up on that.

The Heat faced elimination in their game against the Lakers tonight, down 3-1. The Heat came out strong, surrendering the lead a few times and then only by a point or two. The game came down to the last few seconds, but the Heat managed to hold on. I didn't know much about the Heat's Jimmy Butler before these playoffs, but he's definitely my kind of player. Old-school all the way. He rarely takes a three, plays physical defense, crashes the boards, and drives to the bucket. I could see him playing anytime from the Bill Russell days to today. Tonight, he had 35 points, 12 rebounds, and 11 assists. I thought the Lakers would blast them in this series, but I was so wrong. The series is now 3-2, but it wouldn't surprise anyone if the Heat win the next one. Then, in a Game 7, who knows? I know what I'm rooting for.

I don't care for the Lakers, either, in case you were wondering.

In the French Open, Djokovic beat Tsitsipas. The Greek took him to five sets after being down 0-2, but ran out of gas in the 5th.

Saturday October 10, 2020

We might have a semi-normal Saturday handle.

The day kicked off with Oklahoma-Texas, Florida-Texas A&M, North Carolina-Virginia Tech, LSU-Missouri, Syracuse-Duke, and some lesser games. Don't scoff at Syracuse-Duke; it was one of the heaviest bet games of the morning.

Later today it's Kentucky-Miss State, Florida State-Notre Dame, Miami-Clemson, and Alabama-Mississippi.

One downer, in the NFL, the Chiefs reported a player positive. Their game with the Raiders tomorrow is in question.

It wound up being a terrific day, certainly for the bookmaker, but also for college football fans in general. The Texas-Oklahoma game went four overtimes before Oklahoma scored, then intercepted Texas in the end zone. In between, both teams missed overtime field goals that could have given them the win.

That five-hour fiasco figured to be the game of the day, but it wasn't. Alabama visited Ole Miss in a game that featured Lane Kiffin, a former Bama assistant, going against Nick Saban, probably the greatest college coach of all time. No former assistant has ever beaten Saban; coming into the game, he was 20-0, and he and Kiffin didn't part under the best of terms. Nevertheless, Ole Miss scored first and matched touchdowns with Bama until the fourth quarter when they just couldn't hold on. They covered, though, which was most important to me, but I was rooting until the end for an outright upset. It wasn't to be as Alabama won 63-48.

In other highlights, Arkansas got robbed on a late fumble that wasn't called, allowing Auburn to kick a game-winning field goal. Clemson faced a big test against Miami and dominated. Notre Dame got a bit of a scare from Florida State. Pitt blew an extra point in overtime to lose 31-30 to Boston College. Florida, which harbors national-championship ambitions, lost at Texas A&M. And last year's champs, LSU, lost at Missouri for their second loss in a row.

A day like this is what makes college football such an American treasure. Drama, pathos, fanaticism, athleticism, upsets, domination, and of course the anguish of winning or losing a bet on a referee's call or the fuck up of an 18-year-old. What's not to love?

By the way, we kicked some ass, which doesn't hurt my love for college football Saturdays like this one.

Sunday October 11, 2020

It was typically busy.

I hear different things about one particular outfit here in town—it's a group of poker players, fantasy specialists, or quants. Any way you cut it, they're pretty sharp and have a ton of money. It pains me to admit it, but last year I let them take advantage of me. I've always held the philosophy that if a guy is a gambler, I'll put him on for a big bet. Well, they were sending in different runners all the time late last year and betting big on the NFL, anywhere from $30K to $100K. Unfortunately for me, these guys won a lot more than they lost. It took a while, but I had to cut them way back. What hurts is now, if a stranger walks up to the counter with a big NFL bet, I have to assume he's with this outfit. I know it's just a matter of time before I cut back a guy whose action I should be taking all day long.

Some people don't realize that different individuals or different groups with lots of money have different opinions on games. Even so, many of them do quite well. I get asked, "Who are the wise guys on?" I answer, "There's no wise-guy union." Some like one side, some like the other. After all, there are only two sides in a game.

Sharp money, including the mystery group, came in on the Raiders plus the points against the Chiefs. Not to worry, plenty of Chiefs bettors were out there. Really interesting was that we had lots of money-line parlays with all the big favorites, the Chiefs among them. As the morning wore on, we were losing every one. The only chance we had was the Raiders over the Chiefs. The Raiders did more than hang on, they won going away. We needed the one outright upset and we got it. A real day-maker.

In one of the afternoon games, the Cowboys faced the Giants. The Cowboys won after two (that's right, two) touchdowns were taken away from the Giants on highly questionable calls. But the big story was that Cowboy's quarterback Dak Prescott suffered a horrific compound fracture of his ankle, which could end or at least greatly impact his career. Prescott is regarded as one of the good guys in the league, so folks are rooting for him.

In the Sunday Night game, we had our usual boatload of money on the favored Seahawks over the Vikings. The wise guys came in late taking the dog, mostly with the points, but a little on the money line, too. At kickoff, we were pretty even on the pointspread. The only thing we really needed was the Vikings to win outright. And if we got that, it would be one of the biggest Sundays we'd ever had at South Point. The Vikings controlled the game from the beginning. With little more than a minute to play, the Vikings, up 26-21, had the ball deep in Seattle territory. On fourth and one, they could have kicked an easy field goal to go up by eight. Being up eight with a minute to play, the Seahawks would have to score a touchdown and a two-point conversion just to tie the game. On the other hand, if Minnesota went for the first down and made it, the game would essentially be over. The television broadcast started showing the win probabilities of the various decisions and outcomes. Mathematically, it looked like going for the first down, a mere one yard away, was the right thing to do. Right away I thought, no way. If you miss, you give Russell Wilson the ball and all he needs is a touchdown to beat you. Needless to say, the Vikings went for it, didn't make it, and of course the Seahawks scored a touchdown on fourth down at the buzzer to beat the Vikings and ruin what would have been our monstrous day. We still kicked some serious ass for the weekend.

I do Gill's "A Numbers Game" show every Monday. Gill is big on the analytics and I had to ask, "When they flash those percentages, does it take into account who the quarterback is on the other side of the ball?" I learned, no, they don't. So Russell Wilson would have the same win percentage as JaMaurcus Russell? That makes zero sense, but that's the way they figure it. I've often said, whenever you're doing an analysis, be careful of your assumptions. We all make them. Most are entirely logical, but if one is off in the slightest, it can completely upset the equation. One more tidbit of information from a guy who often had to learn the hard way.

The Lakers won the championship yesterday. They deserved it, taking down the trophy under some very difficult conditions. LeBron James was playoff MVP, a well-deserved accolade, though I would have voted for the Heat's Jimmy Butler.

I have to give huge kudos to the NBA for a variety of reasons. I want especially to congratulate them for the way they conducted business and, in fact, the way they always conduct business. They ran this bubble about as flawlessly as you could ever hope for and it couldn't have been easy. We saw the players, coaches, and refs, but hundreds were working behind the scenes, like cooks, housekeepers, security, maintenance, trainers, and a whole bunch more. Any problems the bubble encountered were small or non-existent. I know the NBA isn't perfect. But it's a lot better than the other leagues.

Joe Morgan, Hall of Fame second baseman for the Astros, Reds, and Giants, passed away today. Morgan's glory days were with the Reds, where he won two consecutive MVP awards. He could have won at least two more. As a young Pirates fan, no one gave me more nightmares than Joe Morgan. Not only could he hit, he got big hits that crushed the Pirates at the most inopportune times. Man, was he tough.

As he was finishing out his career with the Giants, I needed them to knock the Dodgers out of the playoffs. The Giants had been eliminated earlier, but their last series of the season was against the Dodgers. The Giants played their hearts out and beat the Dodgers on the final day, sending them home, too. It was a big decision for me and I was so happy the Giants gave it their all. I remember a quick interview with Morgan as the Giants left the field, celebrating as if they were now in the playoffs. I'm paraphrasing the question, but an announcer asked Joe why they played so hard. I'll never forget his answer. "We ain't going. They ain't going." And he trotted off to the locker room. Now that's a competitor. What a great player. RIP Joe.

Monday October 12, 2020

Betting today was mostly on the underdog Chargers. Now that's a bit of a surprise, needing the dog on Monday night.

We worked on improving our position all day. In the end, we still needed the Saints to win and cover the 7-pointspread. The Saints looked bad for most of the game, down 20-3 at one point, but managed to pull out the win in overtime, 30-27.

In baseball, the Rays beat the Astros and the Braves beat the Dodgers, both excellent results for us.

We wound up losing just a peanut, rare on the best Monday during football season. And don't forget, we actually lost the game. What will I tell Michael? Superior bookmaking, of course.

In our handicapping contests, we still can't make any headway. Two of our entries were 3-2 and one was 2-3. It's slipping away quickly. However, we're still alive with all five of our Survivor entries. But it was close. We had the Saints on three entries. Down 20-3, I wasn't feeling very good. We won that game, but it sure didn't seem like we deserved it. Nonetheless, I'll take it. Survive and advance.

Tuesday October 14, 2020

Tuesday-night football was awfully weird. Even weirder was the betting pattern: the money on the Bills at -3.5, but the Titans on the money line. We were in a position to really score if we could have gotten the Bills to win by 1 through 3. Of course, soon after kickoff, I could see we had no chance. The undefeated Titans, who hadn't played in 28 days, completely dominated the formerly undefeated Bills, 42-16.

Nice day for us in baseball, as the Braves beat the Dodgers 8-7 to go up 2-0 in their series. In the American league, the Rays beat the Astros 5-2, putting them on the brink of advancing with a 3-0 series lead. We need to knock out the Astros because of Mattress Mack, but getting the Dodgers out of there would help, too. We've had a steady attack on them all year. I can see why; they looked like the best team in baseball. But as soon as the playoffs started, the Braves caught fire, going 7-0 so far. If we get the Braves vs. the Rays for the World Series, our futures book is in great shape.

Wednesday October 14, 2020

I thought I might have a few days to unwind. My wife is visiting a friend in San Diego and I'd planned on reading, doing a little writing, listening to music, and not turning on the television. No such luck.

Nick Saban, the greatest college coach of all time, has come down with COVID. Alabama has a big game this week against Georgia, coached by a former Saban assistant Kirby Smart. Saban is now 21-0 against his former aides, but I already liked Georgia in this one. The game opened Alabama -6, but now it's down to -4 with the revelations about Saban.

In baseball, the Dodgers scored 11 runs in the first inning and coasted to victory over the Braves, cutting the Braves' series advantage to 2-1. Clayton Kershaw goes for the Dodgers tomorrow, so this series could very well be tied by tomorrow night.

The Astros held off the Rays to escape elimination. They're still down 3-1, but it's baseball. No clock runs out when you're ahead. You gotta win that fourth game to advance. I hope the Rays can do it. I like Mattress Mack, but I'm not crazy about giving him a couple hundred thousand dollars.

Thursday October 15, 2020

The Astros beat the Rays again. The Astros are now down 3-2 and officially back in the hunt. And I'm officially worried.

The Dodgers, behind Clayton Kershaw, lost to the Braves. They're down 3-1 in a series in which they were heavily favored. Kershaw now has the worst post-season ERA of any pitcher who has thrown a minimum of 100 post-season innings. He's a sure Hall of Famer, but he hasn't been anywhere near the same pitcher in the playoffs. I'm no Dodger fan, but I feel bad for the guy—even though yesterday, a player bet $50,000 on him. So I had to root against him one more time.

Hopefully, the Rays and Braves can win tomorrow so we can go on to the World Series. And of course, put me in an excellent position with our future book.

October 15th is always a weird day for me. It was my mother's birthday and the day my father passed away. That's one hell of a 365-1 shot. Needless to say, the birthday celebrations for my mother were never the same after 1970.

Friday October 16, 2020

The Astros won again. Their 3-0 deficit has now turned into a 3-3 tie. The rubber match is tomorrow. Am I worried? Yyyyyyyeeeeessssss.

The Dodgers beat the Braves tonight, too, for a little more salt in the wounds. The Braves still hold a tenuous 3-2 lead in their series.

Saturday October 17, 2020

Let's start with the biggest news for me: The Astros lost. The Rays beat them to advance to the World Series. Finally. I don't have to sweat losing a couple hundred thousand to Mattress Mack. I can breathe a lot easier.

In the National League, the Dodgers won, forcing a Game 7 with the Braves on Sunday. At least one more day of rooting against the Dodgers and I hope it ends there.

College football was the main event for most of the world. The schedule wasn't great, but we're inching back to normalcy. The Big 12 took the day off, but the SEC and ACC saw some nice matchups.

Clemson showed why it has a claim on the top spot in the country. Georgia Tech scored early to tie the game at 7-7, thought they showed enough, then disappeared. Clemson beat them 73-7. And they looked every bit as dominant as that.

In the biggest game of the day, Alabama hosted Georgia. Georgia has out-recruited Alabama since Kirby Smart was named Georgia's head coach. Georgia led 24-20 at the half and looked like it was in this till the final gun. Wrong. Bama shut them out the second half, capitalized on Georgia turnovers, and won 41-24. Bama's defense isn't as dominant as it has been, but the offense looks better than ever.

In other games, North Carolina lost in a big upset to Florida State, 31-28. Notre Dame slipped by Louisville 12-7. Auburn lost to South Carolina for the first time in forever, 30-22. Kentucky smashed Tennessee 34-7 in an underrated rivalry. Our handle still isn't up to last year's typical Saturday, but no complaints. Plus, we had a huge day.

I hope this is the sign of a new trend (it won't be), but we had a big boxing match in Las Vegas. Teofimo Lopez, a 23-year-old surging lightweight champion, beat Vasilly Lomachenko to unify a bunch of championship belts. Besides being in Las

Vegas, it was also on ESPN, so no pay-per-view—you know, like the glory days of boxing. At least do that, boxing powers that be. Maybe you can get your sport back on the front page of the sports section.

Wait. Are there still newspapers with sports sections? Oh well, you know what I mean.

Sunday October 19, 2020

The action was heavy in the morning, with all the NFL games a go.

The afternoon had only two games, Dolphins-Jets and Bucs-Packers. The Dolphins opened -8.5 and we got as high as high as -10. It was one of the few games with any real teaser action, all on the Dolphins. The Dolphins won in a cakewalk, but the teasers didn't hurt us; there weren't many games for the other side of the teaser.

In the other afternoon game, the Packers opened -1.5 and got all the way up to -3. It was probably the most heavily bet game of the year. No wonder: It featured Aaron Rodgers and Tom Brady. Rodgers has been playing great all year, while Brady has been a bit sporadic. We got flooded with Packers money and early on, it looked like we were dead. The Packers took a 10-0 lead, then Aaron Rodgers threw a pick-six. Rodgers rarely throws interceptions, but that's sports. In fact, his very next pass was intercepted again, this time returned down to the Packer 2-yard line. One play later, the Bucs scored to make it 14-10 and they never looked back, scoring 38 unanswered points to win 38-10. It was huge win for the Bucs and dare I say, even bigger for us.

The late game was Rams vs. 49ers. The public was all over the Rams, but the wise guys were on the 49ers. The 49ers blasted them 24-16 in a game that wasn't really that close. It put a cherry on top of our day—in fact, the biggest win since I've been at South Point, bigger than any Super Bowl. I know to enjoy it. These wins are very fleeting. We can get our asses kicked tomorrow and lose that much back before you know it.

Contest update: Well, we finally lost on one of our Survivor entries. We had three of them on the Dolphins (winner), one on the Colts (winner, barely) and one on the Patriots (loser). We're still in the hunt with four of our five, so I can't complain.

Our handicapping isn't going so good, but we've got one Monday-night game on two of our tickets, so I'll update that part tomorrow.

Monday October 19, 2020

The NFL had two games today, Chiefs at the Bills and Cardinals at the Cowboys.

The Chiefs drew a lot of money and beat the Bills 26-17. The Cowboys lost 38-10. That was the least bad of our what ifs, so somehow we still made a couple thousand for the day. That was nice. But now it's on to next week.

In our handicapping contest, we were 2-3 on all three of our entries. We'll keep plugging, because they have some monthly awards, but we're out of it for the big prize. It's hard to believe for some people, but we have some of the best handicappers and veterans of this industry working to try to take down this prize and we can't pick enough winners to stay in the hunt. It shows you just how tough the NFL is to handicap. At least four of our five entries are live in the Survivor pool.

Tuesday October 20, 2020

It's really hard to believe how little action we book on World Series games. We had one $10K bet and nothing else of note. We still need the Rays to win the Series for the futures bets, but the game attracts nothing. In fact, I'm going out to dinner. I'll get the scores on the internet.

Wednesday October 21, 2020

Last night, I had dinner with some old friends, a couple from Reno. They told me about the passing of a dear friend of ours, Tony Stempeck. The Stempeck-Casale family owned the Halfway Club in Reno. His mother, Inez, passed away three weeks ago. She, her restaurant, and the family were Reno institutions. Inez was in her 90s. Her passing was sad, but not tragic. Tony's death was tragic.

On Monday afternoon, he had trouble breathing. It quickly got worse. He was at the restaurant, which he'd been running as his mother aged. The staff called 911, but by the time they arrived, only minutes later, he'd passed. It happened that quickly. COVID-19. We keep hearing how the disease affects different people differently. Tony was 63, one year younger than me. They told me he wore a mask and was as careful as business would allow, but he tended bar at the restaurant and certainly was in contact with a lot of people. He was a real character, as personable as you can imagine and a bit of a nut. A lot of people came by not only for the food, but to visit with Tony as well. I really loved the guy. I spent years watching every Monday Night Football game at the Halfway Club. On my last visit to Reno, he and I drank together like I'd never left. I had to call my sister-in-law to drive me home. There was no responsible way for me to get behind the wheel of a car after a night with Tony Stempeck.

I'll never drink another shot of Jagermeister without thinking of him. Rest in peace, my old pal. I'll miss you.

The Rays won Game 2 of the World Series tonight, 6-4, costing us a little, but putting us in much better shape for overall Series action. It's still amazing to me how we do more business on the worst NFL game on the schedule than on a stand-alone World Series game.

Thursday October 22, 2020

The NFL moved the Raiders-Bucs game from Sunday night, the featured NBC game to cap off a big day of football, to Sunday afternoon—if it even gets played. Five Raiders offensive linemen have not been cleared; they haven't even been permitted in the facility. Getting it resolved quickly with everyone allowed to play would make my life a lot easier.

To replace the Raiders-Bucs game, the NFL moved the Seahawks-Cardinals game to Sunday night. No way would the NFL blow a big television audience, no matter how much it hoped to feature the Raiders in their new town and the league's newest stadium.

Today, a customer came in wanting to cash a Cincinnati Reds season-win total futures ticket under 84. Well, of course they went under; they played only 60 games. The guy called Gaming, which now has to investigate. I let Tom Blazek handle it; I hate dealing with regulators. I noted earlier that we voided all season-win totals before the season ever started. What's amusing is the guy had a couple of bets on some teams over their win total, which we have records of refunding. So he's taking the money for the refunds, but wants to be paid for what he considers winners, the very definition of a scumbag move. He, along with the Control Board, wants to talk to me tomorrow. So I guess I can't avoid it any longer. Knowing my past good fortune with Gaming, they'll probably make me pay him.

Tonight the 1-5 Giants and 1-4-1 Eagles were the Thursday-night game. If the Eagles had won, it would have put them in a first-place tie, believe it or not. It wasn't much of a decision, but we needed the Giants +4.5. The score made the game interesting, if you had action on it, but it looked exactly like two teams that had two wins between them in 12 games. Fortunately, the Eagles won, but didn't cover, 22-21. And the game managed to stay under the total of 44.5 thanks to a couple missed extra points.

Not much of a win, but much better than losing.

Chapter Nine
October 23-November 21, 2020

"Doctors are great—as long as you don't need them."
—*Edward E. Rosenbaum*

Friday October 23, 2020

This morning, I tested positive for COVID.

I started coughing pretty heavily yesterday evening, then couldn't sleep much, with the coughing waking me up. I got up this morning with a lot of stiffness, then had to run to the bathroom with diarrhea. I took my temperature and it was swinging from a low of 97.0 to a high of 99.9. I got hot, then chilled. I knew something was wrong.

South Point set up a testing protocol with one of the local labs, so I went in to get tested. A few hours later, they let me know I'm positive.

I'm now in quarantine for at least 10 days, after which I can get retested. In the meantime, it's not that bad of a case, not yet anyway. I know it can turn on a dime, but at this point, I plan on working at home as much as possible.

When I told Michael, he said I was the safest person he knew of. I always had my mask on, never ate with anyone, and stayed back in my office. But it's a virus. I still had to walk through the casino. I still had to go to the bathroom. It's impossible to be completely safe unless you're completely quarantined.

Michael ordered the whole crew to get tested. With enough

positives, he planned to shut down the sports book. As of 4 p.m., we have only one additional positive. We'll remain open.

So many events in this book have been completely unanticipated; this is just one more. But I guess I can keep you informed about living through this disease, if indeed I do live through it. If not, I can tell you about how I'm dying with it. I hope that's not how this book ends. I'd much rather it ended with the Super Bowl, like I've intended all along.

We get Big 10 football back tonight, Wisconsin and Illinois for a little Friday-night action. We also have Tulsa-South Florida and Louisiana Lafayette-UAB. And Game 3 of the World Series. I'll have some TV sweat for my first night of quarantine, anyway.

Wisconsin, which had a solid program, but somehow failed to make it to the promised land due to mediocre quarterback play, might have found its savior. Freshman Graham Mertz set a bunch of records in his first start. Wisconsinites had been talking about him for two years and now I see why. They crushed Illinois 45-7. Look out Big 10; this team will be tough.

We finally booked some big action on Game 3 of the World Series. The Dodgers won 6-2, but the Rays hit a two-out no-one-on home run to put the game over. That cost us a few thousand. It's never under until it's over.

Gaming ruled in our favor in respect to the bettor who was trying to cash on the Reds under. Hallelujah.

Saturday October 24, 2020

Day 2 of COVID. This is not the flu. And what kind of permanent damage it might do to my—or anyone's—heart, kidneys, and liver isn't clear. People are telling me it's a 95+% survival rate. That's great if you're one of the survivors. But right now, we have more than 220,000 deaths in this country. Those 220,000 would tell you to stick that survivor rate up your ass.

Yesterday was the biggest day of new positives: 83,757. I'm so happy I got to contribute to that. Yeah, right.

I haven't announced my condition on Twitter yet. But it seems like a matter of time before it leaks out.

Pam got her results this morning: negative. That's a huge relief. With all the breathing problems as a lingering result of her brain tumor, she'd be in much more danger than I am.

We have a really good schedule today, easily the best of the year so far. I can't believe I have to stay home. Since I'm under quarantine, I can watch only one game at a time. And let me tell you, if you're used to watching nine at a time, like I do in my office, it really sucks. Anyway, I took in the Penn State-Indiana game. As a Penn State fan, I was unhappy with their performance. They had two interceptions, two missed field goals, and a fumble, and that was just in the first half. They fought back in the second to take a 21-20 lead, but the game went into overtime and Indiana got a good call to win the game.

Elsewhere in football, Greg Schiano is back at Rutgers and they suddenly have a team again. Northwestern bolstered its coaching staff and they're real contenders in the Big 10. Alabama won by a million, Clemson struggled a bit as a 46-point favorite, but pulled away late. Michigan won big over Minnesota in a major test for both. Ohio State beat Nebraska, which already puts them in the playoffs. They're like Alabama. They don't have to win their conference or even their division; they get voted into the final four because "everyone knows they're one of the best." Otherwise, it was mostly business as usual.

But baseball is a completely different story. It was one of the most dramatic endings of any game you'll ever see, let alone in the World Series. Down 7-6 in the bottom of the ninth, the Rays had men on first and second with two out when Brett Phillips looped a hit to short center. Kevin Kiermaier was running all the way. It was obvious he was going to score to tie the game. But Chris Taylor misplayed the ball, letting it get away from him briefly. By the time he tracked it down, Randy Arozarena was coming around to try to score as well. It looked like there would be a play at the plate. But Arozarena stumbled and fell all the way to the ground. Taylor's throw came in to catcher Will Smith, who thought he would need to make a swipe tag, but in his rush, he misplayed it. The ball got far enough away that Arozarena had time to regain his feet and slide home headfirst with the winning run.

Just an amazing ending that you'll see film clips of for years. We needed the Dodgers for the game, but since we need the Rays for the Series, I was happy to see it. Now we're tied 2-2 and heading for a dramatic finish.

Sunday October 25, 2020

In many ways, it was a typical NFL Sunday. But since I had to monitor it from afar, it seemed awfully strange. As I watched the action, the crew did everything I would have, so there was no reason to bother them. They did call me to see how I wanted to handle one of our big players. Other than that, I let them handle things and they did fine.

The results were a different story. We lost four games on essentially the last play of the game. We didn't get the best of any of those. But I kept in mind the inordinate amount of money we won last week. One week it falls great, the next it doesn't. If you can't live with it, you have to find a new profession.

The afternoon results were even worse. Last week, everything lined up perfectly for us; this week everything lined up against us. The only difference was we didn't have a shot in any of the late games. It started bad and just got worse.

As an aside, the Dodgers won World Series Game 5, 4-2, which didn't cost us much, but did push forward a bunch of live parlays.

All the early football winners were funneled into the late game between the Seahawks and Cardinals. So we were going to be a big loser no matter what. In the end, it was pretty bad.

We gave back about half of what we won last week.

There are times when you'll blow it and right where the world can see it. What do you do? Are you the kind that takes days to recover while you sulk? If so, get out of this business. You have come back tomorrow and do your job. And you might lose again. Then what? You stand up and get back in the game. It's not easy, it can really wear you down, but that's the job. And hopefully you have bosses who understand. And if they don't, they should get out of the business.

Above all, tap into your inner Jimmy Vaccaro.

COVID Day 3.

Last night, sleep was hard to come by. The coughing wakes you up too often to get into anything deep.

My throat hurts, my head hurts, my body hurts. I swing between sweats and chills. I wanted to do Gill's show tomorrow morning, but I can hardly speak, my throat is so raw. So I have to pass. Gill will tell his listeners that I'm COVID positive. I expect a bunch of political horseshit. It seems inevitable. I'm not looking forward to that.

Nonetheless, if you're too arrogant to wear a mask for your own safety, how about wearing one in compassion for your neighbor, your fellow man? Coronavirus survivors might tell you how this isn't any worse than the flu and for many it's not. But the dead speak very eloquently, too. You just have to know how to listen.

Monday October 26, 2020

Late last night, a customer wanted to bet the Bears money line (+220) to under 44.5 for $20,000. I'm not crazy about taking big parlays on the same game. I never know if the guy has an angle worked out or not. I know he certainly thinks he does. So I gave him $10K at those numbers, moved the money line to +210 and the total to 44, and told him he could bet it again at the new numbers. He did. Right now, that's the worst combination, so I've got to beat that. But every combination is lousy; some are just worse than others. All we can do is keep booking the action and see where we wind up.

The Rams beat the Bears 24-10. Both defenses looked pretty good, but the Rams' offense looked competent. The Bears' didn't. We actually won a little, which is remarkable for any Monday, especially coming off the NFL Sunday we had.

On our contests, we went 4-0 on Survivor. One other guy still has five entries alive. We were 3-2 on all five of our Circa entries. We went 4-1 on one DraftKings entry and 3-2 on two of them. They have some weird rules on DK, but we're 63% on two entries and 60% on the other. I know we're still in it for the Survivor, but I think we're just out of the money on the others.

COVID Day 4: Slept pretty good last night. Pam got me a humidifier, which helped a lot. After 40 plus years living in the desert, you'd have thought I had the brains to do that already, but of course I didn't.

The number of phone calls, texts, emails, and tweets I received after Gill announced that I was positive was incredible. It really warmed my heart. If any of you are now reading this book, thank you very much. And if I missed replying to you, my apologies.

Feeling a little better today, even though the coughing jags come occasionally and the sweats and chills are taking their turns tormenting me. It's now 3:30 p.m., I've been up since 6 a.m., and I'm beat.

Tuesday October 27, 2020

COVID Day 5: I continue to feel much better. Still not sleeping as well as I should. I'll probably need a nap sometime today. But I hope this trend continues.

Surprisingly, so far I've had to mute only five people on Twitter for saying stupid and hateful shit. I thought it would be a lot more. To be fair, I might have already muted a lot of guys for saying totally ridiculous things about COVID, so who knows. By the way, very rarely do I "block." Too many assholes take being blocked as a badge of honor, so I just mute them. That way, they don't know that I'm not getting their messages. Not that I give a shit what they have to say, just the world is full of enough negativity, no reason to hear it from someone anonymous.

In college-football COVID news, Florida hasn't played or practiced in two weeks because of the virus, then had six new positives today. That brings the total to 37 for the month. I'm not sure what's next for the Gators, but they're scheduled to play Missouri this week.

The New Mexico-San Jose State game had to be moved from Albuquerque to San Jose because of pandemic fears. The Marshall-Florida International game was canceled due to excessive cases on FIU. The North Texas-UTEP game was also canceled. Wisconsin is down to its fourth-string quarterback after the top three all tested positive. Just another brick in the wall.

The Dodgers won the World Series tonight. As much as I loved the game on Saturday night, tonight's game was why I don't like baseball the way I did as a kid. At one point in the game, there were 33 outs, 21 by strikeout. I tweeted that it was like an Eddie Feigner game. Google him; it'll be interesting.

Analytics also reared its ugly head when Rays' manager Kevin Casey lifted Blake Snell with one out in the 6th inning. Snell, a former Cy Young Award winner, was dominating. He'd given up one hit and struck out nine. Nine! He then gave up a bloop hit to center and got yanked. Snell was visibly upset, which you can understand. But more important, you could see the Dodgers were elated. They showed the Dodger dugout and they were all smiles. The Dodgers scored two runs with Snell's replacement, Nick Anderson, on the mound, then scored one later to win the game 3-1 and the Series.

As a bookmaker and oddsmaker, I appreciate analytics. It's a valuable tool. But if we take away the beauty of the game, what's the point? Someone pitched a no-hitter a couple years ago, but he walked five batters. The analytics guys were on a rant, saying it wasn't that great of a performance, because he allowed five base runners. There had been a recent one-hitter pitched by someone who had only given up one walk, and the point they were making was the one-hit pitching performance was actually better. Really? It was a no-hitter! There's something special about that. Don't take that away. If we lose what's actually enjoyable about watching the game, we'll lose it altogether.

We wound up okay on the Series. We'd taken back action on the Rays, where we already had a good position. So now it's goodbye baseball for ... I have no idea how long. I hope pitchers and catchers report in late February. I wouldn't bet on it, but I'm hoping. When will we see college basketball? NBA? NHL? I have no idea. Right now, we have college and pro football. That's our bread and butter, but we need a little more. We do have soccer. I hope that keeps the fires burning on a daily basis.

Tonight was a huge event, probably the social event of the year in the Las Vegas casino industry: the opening of Circa. The owner, Derek Stevens, as well as his top assistant Mike Palm, have become friends. I'm really anxious to see the sports book, which is getting reviews as tops in Nevada, if not the world. I hope they make it—without taking too much business from me.

It was black tie, with casino execs from all over the country well represented. I was invited, but obviously I couldn't attend. Too bad. It looked like a hell of a party. They went all out. Even my invitation had to cost a couple hundred bucks. Oh well.

Wednesday October 28, 2020

COVID Day 6: This is going to be boring. I feel pretty good. I still have the occasional coughing fits and my stomach isn't exactly right, but overall not too bad. I talked to my doctors at

USC today; they think everything is going well, but I have to stay vigilant. I hope to keep the news very boring until the test comes back negative.

In sports, we had some soccer today and NASCAR that had been postponed daily since Sunday. Otherwise, a bet here and there. The biggest news of the day was that the Wisconsin-Nebraska game was postponed due to numerous positive tests for Wisconsin. The game won't be made up, which could have a huge effect on the Big 10 championship.

Somehow, we still managed to lose $6,000.

Thursday October 29, 2020

COVID Day 7: Still getting a little better every day. Same issues as yesterday, so I'm not there yet. But I found out I can retest on Monday. If I'm negative, I can resume my normal life.

At 9 a.m., we put up the Cowboys-Eagles. Now that it appears that Andy Dalton is out for the Cowboys, who'll start Ben DiNucci, a rookie from James Madison. Meanwhile, the Chargers-Broncos and Monday-night Bucs-Giants are both possibly postponed for this coming weekend.

Later in the day, we learned that Trevor Lawrence, the number-one player in the country for the number-one team in the country, Clemson, has tested positive.

Lawrence will certainly miss this week's game against Boston College. Clemson is scheduled to play Notre Dame next week. The ACC COVID protocols call for a player to sit out 10 days before he's allowed to practice or play. If Lawrence tested positive Thursday for the first time, he won't play Notre Dame. Well, what do you know? He actually tested positive on Wednesday, even though they didn't announce it until Thursday, thus making him possibly available for Notre Dame next Saturday. Amazing how that all worked out.

We did have two college games and the Falcons-Panthers. Money started coming in Tuesday on the Falcons, who won

25-17. The Falcons have blown three fourth-quarter leads so far this season and a lot of fans were ready for them to do the same, but they held on. It wasn't a great game for us, but along with the college results, we wound up making decent money for the day.

Friday October 30, 2020

COVID Day 8: I'm almost there. Not quite, but almost.

I woke up this morning to news that no news for the New York Giants was good news. No new players tested positive. That bodes well for the Monday Night Football game, which I'm sure the NFL and ESPN will do all in their power to play.

The good news didn't last long. Shortly afterward, it was announced the Vikings had some positive tests and their game with the Packers is now questionable this Sunday. Not long after that, we heard the Chargers-Broncos game is still under question with positive tests on both teams.

Travis Roy passed away today. If you don't know his story, he was a freshman hockey player at Boston University. Eleven seconds into his first shift as a collegian, he was checked and fell awkwardly, tore his spinal cord, and was a quadriplegic for life. As a father and grandfather, those tragedies are my biggest fears. He seemed happy with his new life. It was incredibly heartbreaking, but Roy took the high road, helping to raise money for spinal-cord research. He was 46 years old. Rest in peace. You really made a difference.

It looks like the Packers-Vikings and Chargers-Broncos will both be played as scheduled. That's a relief.

Saturday October 31, 2020

COVID Day 9: Feeling good. Just about through this thing. But on days like this, I really hate working from home. I talked to the crew throughout the morning, but it's just not the same as being there.

We had a pretty good schedule. The PAC-12 is the only major conference that isn't playing. A few moves showed up during the run-up to the 9 a.m. starts, always the busiest part of the day. At about 8:45, some of our biggest players started coming in. These aren't wise guys, but they bet big money and can really hurt you. On one hand, I like them playing this late; I know they're betting into solid numbers. But when they do bet this late, I have nowhere to go to get some action the other way. I wouldn't mind getting a little something back, but I do like booking their action and just sticking it in our pocket. Except when they win. Because, like I said, they can put a hurting on us.

In college, there were a few upsets, but overall, the main competitors for the national championship played well and stayed in the playoff hunt.

Alabama beat Miss State 41-0. Clemson struggled early without Trevor Lawrence, though his replacement, DJ Uigalelei, played well enough. But the defense was less than spectacular and Boston College returned one fumble 97 yards for a touchdown as Clemson was about to score. DJ completed 30/41 for 342 yards with 2 TDs and no interceptions. He was the number-one passing quarterback coming out of high school. He's a big strong kid and will be a star once Lawrence moves on. Meanwhile, Clemson has already announced Lawrence won't play in next week's game at Notre Dame. Interesting. I thought they'd hurry him back as quickly as possible. I'm glad they're taking his health and recovery seriously.

Notre Dame had a methodical win 31-13 over Georgia Tech to set them up for next week's showdown with Clemson.

In the biggest game of the day, Ohio State beat Penn State. Ohio State was up 7-0 1:27 into the game, then 14-0 after another possession. Penn State tried to get back into the game and I was impressed by their fight, but they were outclassed by a much better team. What's the best team in the country? I'm not sure, but Ohio State is right there.

In the second biggest game of the day, Michigan State beat Michigan, 27-24. We closed Michigan a 21.5-point favorite. Things aren't looking particularly great for Jim Harbaugh. Opposing fans are even to the point of outwardly encouraging Michigan to sign him to a long-term contract. Of course, I fell into the "Michigan should be in the national championship hunt this year" crowd, like I do almost every year. That and overrating Oklahoma are annual rites of fall for yours truly.

In news only Nevadans care about, Nevada beat UNLV 37-19 to take the Fremont cannon back to Reno and paint it blue, as it should be. I might live in Las Vegas now, but I root for the Wolf Pack, not the Rebels.

And it's Nevada, not UNR, you heathens.

The sports book had a decent day, grinding out a nice win. I'm sure it will be busy tomorrow.

Sunday November 1, 2020

COVID Day 10: Feeling good. Wish I were at work, where no surprise, we had great action all day. The Steelers-Ravens game was the biggest of the morning. We had great two-way action and like many games of the day, I'm not even sure who we needed. The Steelers managed to pull it out when the Ravens' last pass fell incomplete in the end zone; a completion would have won them the game.

The Chargers did the (almost) impossible. They led 24-3 over the Broncos and blew it on the last play. That's bad, but in the last three weeks before losing this one, they lost leads of 16, 17, and 17. Four weeks in a row of coughing up leads like that is unheard of. In fact, no team had even done it three times. Not a record to be proud of.

Tua Tagovailoa made his starting debut for the Dolphins. With a fumble return for a touchdown and a punt returned to the end zone for the Dolphins, Tua didn't have to do much. The

Dolphins beat the Rams 28-17 without a lot of help from Tua, which is a nice debut for rookie quarterback. Let him get his feet wet. Are good or even great things to come from Tua? Maybe. But you couldn't ask for an easier way to get his career started.

Different sides were getting bet by different groups of wise guys, often against each other. That's great for business and on days like this, we just need the proper split to have a big day. We got the proper split and had a huge day.

The Eagles-Cowboys game that got moved to Sunday night due to COVID was one of the worst games I can remember. The Eagles won 29-3 with Ben DiNucci quarterbacking America's Team. The Eagles looked horrible and only the Cowboys ineptitude allowed them to cover. I continue to hear how the Eagles can make a real run once they get healthy. They'll have to prove it to me.

Today's win will go on November's figures, which gives us a nice start to the month, but we wound up with a terrific October. Without the NHL, our handle was down slightly, but the win was up 50% over last year. I'm just trying to keep Mr. Gaughan happy.

Monday November 2, 2020

COVID Day 11: I feel fine. I could have gotten tested today, but I'm waiting until Wednesday. If I test positive, I have to wait another 10 days before getting tested again. I'd rather give it a couple more days for a better chance to test negative. So Wednesday it is.

I did Gill's show remotely this morning. It felt good getting back to it after missing a week. I had a lot of well-wishers. Much appreciated, folks.

Decent action on tonight's Bucs vs. Giants game. Of course, the Giants have gotten the best of Brady more than any other team. The Bucs opened -10.5 and we went as high as -13 before getting any serious money back on the Giants. Naturally, the book needs the Giants, outright preferably, but even with the number would be okay.

The Giants led 14-6 at the end of the half for a big score for the sports book. One of the best first halfs of the year.

Daniel Jones, who really needs to learn to take care of the ball better, threw two second-half interceptions that the Bucs capitalized on. Late in the game, the Bucs led 25-17. The Giants got the ball with a little more than two minutes to play and converted two fourth downs. Then Jones hit Golden Tate in the end zone to cut the lead to 25-23. The Giants went for two, but the Bucs stopped them and ran out the clock to win the game. It would have been nice for the Giants to win, but it was still a huge Monday night for us in the sports book.

In our contests, we went 3-2, 2-3, 2-3   and 1-4. Not good, but we stayed alive with all four of our Survivor entries. A Bucs loss would have knocked out a few guys, which would have been nice, because we didn't have them. We're still in decent shape with half the season to go.

Some big news off the field. The 49ers lost their two most valuable offensive players, starting quarterback Jimmy Garoppolo and tight end George Kittle, for the season. They've had some huge injuries this season, but these just about sink them.

The Packers running back AJ Dillon tested positive. He was placed on the injured-COVID list, along with two other players just out of precaution. The Packers are in the Thursday-night game this week, so some decisions need to be made quickly.

The NFL is contemplating expanding the playoffs to 16 teams this year, partially in response to the potential of games being missed by COVID. Great. I booked every team in the league with a yes/no to make the playoffs. That might cost me some, but I'll probably make up for the losers with an extra weekend of the playoffs.

In college football, the MAC is coming back this week,

opening its season on Wednesday night. It's brilliant marketing. They have the night to themselves. All their games will be on TV in one form or another. I love it.

Tomorrow is Election Day. It's going to be a long day. And even a longer night.

Tuesday November 3, 2020

There wasn't a single sporting event to bet on yesterday, but there was betting. Oh, there was betting.

The presidential-election betting was some of the wildest action I've ever seen in my life.

Now, just a reminder, kids. There's no "official" line. Different places have different prices. Please keep that in mind.

Joe Biden started the day as a -200 favorite. The odds shifted slightly toward Trump as the day went on. As the polls began to close, the odds had dropped to Biden a very slight favorite, somewhere between -120 and -140.

Somewhere around 3 p.m. Pacific, Trump went to a slight favorite. By 3:30 p.m., he was up to -300. What probably opened the floodgates was Trump taking Florida. Bettors immediately thought, "It's just like 2016!" It wasn't. Biden expected to lose Florida. Those in the know, and not just the Biden camp, were well aware of it. You could see by the last few days of the campaign, neither Biden nor Kamala Harris bothered to go to Florida. If they thought it was in play, at least one of them would have campaigned there.

As Trump supporters poured money into the markets, at least one bookmaker had the price up to Trump -700. I fell asleep at one point relatively early in the evening. The odds had dropped to Trump -200, still a fairly significant favorite. At that time, following all the information and misinformation from the news and betting markets, I thought Biden had a very slim chance of becoming president.

Biden spoke to the nation. His message was short and simple,

181

even though he's known for being long-winded. To paraphrase, he said we're still in this. All the votes need to be counted and when they're finished, we're going to win.

Conversely, Trump declared victory. He wanted some states to continue counting votes and others to stop.

Wednesday November 4, 2020

I woke up this morning at six. The first thing I saw was Biden -400. What the hell happened? Oh, I see. They counted the votes.

Last night, many of my compatriots from our business said how much more accurate the betting markets are than the pollsters and pundits. I haven't heard much from them this morning, since Trump has gone from a -700 favorite to a +400 underdog.

I was briefly out of gaming and involved with an investment firm. A Wall Street veteran told me that the wisdom on the Street is that the betting markets are the most efficient markets known to man. I told him he was nuts. I've seen it every day for 40 years and they're tremendously inefficient.

Everyone needs to understand, news organizations declare winners based on some analytic metric. They want to be right, but they also want to be first. Nevertheless, they don't do the count. States don't declare results until all the votes are counted. Then they certify the election as official. That's how it works. That's how it always worked. And the president isn't actually officially elected until the Electoral College votes, which is on the Monday after the second Wednesday in December, this year December 14. It's not official until then.

As I'm writing this Wednesday morning, Biden leads in Wisconsin and Michigan. He's behind in Pennsylvania, North Carolina, and Georgia. Nevada is rated a tossup. The race could come down to Nevada.

It's now Wednesday afternoon. The straggling votes are coming in for Biden. By the way, this is what had been predicted for weeks. Trump would probably lead on Election Night, but when all the mail-in and early votes were counted, Biden would be ahead.

The latest odds have Biden -500 in Pennsylvania, -190 in Georgia, -850 overall. Arizona, Nevada, and North Carolina are still up in the air. Some election betting is still going on, but it has slowed to a trickle compared to yesterday.

COVID-19 has slipped off the front page for a day, but it's still raging. Positive test results surpassed 100,000 in the U.S. today for the first time, with more than 1,000 deaths. In sports, Lions quarterback Matthew Stafford was exposed to the virus and will likely miss this week's game against the Vikings. Also, due to multiple positives on Louisville, their game with Virginia has been pushed back a week. The 49ers now have four players positive. Their Thursday night game against the Packers is still on, but it moved from Packers -4.5 to -7.5. It might even go higher.

In sports broadcasting, Fox's entire early college-football TV team, Urban Meyer, Reggie Bush, Matt Leinart, and Rob Stone, have been put under quarantine for COVID protocols and will not be on the air Saturday morning.

Personally, my COVID test came back negative today, but Pam's came back positive. She's completely asymptomatic, but her test results contributed to that record number of cases. I'm not sure what's next for us. I want to go back to work, but I don't really want to abandon my wife right now. Plus, I might not be allowed to return to work until she's negative.

Thursday November 5, 2020

Late yesterday, the UTEP-Florida International game was canceled. Now Navy-Tulsa and Army-Air Force are off the board, along with Washington-California and Louisiana Tech-North Texas.

In the NFL the Texans shut down their facility due to a positive test.

Earlier in the week, I talked about the MAC having a captive audience on Wednesday night. We didn't do much business. After talking to other bookmakers abound town, that was the consensus. I'm disappointed. I think they play a good brand of football.

Tonight, however, the action was sensational. We opened the Packers -4 over the 49ers, went as high as -8, then back down to -6 at the close. We opened the money line at -280, went as high as -380, then closed -290.

The action spilled over into the college, too. We had two Mountain West Conference games, Nevada-Utah State and Wyoming-Colorado State, but neither was anything special. Nonetheless, the action would compare to our most heavily bet games on a typical Saturday.

I was rooting for the Packers tonight for two reasons. First, I liked them after seeing the mountain of injuries for the 49ers. I just didn't think the 49ers could compete. I stayed ahead of the number as it rose. Second, the wise guys bet the hell out of the 49ers all the way to post time. When the wise guys are all over the dog and the public is on the favorite, I'll always root for the public. The wise guys never seem to run out of money.

The Packers won 34-17, but the game went over with four seconds left when the 49ers scored from the 1-yard line. Oh well. So it goes sometimes. We still wound up with a pretty decent day.

In election betting, I saw one site has Biden -2000/Trump +900. But I sure don't see anyone betting anything on Trump and I wouldn't expect any bookmaker taking a serious bet on Biden. It's pretty much over at this point.

Since Pam tested positive, it turns out I can't go back to work for at least 10 days. This really sucks. But I don't want to get anyone else sick.

Friday November 6, 2020

Pam is doing well. Thank goodness.

First day of the Breeders Cup today. I did Ron Flatter's podcast the other day with Vinny Magliulo, Duane Colucci, and Johnny Avello—three New York Italians and me. My kind of crowd.

Nonetheless, I didn't cash a ticket. What happened to me? I used to be a great horse handicapper. In my first book, I tell the story of winning a handicapping tournament. I was following it every day, playing every day, and winning.

Now? The game has changed and I haven't changed with it. Horses, especially the best, run an average of only six times a year. When I learned to handicap, horses ran much more often. One of my mantras, horses run themselves into shape and they run themselves out of shape, no longer applies. Maybe it does with cheap claimers, but that's not the kind of races I bet. I bet the big races and almost none of those horses have run themselves out of shape coming into a particular race. So there goes my sharpest angle.

If I were at a track where the horses ran fairly often and I got to know the jockeys, trainers, and condition book, I could probably do as well as I did in the past. But right now, that doesn't look likely to happen.

I've learned to manage my money a little better. I used to bet a couple hundred a race. Now it's not more than $50 and usually a lot less. Oh well. I enjoyed it immensely when I had it going my way. One more concession to age.

Only three games tonight, but we still managed to have a really good day. The big game was BYU-Boise State. BYU throttled them. They'd be a strong opponent for anyone in the country.

Saturday November 8, 2020

In spite of losing 10 games to COVID, we still had a pretty full schedule.

There were no really big plays early, but as the day advanced, some of the bigger players developed opinions. Big steam games were Virginia Tech over Liberty, Houston plus the points vs.

Cincinnati, North Carolina over Duke, Michigan over Indiana, Ohio State minus a million over Rutgers, Penn State minus half a million over Maryland, Oregon over Stanford, Oregon State over Wash State, Oklahoma minus a million over Kansas, Oklahoma State over Kansas State, Texas A&M over South Carolina, West Virginia plus points vs. Texas, Northwestern over Nebraska, Arkansas vs. Tennessee and Clemson over Notre Dame.

Now that I look at it, we had a lot of big decisions. We lost a bunch and won a few. While the results were rolling in, I thought we were in for a really rough day. We made a little money, just a nice grind.

Pam continues to do well.

And the powers that be finally determined that Joe Biden won the presidency.

Sunday November 9, 2020

We didn't lose any games. That was victory number one.

After that, we had an excellent handle with a good slate of games. Just about every NFL team is still harboring hopes of making it to the playoffs. (The Jets don't play until tomorrow, so they don't count.) We got through the early games with a mix of dogs and favorites. We went into the afternoon with a lead and managed to extend it by winning two of the three.

The Sunday Night game was slated to be a classic with two old warhorses, Brady and Brees, squaring off in a divisional matchup. The two future Hall of Famers have been trading positions as the all-time leader in touchdown passes and probably will continue to do so for the rest of the season. It had all the makings the best game of the week, if not the year. It was anything but. Brees and the Saints took an early lead and won 38-3. The Bucs kicked a late field goal to save face by not being shut out. It was a total beatdown.

I thought the Bucs and Brady were heading to a Super Bowl. Instead, they got throttled in every aspect of the game. An aberration or a sign of things to come?

In other games, Josh Allen of the Bills beat Russell Wilson and the Seahawks with 415 passing yards. After a few mediocre games, Allen is right back in the MVP conversation.

Two young future stars, Kyler Murray of the Cardinals and Tua Tagovailoa of the Dolphins, matched scores until the Dolphins pulled out a late victory with a 34-31 win.

The Chiefs were heavily favored over the Panthers and squeaked by 33-31. The Steelers were two-touchdown favorites and managed to stay undefeated, though barely, with a 24-19 win over the decimated Cowboys. The Chargers lost on the last play of the game, again, to the Raiders, 31-26.

Just a typical day of NFL football. The gambling gods smiled down on us again.

Monday November 9, 2020

The action today was snail-paced, with a lousy matchup between two division rivals, the Patriots and Jets. I'm sure the game looked attractive before the season, but boy, are these two teams disappointments. The Pats post-Brady have been a letdown and the Jets are to the NFL what the Titanic was to White Star Lines shipping.

The Pats still went off as considerable favorites. We opened the Pats -7.5, while some -7 was out there. The +7.5 is an automatic take for the wise guys, which was exactly what I wanted. We went to -7, then the money started pouring in on the Pats. We didn't get up to -10, but others did. We closed Pats -9. We needed the Jets, but only for a little. A Jets outright win would be a good result, but like typical Monday nights, we were probably losing no matter what.

The lousy game on paper wound up being pretty good on the field. The Jets led throughout most of the game, looking to get their first win. The Pats tied it late, then after a 3-and-out by the Jets, got the ball back with less than a minute to play. They managed to get their kicker in position for a 51-yard field goal attempt and he converted, giving the Pats a 30-27 win.

The Pats managed to save face. Nice for them, but even better for me. Our group has four entries left in the Survivor contest and we put two of them on the Pats. We had the Steelers and Chiefs on the others, so we're still in pretty good shape. A huge decider this season will be Thanksgiving, with three games, considered a separate week. We've kept some powder dry to make decisions that day and I'm hoping others didn't have that foresight.

The rest of our contest entries were total garbage. We went 1-4 on our three entries. Guys who've been in this business for 40 years or so look more at line value than picking winners. I can't complain. My picks were as bad as everyone else's. So it looks like we're out of the handicapping contests. But if we can still win the Survivor, well, that will be pretty darn good.

Tuesday November 10, 2020

Big news for the league's only unbeaten team: Steelers' tight end Vance McDonald tested positive and five of his teammates, including Big Ben Roethlisberger, have been put on the watch list. We had to take the Steelers-Bengals game off the board. Once you're on the list, you have to pass five COVID tests in five days before you can be cleared to play.

The SEC canceled LSU-Alabama and Texas A&M-Tennessee. The college players just aren't following the protocols the way they're supposed to.

In defense of the players, they're just kids. They've been asked to follow these restrictions when for some of them, it's their first time away from home. And once they're out doing what kids do, it's almost impossible not to pass this disease around.

On the bright side, Pfizer, one of the biggest pharmaceutical companies in the world, announced a COVID vaccine that apparently has a 90% success rate. But we're still months away from delivering it around the country, let alone worldwide.

Wednesday November 11, 2020

More postponements in the SEC. Nothing official yet, but it looks unlikely for the Cal-Arizona State game. Cal's entire defensive line is under quarantine, which the city of Berkeley said won't end until November 17. Then the Ohio State-Maryland game was canceled due to an abundance of Terrapin positives.

One thing I got right this season was home-field advantage is essentially meaningless. According to Andrew Siciliano of the NFL Network, home teams are 65-67-1 straight up and according to Dave Tuley of VSiN, home teams in the NFL are 61-70-2 ATS. I've been making my numbers with no home-field advantage built into the line. It looks like that's the way to go.

Another night of MACtion. We blew a little. Nothing more than a peanut. Mr. Gaughan won't have to sell the plane.

Thursday November 12, 2020

The Masters action was incredible this year. It's unquestionably the biggest betting event of all the golf majors, but I wasn't sure how the November date instead of April would affect it. Part of it is very little competition from the NHL or NBA; other than football, it's the only game in town.

Paul Casey leads by 2 strokes after a first round shortened by darkness. Six figures in our pocket if he holds on. That's almost a joke. I don't start looking hard until Saturday at the earliest. Long way to go.

We lost three more college games today. Paul Finebaum, one of the leading voices in college football, made a significant point that the teams doing exactly what they should be are the ones being punished because of their opponents. He's right.

In the Thursday-night game, Titans and Colts in a division

game, we opened Titans -1.5. While the public is on the Titans, the wise guys are on the Colts. We got to the Colts -1 at one point before the money started coming back from the public to overpower it.

We closed the game at a pick 'em. The Titans took the lead, but the Colts slowly ground them down. They outgained them 430 to 294 and returned a blocked punt for a touchdown. I didn't see it coming, but you have to respect the wise guys who did.

In college, Boise State faced off against Colorado State. Our one big money-line player bet Boise -550 to win $10,000. The wise guys came back on Colorado State +14.5 once it was announced Boise would be missing a total of 14 players. Nine were positive and another five sat because of contact tracing. We booked a little on the money line, but not enough to offset the $10K. We're okay on the pointspread, but straight up we needed the big upset. We didn't get it. Boise crushed them.

We still wound up with a pretty good bottom line for the night.

Early in the day, I sent out a tweet about who the wise guys were on in the Colts-Titans game. It got a positive response. Jeff Fogle, my Twitter and VSiN buddy, told me I should do it a lot more often. Jeff is a smart guy. I think I'll take his advice.

On another personal note, my doctors at USC liked the results of a recent blood test. It was a big relief, because my last test results weren't so good. My doctor told me it was probably an aberration, which it was. But I was less than confident. This confirmed it really was just one of those things. Phew.

Friday November 13, 2020

I don't know why, but the wise guys love betting against Cincinnati. Unfortunately, the public overpowers them. They keep winning and tonight they blew out East Carolina and poured it on at the end. Last week, they won by 28 and lost in the polls, so they made sure that wasn't going to happen. They won 56-17 and even had a fourth-quarter fake punt. Another chalk winner was Florida Atlantic, winning 38-19 as 10-point favorites over Florida International. Iowa-Minnesota was fairly evenly bet, but Iowa blew them out 35-7.

Saturday October 14, 2020

Pam went in to get retested. She's been completely asymptomatic the whole time, more than 10 days. When she tested positive, I couldn't believe it. The lab told us she might test positive for months, even though she doesn't really have it.

Well, shit. You couldn't have told me that before I blew another $150 to get her tested? They said she should consider herself COVID free now that she's had that much time with no symptoms.

I called our HR director and she said it's okay for me to go back to work tomorrow. Things like this make you realize how much you love your job. I know for me, it's not just a job. It's a huge part of who I am. I know that's not the right thing for a lot of people, but it is for me.

Late Friday night, I got a text from a good friend in the Chicago media who has excellent information on the Big 10 teams. He told me four starters and a cluster of others were out for Michigan. They had a big game with Wisconsin, which hadn't played in weeks. We opened Wisconsin -4 and were getting play on the favorite. I called the book and went to -6. I thought maybe I could get ahead of it, but no such luck. We went as high as -7.5 before we got some play back on Michigan. It's probably the biggest action game of the year for us so far and Wisconsin beat them 49-11.

The rest of our day went like that, too. It seemed like every side we got steamed on got there—Florida over Arkansas, Indiana over Michigan State, Nebraska over Penn State, Houston over South Florida, Virginia over Louisville, Notre Dame over Boston College, Oregon over Wash State. All winners. We won a couple, but I forget about those pretty quick. I'm like every other bettor in the world: It's my God-given right to win every bet I ever make (or book).

Well, not today. Our butts got kicked pretty good. I keep telling myself I'll still have the same breakfast in the morning. But it tastes a lot better after a winning day.

Sunday November 15, 2020

By losing yesterday, we started the day behind the eight ball. The one bright spot was The Masters tournament. Dustin Johnson, already the number-one-ranked golfer in the world, started the day with a 4-stroke lead. We did well with Johnson and I was confident he would hold on and win the tourney.

The downside was there wasn't much drama; Johnson was never really threatened and coasted to victory. He shot 20-under par for the four days, breaking Tiger Woods' Masters scoring record and tying for the best round in the history of the majors. Any of them.

It wound up we needed that cushion. The rest of the day wasn't so hot.

Because of The Masters, shown on CBS, the football schedule had five early games and six games in the later slot. It was awesome. Why they don't do a relatively equal split every week is beyond me. Obviously, it has something to do with TV ratings.

The big early steam was on the Browns, who got bet from -3.5 all the way up to -5, plus big money-line play, over the Texans; the Eagles, who also were bet from -3.5 to -5 over the Giants; Washington, which opened as a 4.5-point dog and went as low as +2.5 before we got money back on the Lions and closed the game at +3. We also had smart money on the Jaguars +14 against the Packers and big public play on the Bucs -6 over the Panthers.

The Browns won by 3, so we beat the spread play, but lost pretty big on the money line. The Giants won outright, a good game for us. The Lions won by exactly 3 with a 59-yard field goal on the last play of the game. That was disastrous, a clean middle for the players. The Packers won by 4, so the wise guys cashed on that game. The Bucs won by a million, so the public kicked our asses there.

Not a good morning, to say the least.

In the afternoon slate, Steelers against the Bengals, the wise guys were all over the Bengals, but the public was firmly on the Steelers. The Raiders opened -5.5 and got bet down to -3.5 over the Broncos. The Bills squared off against the Cardinals; we had good two-way action on that game—unfortunately, which I'll go into later. The wise guys loved the Rams, who opened -1.5 over the Seahawks and pushed the line up to -3. No major moves on the Saints, -9.5 over the 49ers, but the public was on the Saints just as you'd expect. The Dolphins opened -2.5 over the Chargers. It was one of those games where they took away your wise guy membership card if you didn't take the short price on the 2-6 Chargers over the 5-3 Dolphins, one team that hasn't figured out how to win against a team that finds a way to win most weeks.

The Steelers trounced the Bengals, so we beat the wise guys, but got hammered by the public. The Raiders annihilated the Broncos, beating the wise guys again, but giving the public a nice win. The Rams beat the Seahawks 23-16, a win for the wise guys, though there was plenty of public money on the Seahawks. The Saints beat the 49ers 27-13, more due to 49ers' ineptitude than Saints dominance. And no surprise to me, the Dolphins beat the Chargers 29-21; that crushed the wise guys. The public used actual common sense and had the team that likes to win against the team that finds it a mystery to score more points than their opponents.

All in all, the results weren't very good. The parlay cards that hit lost mostly to the public and split with the wise guys. We went into the Sunday-night game needing the Pats, a 7-point underdog, to beat the Ravens. I didn't like our chances. I cut the potential loss down from mid-six figures, but if we couldn't pull out the outright win, we were looking at a pretty sizable loss for the day.

Bill Belichick came up with a brilliant game plan (big surprise) and the Pats upset the Ravens 23-17. It was a huge win for the Pats, still in the playoff race, and a monstrous result for us. We beat the parlays and teasers on the Ravens, though I did have to give some back to the wise guys who I got to bet the Pats and take some of the risk off my hands.

The bottom line was we wound up okay for the day, winning the theoretical percentage we're entitled to hold. By the way, that rarely happens. It smooths out over the long run, but it's a bumpy ride getting there.

Now for the Cardinals-Bills game. We opened the Cardinals -1.5, went to -3, then back and forth from -2 to -3 all week.

The Bills scored on a Josh Allen pass to Stefon Diggs with 34 seconds to play, taking a 30-26 lead. It was all over but the shouting. Right?

Wrong. The Cardinals got the ball back and after three plays chipping away modest yardage, Kyler Murray started right, then rolled left, and launched a 43-yard Hail Mary to DeAndre Hopkins, who made the soaring catch in the end zone with three Bills leaping along attempting to stop him. Hopkins' two hands snatched the ball over six Bills hands and won the game for the Cardinals. With a 32-30 lead and 2 seconds left on the clock, the Cardinals took a knee on the extra-point attempt, rather than kicking. It made sense. The only way they could lose at that point was if the Bills blocked the extra point and ran it back for their own two-point conversion, thus tying the game and winning in overtime. Not likely, but they did the right thing by kneeling.

Winning by 2 killed us, though I have to admit winning by 3 would have been even worse. Nonetheless, not a good result for the house.

The Murray-to-Hopkins play is one you're likely to see for years. I was slow to come around on Murray. I thought he was just too small. But he, and maybe one or two others — I'm thinking Rodgers and Mahomes — have to be the only ones in the league (make that on Earth) who could have made that throw. For a right-handed quarterback to roll left, swing his hips into place, and make an accurate 40-plus-yard pass to the end zone is damn near impossible. But he did it.

And DeAndre Hopkins, who wound up on the Cardinals in one of the stupidest trades of all time, has to be one of only a handful of receivers who could make such an effort and come down with the catch. A truly incredible play.

Monday November 16, 2020

Will Muschamp got fired as South Carolina head coach yesterday. He gets $13.3 million to leave. Amateur athletics at its finest.

I hate to speculate on people losing jobs, because I know firsthand how traumatic it can be. But a few others might bite the dust before the season is over. I didn't post them when they happened, but Gary Anderson of Utah State and Jay Hopson of Southern Miss were let go earlier in the season.

Some big injury news in the NFL. It looks like Drew Brees will be out a while. He has multiple broken ribs and a punctured lung. The Saints have Jameis Winston and Taysom Hill backing him up. I think Winston gets the start, but we'll have to see what Coach Payton decides.

Lots of key injuries—Matthew Stafford of the Lions, Teddy Bridgewater of the Panthers, Andy Dalton of the Cowboys, and Drew Lock of the Broncos—and question marks I have to work around this week.

In tonight's game, the Vikings are -3 and the Bears +3.5. The game wound up perfect for us, even though because of a missed extra point by the Vikings, it flirted with falling Vikings by 3. Once the final bet was made, we needed the Vikings -3.5 and under 44. They came through for us, beating the Bears 19-13.

Mondays can be tough, mostly based on how the accounting works, but the whole industry does it the same way. Well, we wound up with one of the best Mondays we've ever had. I honestly didn't see it coming. The weekend was less than stellar overall. But I was very happy for the pleasant surprise.

In our contests, we won our four Survivor plays, so we're still alive. In our handicapping contests, our entries went 3-2, 3-2, and 4-1 locally and 3-1 in our New Jersey contest. I didn't even know we had that at the beginning of the season, so I was probably remiss in updating you for a while. My bad.

Slow day with just a couple MAC games. Today was more like MAC-inaction.

Thursday November 19, 2020

Today is a big COVID-testing day for college teams. Only Michigan State-Maryland got canceled, but UCLA's quarterback and some other teammates are under protocols. The game went from Oregon -13.5 to -17.

Two games tonight. Tulane vs. Tulsa opened with Tulsa a 6-point favorite. I've rated Tulane higher than anyone all season. I like their coach, Willie Fritz, who turned around the moribund program when he got there three years ago. When the wise guys took Tulane +6, I went straight to -5 to get money on Tulsa. I wanted to go into the game needing Tulane. Mission accomplished.

Tulane was up 14-0 when Tulsa lost its starting quarterback. Then it lost its second-string quarterback. I was patting myself on the back for being the smartest bookmaker in the world—until the third string quarterback brought them back, first to 14-7, then after Tulane went up 21-7, he led a touchdown drive with

1:38 to play to cut the lead to 21-14. He wasn't done yet. He hit a receiver on a 37-yard pass to the end zone to tie the game 21-21 with 0.00 on the clock. Do I have to tell you what happened in overtime? After an exchange of field goals, Tulane got the ball and threw a pick-six to win 30-24. We got it stuck right in the … well, you know. I was the ex-smartest bookmaker in the world.

In the NFL, the hot Arizona Cardinals faced the stumbling Seattle Seahawks. The Cards were coming off a game they won with the best play of the year so far, Kyler Murray's last-second Hail Mary to DeAndre Hopkins.

Monday on Gill's show, I said my power ratings make the game a pick, but the situation favored the Seahawks. In these Thursday games, I like a veteran coach and an experienced quarterback. The Seahawks have both, the Cardinals have neither. Then, on "Get Up," ESPN's morning show, every pundit picked the Cardinals. I shouldn't call them pundits. They're journalists and former players, definitely not handicappers or bettors. Now if that doesn't tell a bookmaker, who has to be contrarian whether he likes it or not, who the winner is, I don't know what does. Man, would I love to book these guys for a living. I know they all make big big money.

We had the Seahawks at -3 and all the money was on the Cardinals. I decided we were sticking with the number, no matter how high on it we got. Well, we got pretty damn high and I still refused to move the number. The flood stopped late in the afternoon, but we never got close to even, we just plateaued.

The Seahawks won a close game 28-21. They led all the way, though the Cards were throwing the ball in the endzone in the last seconds. When the gun finally sounded, I was back to being the smartest bookmaker in the world. And the Tulsa-Tulane game didn't hurt us too bad. So we wound up with a fine bottom-line plus for the day.

Friday November 20, 2020

Only four games are scheduled for today, but lots of action, particularly on the Purdue-Minnesota game.

Yesterday, my connection in Chicago texted that the Purdue quarterback, listed as questionable, would definitely not play. Purdue was a 2.5-point favorite, but by this morning, the line totally switched and Minnesota was now -2.5. We stayed ahead of the move the whole way, so even though the money showed for Minnesota, we were pretty even on the game.

Then the word came that Minnesota would be missing 20+ players due to COVID and a variety of injuries. Money poured back in on Purdue. At that point, I didn't want to move on information, but on money. At kickoff, we'd gone back to Purdue -2.5 at the close. We needed Minnesota.

It wound up being a pretty good game, back and forth with a couple lead exchanges. With under a minute to play and Minnesota leading 34-31, Purdue threw a pass into the endzone caught by their tight end. Wait, offensive pass interference. The next play, an interception, effectively ended the game.

I needed Minnesota and right away I said what a horrible call it was. The tight end didn't push off. There never should have been a flag thrown for offensive pass interference.

I once asked a referee friend of mine, what's worse? Missing a call that happened or calling something that didn't? He said calling something that didn't happen was worse. You can only call what you see. If you didn't see it, you can't call it. You can't see every single thing every single time. Maybe you were out of position or watching something other than what you were supposed to, but that happens. If you call something that never happened, you're making stuff up. This ref made stuff up.

Twitter went crazy, calling for this guy's job or a suspension for the whole crew. That's what Twitter does. Fortunately, I felt above the fray; I had the winner. But the complainers had a valid point. That call absolutely cost Purdue a game they should have won. It's unfair to the players, coaches, administration, and alumni.

I do hate when games are decided unfairly. It's not good for the sport. And if it's not good for the sport, it's not good for me.

Regardless, we had a pretty good day. The Minnesota win was the biggest decision and the rest of the schedule was pretty much breakeven.

To tell you how COVID has affected college football, Texas State is playing its 11th game on Saturday and Utah is playing its first.

The U.S. death total is up to 240,000. The worst cases are the rural states: North Dakota, South Dakota, Wyoming, Iowa, Nebraska, Minnesota, Wisconsin, Montana, Utah, and Kansas are the top ten. They're running out of hospital beds, nurses, and doctors. The vaccines look promising, but they have to be manufactured and distributed. Snapping fingers won't get the job done.

Saturday November 21, 2020

We lost only one game today, but COVID had a noticeable effect of the betting.

It was reported that Pitt was missing up to 25 players. Naturally, the number moved from Va Tech -3.5 up to -6.5. Then, right after kickoff, it was revealed Virginia Tech had 10 players out themselves. Too late for bettors. Pitt killed them 41-21.

Missouri is missing a bunch of players. They already had their hands full playing Georgia as a 25-point underdog. We moved the number to Georgia -26, but wound up getting money on the dog. Georgia won 31-24, so Missouri got the dough.

Cincinnati, laying -4 to Central Florida, was up 36-33 with time running out. Cincy had it deep in UCF territory when the runner broke free for an easy touchdown. He stopped at the 1-yard line rather than scoring, so Cincy could run out the clock. Lots of groans from the crowd, who were largely on the favorite. They knelt three times. Smart. Then for some unknowable reason, they went into shotgun formation for fourth down. The snap got away from the quarterback. UCF broke through the line and had a chance to scoop and score, winning the game on a defensive touchdown. They didn't recover the fumble, but they did get the ball on downs with one second left on the clock. Now it was all or nothing. They started doing one of those lateral plays and right away I thought they would either get caught for a safety or Cincy would intercept and score a late touchdown. Fortunately for us, neither happened, but the collective blood-pressure readings of those of us involved probably would have exploded the meters.

The bottom line is we won a lot of games. And even though we lost a total of 16 games to COVID, we still had a pretty good handle. A big plus figure for us in the end.

Chapter Ten
November 22-December 31, 2020

"They say every day is a gift, but why does
it have to be a pair of socks?"
—*Tony Soprano*

Sunday November 22, 2020

We didn't have too much running from yesterday into today. Of course, once we opened the gates for Sunday's NFL action, we wound up with plenty of risk. It's been that way since the day Bugsy Siegel had the crazy idea of putting a lavish hotel in the middle of the desert.

In the early round, wise guys and the public were on the Eagles +3 over the Browns and the Falcons +3.5 over the Saints. The Browns won 22-17, the Saints won 24-9. Two very nice results.

Except for the Lions-Panthers, the other games were pretty split.

The Lions-Panthers were off the board all week. Lions quarterback Matthew Stafford had a problem with a ligament in his thumb from an injury the week before. The Lions were also missing three key receivers. Teddy Bridgewater, the Panthers QB, was also questionable all week with a shoulder injury. The way I was reading the information, I just assumed Teddy was out. About 8:30 a.m., the word came out that Stafford would play, but Bridgewater wouldn't. It was P.J. Harvey time for the Panthers. I opened the game pick 'em; I couldn't make either side the favorite.

Well, the world saw otherwise. We took limit bets on the Lions at pick, -1, -1.5, -2, and -2.5. Finally, at Lions -3, we wrote even business, but never got enough to offset the action that got us to -3. This shit game wound up being one of the biggest decisions of the day.

The Lions were totally inept on offense, as bad a team as I could remember. They had the ball for 23:12, gained 185 total yards, converted 10 first downs, and were shut out 20-0. Pitiful. But fantastic for us.

A good mix in the other early games gave us a pretty good start to the day.

In the late-afternoon slot, the wise guys were on the Colts over the Packers and the Broncos over the Dolphins. The public was firmly on the other sides. The Colts, laying from -1.5 to -2.5, looked like they were dead, down 28-14 at halftime. They came back to win in overtime 34-31. The Dolphins were never in the game, even though the Broncos won by the deceiving score of 20-13. In spite of the wise guys, both games were big decisions in our favor.

The Cowboys beat the Vikings as a 7.5-point dog and the Jets lost 34-28 to the Chargers, covering the 9.5-pointspread even though they couldn't win the game.

We were batting 1,000 going into the Sunday-night game, a rematch for the Chiefs, who suffered their only loss of the season to the Raiders. The Raiders had all sorts of COVID implications all week, so the opening number, Chiefs -6.5, got bet up to -8.5 before the dog players started to come in on the Raiders. At post time, we didn't need much. In a hell of a game, the Chiefs just held off the Raiders 38-34.

In a game like that, with a day like we had, we cleared out a lot of crap that hadn't gotten accounted for yet. I told Michael we needed the Sunday-night game under 56. Even though it went over, we had the second biggest Sunday win of the year.

However, Nevada Governor Sisolak announced enhanced COVID restrictions this afternoon. He cut capacity everywhere from 50% to 25%. Right before Thanksgiving. South Point already had all its restaurants filled for Thanksgiving at 50%. How do we cut that to 25%? We'll be jerks to half our customers no matter what we do. Also, dining parties are limited to four people per table. And no one can just walk into any restaurant in Nevada; they must have a reservation.

Also, no gatherings can have more than 50 people. That's where it affects me. We've done our best to spread things out. The sports book can hold about 250 people. We cut it to 60. Now we have to cut out 10 more seats. Ordinarily, this is one of the book's biggest weekends of the year.

South Point had a big rodeo event lined up for December. I'm sure that's a no-go.

To slightly defend Sisolak, he was dealt a bad hand. No way he could play that into a winner. But he never should have done it on the Tuesday before Thanksgiving. He should have done it two weeks ago or not at all.

Michael called me after Sisolak's news conference just to vent. I'm sure he does that with a few people, but I'm still happy to be one of them. After he went through all the things we're going to have to do as a company, he gathered himself and asked, "By the way, how are we doing today?"

I gave him the figure.

He laughed. "Well, I guess it's not all bad news. Good job, Chris."

I'm glad I could put a smile on his face, even if it was only momentary.

Monday November 23, 2020

Once again, we didn't have a whole lot running from the weekend into the Monday-night game. That makes bookmaking so much easier.

The game was good on paper and the field. We opened the Bucs -3, went as high as -4.5, then closed -4. We needed the Rams a little, but it wasn't a big decision either way.

The Rams won 27-24, but the bigger story was Tom Brady. Once again, he looked awful. They're throwing the ball downfield, which is Coach Bruce Arian's game, but it's definitely not Tom Brady's game. The only time it was his style was in 2007 when he had Randy Moss, one the greatest deep-threat receivers of all time, as his top wideout. Otherwise, throughout his career, and his is one the best ever, he concentrated on accuracy in the short game. If the Bucs don't adjust, they'll either get bounced out of the playoffs or not even make them at all.

After the game, Brady walked off the field without shaking hands with Jared Goff, the opposing quarterback. A total scumbag move. I said for years I should hate Brady a lot more than I do, but he's won some big games for me.

In our Survivor contests, we went 3-1, losing on the Vikings, but winning two with the Chargers and one with the Steelers. We live to fight another day.

In our handicapping contest, we were 1-4, 3-2 and 2-3. Not very good, but I guess we'll keep plugging to the end.

Tuesday November 24, 2020

Not a very fun day at the South Point. Michael had to make some cuts in the restaurants, special events, arena, bowling. All the salaried executives took a cut in pay. We've been asked to watch overtime in all departments. In the sports book, we're coming into one of the busiest times of the year. Our hourly employees, including all the supervisors, stay at the same rate. There won't be a lot of overtime, but at least they'll get paid the same for their work. It's awful, but we have to keep the doors open. Speaking for myself, I'll be okay. I would say the same is likely for the rest of my department. I'm hoping the best for the rest of the employees.

In college football we lost 15 games so far. Like I said, this is traditionally a huge week for us. It might still be, but losing that many games doesn't help.

We put up lines for college basketball, which opens tomorrow. It's a big schedule, but we've lost 20 games so far. It's probably more; a bunch of tournaments got reconfigured. Honestly, I can't keep track.

Sports is just the tip of the iceberg. ICU beds are filled up to and beyond capacity throughout the country. Cases are rising and so is the death rate. With more than 2,000 lives lost yesterday, it's now over 260,000 dead in the U.S. And it's getting worse by the day.

Personally, someone else I know died of COVID. He was about 75 and had heart issues. But without this virus, he'd still be alive.

Wednesday November 25, 2020

Opening day of college hoops with all-day action. I wish I could say how well we did, but it looks like they got us today. What can I say? It's college basketball. Winning in the early season would take a miracle.

When I started in this business in 1979, we didn't book college basketball until after the new year at the end of the football bowl games. No schedules were readily available and no lines to be had.

Thursday November 26, 2020

It's Thanksgiving morning and even though I bitch a lot, I have a lot to be thankful for. First, I survived MDS and a bone-marrow transplant last year and COVID this year. I'm very thankful that Pam also came through fine. My grandson and all my kids are doing well. I have a job and I'm thankful for my crew at South Point, Michael Gaughan our captain, and for my gig at VSiN, especially Gill Alexander. There are so many more people and things I'm thankful for, but I'll cut it off here. Check the Acknowledgements for the rest.

In college basketball, we lost 10 games today, in college football, 16.

We had good action on today's football, but it seemed less busy than the last couple years. No doubt the restrictions had a lot to do with it. Without a night game for everyone to get even (or get even worse) with, there's no way we can match the handle from last Thanksgiving.

In the first game of the day, the Texans beat the Lions 41-25. At one point, the Lions turned the ball over on three straight offensive plays. I'm so tired of rooting for the Lions every freaking Thanksgiving for the past 40 plus years. It's been brutal. I'm sure we've won a few, but I don't remember many.

In the afternoon slot, Washington beat the Cowboys 41-16. We lost a little on the first game, won a little on the second. We also ground out a small profit in college basketball. At the end of the day, we'd done way better than some of the Thanksgivings in the past.

In our Survivor contest, we had three entries left. There are eight of us, so I had 12.5% of whatever we made. One partner had another three entries, so we put them together. Now I have 6.25%. It cuts my win in half, but I have a much better chance of getting the first-place purse. Today is a perfect example. We had two close games and we were forced to make selections on them. (Thanksgiving was ruled to be a separate week. We knew this from the beginning.) The Texans were 3-point favorites over the Lions and the Cowboys were 3-point favorites over Washington. Tough games. So we put two on the Texans and one on the Lions. In the late game, we put two on the Cowboys and one on Washington. This way, we ensured having at least two entries moving forward.

The way the live entries broke down, we were probably better off "losing" the opener, leaving us one entry coming out of that game. That might be okay, because 11 players have the Lions and 76 have the Texans, so we'd K-O a lot of the competition. The second game mix isn't as dramatic, but 90 people have the Cowboys and 29 have Washington. Even if we lose both, we'll be live with only 40 left in a contest that started with over 3,000 players.

It ended up with 105 people live going into the weekend. We're three of the 105. We've got a shot.

Friday November 27, 2020

It was a little slower today than in past Fridays after Thanksgiving. Five of the games we lost were scheduled for today. We lost three more for tomorrow. We also lost eight college basketball games today. It's not ending anytime soon. People gathering for Thanksgiving will probably make it even worse in a few weeks.

the head coaches of two of college football's most prominent teams are expected to miss tomorrow's games. Both Nick Saban of Alabama and Ryan Day of Ohio State tested positive. Alabama plays instate rival Auburn. The game will go on without Saban. His assistant Steve Sarkisian will assume command. Bama is still a significant favorite, -24.5 as of this writing.

It was a different story for Ohio State. Day wasn't the only positive. They aren't saying how many, but it was enough to get the Illinois game canceled. Ohio State was another big favorite. The problem is Ohio State might not have enough games to qualify for the Big 10 championship. And though the college-football playoff committee has a bit more leeway, they might not qualify for the playoff either.

Let's be honest. The Big 10 is the Big 10. They've been as steadfast about COVID as much as anyone outside the Ivy League. Moses would have been proud to descend Mount Sinai with the Big 10 rules so magnificently chiseled in granite. Ohio State might be out for the particular accolade of a Big 10 title. But the playoff committee is another subject. Their rules are written on flash paper. They could disintegrate with a stiff Barry Alvarez fart. The committee will do every twist and turn, flip and flop, and tantric yoga position it can channel to find a way to get Ohio State into the playoff. Neither Ohio State nor Alabama has to win its conference or even division to get there. They'll still be viewed as one the four best teams and get voted in by the committee. It's happened before (with those two schools) and it will probably happen again if it's necessary. And it might be this year.

Business-wise, we had a good Friday. Like Michael reminded me the other day, it's not all bad news.

Saturday November 28, 2020

I would love to get back to the days of waking up and checking the numbers while I have my coffee, instead of seeing how many games have been canceled for the day.

The highlight of my morning was getting a mention on ESPN's "Game Day." I made some theoretical numbers on BYU vs. all the teams rated above them and Chris Fallica gave me credit for it. Bear has become a good friend. We usually call or text a few times every week. Wonderful guy.

On the field, the biggest news came when Sarah Fuller kicked off the second half for Vanderbilt—the first woman to play in a Power 5 football game. We knew before the game Fuller was their kicker. A kicker will always get at least one play, kicking off either for the game or the second half. Vandy got shut out 41-0 against Missouri, so that's exactly what Sarah Fuller got, one kick. Maybe next game, we can see her kick off a few times and try an extra point or a field goal. I like interesting things she's one of them.

On the field there wasn't a whole lot to report. Alabama and Clemson both won by more than four touchdowns. The one big upset of the day was Michigan State beating Northwestern, which had the inside track to the Big 10 championship game and even a chance for a spot in the college-football playoff. That all went out the window with a 29-20 loss.

The star of the day was Jaret Patterson of Buffalo, who had one of the best games I've ever seen from a small running back. Patterson, listed at 5'9", had 409 yards rushing with 8 TDs. I had the game on one of my TVs and every time I looked up, that kid was running wild. Buffalo wound up winning 70-41 over Kent State. Kent State was hanging in there for most of the game, so Buffalo needed to continue to put up points in order to fend off a tough competitor. Patterson has some of the quickest feet I've ever seen. Could he be a pro? Who knows, but I'd love to see it.

In the NFL, COVID caused the craziest quarterback situation in the history of the league. Four quarterbacks for the Denver Broncos have been ruled ineligible for Sunday's game against the New Orleans Saints. Starter Drew Lock, backups Jeff Driskel and Brent Rypien, and practice-squad quarterback Blake Bortles all violated the COVID protocols. Driskel is reported as the one who tested positive, but the others were all together in a meeting room not wearing their masks. I was afraid something like this would happen. COVID might not kill athletic young people, but it does infect them. If one guy in that group gets it, they all will, or at least fall under the protocols. It looks like the Broncos are going to start Kendall Hinton (yeah, I never heard of him either), a practice-squad wide receiver who played a little quarterback at Wake Forest before switching positions.

The Detroit Lions finally had enough of head coach Matt Patricia and GM Bob Quinn. Quinn fired the best Lions coach of my lifetime, Jim Caldwell. Caldwell was a good coach, maybe not great, but had them in the playoffs on multiple occasions. Quinn was one of those guys who wanted "his own man" as coach. So he hired Patricia, a great assistant coach, but awful as the head man. What a horrible franchise.

Sunday November 29, 2020

The Broncos-Saints game that never should have been played was as big a cluster fuck as we thought it would be. Kendall Hinton, the practice-squad wide receiver promoted to NFL starting quarterback overnight, performed about how you figured he would. He completed one pass and threw two interceptions. His QBR was 0.1 (out of a possible 100.0). It was the most preposterous NFL game I have ever seen. The NFL talks about integrity (remember they tried to charge bookmakers an integrity fee?). I've seen plenty of NFL mismatches in my day, but this game should have been like Alabama playing Massachusetts.

The line opened Saints -6 with a money line of -280. After we figured out what was going on, we reposted the game at -15 and the money line -2000/+1000. Bettors put their money on the pointspread, back and forth, until we closed the game at Saints -17. But people were taking +1000 on the Broncos. It should have been +1000000. The Broncos had less of a chance of winning than I'd have in a game of one-on-one with LeBron James. The Saints won 31-3, but laid off the gas the whole game.

Monday November 30, 2020

I was surprised so much remained alive going into the Monday-night game. It was all on the Seahawks over the Eagles. If the Seahawks won and covered, it would be pretty bad for us. The Seahawks were a blanket -6.5 when I got the what ifs for the game. I went to -7 just to make sure I got something back in case everyone went to -7 later, which I thought was a distinct possibility.

The trend never really stopped all day. It was all Seahawks. When I did go to Seahawks -7, the wise guys jumped on the

Eagles +7. It took mere minutes for me to get enough to go back to -6.5. I had to go to -7 once more later in the day to get a little more back on the Eagles. We still needed the Eagles pretty good at kickoff.

The Seahawks went up 14-0 and the Eagles were lucky they were only down two touchdowns. The Eagles scored late in the half, but blew the extra point. They were down by 8 and looked like crap. It wasn't promising.

Three Seahawks field goals and one by the Eagles left the score 23-9 with only seconds to play. After the last Seahawks field goal put them up 23-9, I went to the bathroom, knowing the game was out of reach. Then it dawned on me, if the Eagles score now, it'll cut the lead to 7, which would be disastrous for us. Like a B-movie script, just as I got out of the bathroom, I heard an excited Steve Levy announcing a miracle touchdown by the Eagles. You've gotta be kidding me. This team couldn't move the ball all night and now they score late enough to kill me by cutting the score to 23-15? All I could think was, please go for two. A 2-point conversion would get me off the destruction of a 7-point final. If the Eagles get stopped, a Seahawks 8-point win was no bargain, but no worse than a lot of other losses I've suffered over the years. If the Eagles could manage to convert, a 6-point spread would be a thing of beauty.

The Eagles did go for two, for no other reason than, "What the hell?" The gambling gods smiled on me and my fellow bookmakers when the Eagles' Miles Sanders walked into the endzone for a score. Seahawks 23-17 final.

We wound up breaking even for the day. Now that was a miracle.

Wednesday December 2, 2020

The Steelers finally got to play the Ravens today. Pittsburgh looked mediocre, doing barely what they had to on offense to win, but controlling an ineffective Ravens offense for a 19-14 win.

The Ravens scored their second touchdown on an 84-yard pass with 2:58 left in the game by third string quarterback Trace McSorely. Otherwise, it was the most boring Steelers-Ravens game I can remember. The play on the field was nap-worthy, most of the Ravens' lineup was missing, the Steelers played down to the competition, and no fans in the stands waved Terrible Towels and curse out the hated invaders from Baltimore.

The Steelers went to 11-0 with the win, but lost Bud Dupree for the rest of the season with a torn ACL. They lost Devin Bush earlier in the year, their best inside linebacker and now Dupree, one of two Pro Bowl outside linebackers along with T.J. Watt. Every team has injuries, particularly at this time of the year, but these are big ones.

We had a decent day, nothing special. It would have been better, but a guy hit a 7-teamer to more than wipe out our win on the Steelers-Ravens game. And so it goes.

Reported today were 2,760 deaths, the most ever. More than 100,000 people are under hospital care right now in the U.S. That's twice what it was only a month ago. Deaths are a lagging indicator; they're certain after all the Thanksgiving recklessness. Then it's Christmas, another potential super-spreader event, especially in Vegas. Then New Year's Eve/Day a week later. Oy.

The vaccine can't get here quick enough.

Thursday December 3, 2020

College football and basketball continue to be a mess. But both are doing their best to fix the problems as they present themselves.

A number of basketball teams have been quartered at the Mohegan Sun in Connecticut. As one team comes up with enough positive tests to postpone a game, the still-negative opponent has asked other teams if they want to play. Why not? They're all here. The players want to play and the coaches and administrators know the experience is good for the team; come March, if they keep on winning, they'll be in the NCAA Tournament. And if they lose, no big deal. So they're better off playing whoever is available. Just like on the playground.

"Wanna play?"

"Sure. You got your team?"

"Yep."

"Okay. Let's go."

Good for them. They're adding games almost as quickly as they're canceling them. Then we throw together a number and put it up for the world to bet on.

Football isn't nearly as simple. But they're doing their best. Originally scheduled for this week are 18 games that have either been canceled or postponed.

All leagues are scrambling now to make up any games they can with teams that can clear COVID protocols. The Big 10, in particular, is doing its best to get Ohio State enough games to qualify for the four-team playoff. Other schools and leagues are doing the same. Good on them, as long as they can do this all safely. I want as many games as possible.

It's 2020. Nothing is normal and there are very few rules.

Friday December 4, 2020

Jimmy Vaccaro, Nick Bogdanovich, and I were invited by Mike Palm to lunch today at Circa.

All I can say is, wow. It's one hell of an operation, including the greatest swimming-pool setup in Nevada and an incredible sports book. That's just scratching the surface. Mike is executive vice president. He mentioned a couple of investment numbers to me. I've been around a while, so I can take a guess at their daily operating expenses and I would conservatively say they're high as all fuck. But Mike, and Derek Stevens, are smart guys and Derek is a true visionary. I hope they do really well, because if they do, it means the whole town—hell, the whole state, the whole country, and the whole world—is recovering and doing well. Still, it's got to be tough for them, because it's tough for all of us right now. I'm keeping my fingers crossed for them. And all of us.

Pretty good football game tonight between Louisiana Lafayette and Appalachian State. I've had my eyes on Louisiana all season. It's a good program filled with guys who were maybe not quite good enough to play for an SEC or ACC team. That's still some solid talent. They were the better team, but they had never beaten App State, which recruits off a similar talent base.

Money showed for App State at -2, -2.5, and -3. I never moved off the 3. I figured, what the hell, it's the only football game on a Friday night. Let's gamble with it.

It was so windy, Louisiana had three completely biffed long snaps for punts and field goals. With a minute to play facing fourth down, they were up 24-19 deep in their own territory. They took a safety rather than risk another long snap, making the score 24-21. Huh? I guess I can see it. But now a field goal by App State would put the game in overtime. It's like intentionally walking a batter to put the tying run on base. Pretty much unheard of.

App State got the ball after the free kick, then marched into what would ordinarily be easy field goal range. This time the vicious wind helped Louisiana as App State's field goal attempt never came close. I was okay with it. It was a six-figure swing for us.

Saturday December 5, 2020

Fine day, good action, in spite of all the cancellations. I really enjoyed the BYU-Coastal Carolina game that went down to the last second before Coastal hung on for a 22-17 win.

Other than that, there wasn't any unusual drama. Clemson, Ohio State, Alabama, and Notre Dame (the playoff committee's top four) all won easily. Texas A&M, just on the outside, also won. Same with Florida. It was nice having some late action via the PAC-12 and Mountain West Conference. That boosted the action for guys who were looking to get even or get even worse.

The biggest failure of the day belonged to Marshall, a 24-point favorite, getting shut out by Rice 20-0. Rice! That's bad.

The handle was no bargain, but the win was sensational. All things considered, I'll take it.

Sunday December 6, 2020

Another huge day. I don't know how long we can keep this going, but I hope it lasts for at least another couple of weeks. I've been around long enough to know these things have a way of evening out, so I'm not one to get cocky. I've just got to do the right thing bookmaking-wise and let the chips fall where they may. But the pressure is on a bit. The rest of the casino is having serious issues because of COVID.

It wasn't a day of huge decisions or upsets, we just happened to fall on the right side of a lot of games. Seven underdogs covered versus five favorites. Four of the underdogs won outright. It wasn't a massive convergence of luck. We just chopped wood all day.

The only huge upset was the Giants beating the Seahawks as an 11-point underdog. That alone was a six-figure win for us, crushing all the teasers and money-line parlays. Another big result was the Patriots beating the Chargers 45-0 as a slight 2-point underdog. Prior to the game, it was billed as the biggest coaching mismatch in the NFL: the Pats' Bill Belichick vs. Anthony Lynn of the Chargers. I don't know if Bill is 45 points better, but it sure made one hell of a difference. I can't believe we needed the Pats.

Another notable event was the end of the Jets-Raiders game. The Jets took the lead 28-24 with a few minutes to play. After an exchange of possessions, the Raiders got the ball back with less than a minute, needing a touchdown. The Jets were still winless on the season; how head coach Adam Gase and defensive coordinator Gregg Williams were collecting paychecks from an NFL team is beyond me.

From a defensive standpoint, all Williams knew was to blitz. Blitz, blitz, blitz. The blitz should be a surprise to the offense, but when it's your basic defensive strategy, it loses its effectiveness. With 20 seconds left in the game and the Raiders 45 yards from the endzone, Williams called for a blitz. Nelson Agholor got behind the defense and would have scored if the Raiders QB Derek Carr had hit him with the pass. Carr overthrew Agholor, so the Jets lived to see another play. This time, Williams sent an all-out blitz, known as zero coverage, so all his defensive backs were in one-on-one situations. Henry Ruggs III, arguably the league's fastest player, got behind undrafted rookie free agent Lamar Jackson and Carr connected with him for a 45-yard touchdown and the game winner for the Raiders.

It was hard to blame Jackson. No undrafted rookie should be put into that situation. Ruggs gave one tiny head fake and that was all he needed to blow by the rookie. Carr made the pass and it was all over.

ESPN broke down the situation by time left, yardage, and scoring deficit. No defense in their database had ever gone with such a defensive strategy. No wonder. Needless to say, a Jets outright win would have made a great day even better.

I talked to Michael. He knows we can't keep this up. But we'll take it while it lasts.

Monday December 7, 2020

Gregg Williams got fired this morning. Too bad they didn't term him with 15 seconds left in the game. Might have saved me some money and knocked a few guys out of the Survivor contest.

We had a massive handle on both of today's games. We opened the Steelers -10 over Washington and it got bet down to -6 before we bounced up to -6.5, then back to -6 at the close.

So we wound up needing the Steelers pretty bad.

It was a perfect storm against the Steelers. They played with five days' rest, while Washington had 11. The Steelers looked good early, but faded late. Washington won 23-17, a rejuvenated team with likely comeback player of the year Alex Smith at quarterback. Actually, I'm pulling for them to win their division. If they make the playoffs, we make a nice little score. We took a big bet on them to not make the playoffs before the season started. I had pretty much written it off a few weeks ago, but now we have a pretty good shot. They're tied for first place with the Giants, but behind on tiebreakers.

The Bills-49ers game had one of the craziest betting patterns I've seen in a while. We opened Bills -2.5 and before the paint could dry, we were bet up to -3. That unleashed the floodgates for 49ers bettors, who went from 3-point dogs to 2.5-point favorites. I could see the reason for the move. The 49ers this season have had one of the worst injury situations ever. As the team started getting players back, they looked like they were ready to emerge as one of the league's best teams, like the one that had a double-digit lead in the fourth quarter of the Super Bowl.

Fortunately for your favorite bookmaker, that top-notch 49ers team is still at least a week away. The Bills dominated and looked like they were much more of a threat to the Chiefs to represent the AFC in the Super Bowl than the Steelers. We'll find out soon enough; the Bills and Steelers square off in the Sunday-night game.

Earlier, I mentioned the massive handle, which enabled us to win a little, often hard to do on a Monday. Even though we split, losing on the Steelers and winning with the Bills, we turned a modest profit for the day.

To update you on my contests, we lost one entry on the Seahawks, but advanced with two plays on the Vikings. At least the Seahawks loss eliminated 11 other contestants. The Steelers loss also eliminated two contestants. We've got two left, which is nice, but my confidence is waning daily.

We went 3-2 on our handicapping contest entries. Meh.

Off the field, the biggest news was Michigan and Ohio State canceling their game this weekend over Michigan's multiple COVID cases. Besides being one of the most intriguing rivalries in college football—I hate to say this, but it's barely a rivalry anymore; Michigan hasn't beaten them in years—the cancellation leaves Ohio State with only five games (five wins), which would eliminate them from the required number to qualify for the Big 10 championship game. The six-game minimum was a rule the Big 10 imposed on itself, when there really is a paucity of rules and absolutely no precedent for what we're experiencing this year.

If they don't get the sixth game and lack the qualifications to compete for a championship, Ohio State supposedly wouldn't qualify for the college football championship. Supposedly. The powers that be will do everything humanly possible to get Ohio State into the Big 10 championship and/or the college football playoff. Trust me.

Wednesday December 9, 2020

To the complete astonishment of absolutely no one who has followed college football at any time in the past 100 years, the Big 10 green-lighted Ohio State to play in the Big 10 championship game.

Off the field, but on the court, the NBA is starting on December 22. Christmas Day has been a big event for the NBA for years, so it was important to hit the ground running shortly before that.

On the ice, the NHL has nothing firm in place, but is targeting January 13 for the start of the hockey season. It looks like some contractual hurdles still need to be negotiated, including jumbling the divisions for the season. Do we dare have faith they can get this together sooner rather than later?

Thursday December 10, 2020

I have to admit to a bit of *schadenfreude*. I heard my old haunt, the Golden Nugget, has gone to -115 on football straight bets. I don't know what they've been doing the last couple of months, but our October 2020 bottom line was 50% above October 2019. And November 2020 was 120% above November 2019. I can't imagine the bad decisions that led them to book a 30-cent line A friend sent me a picture of their sports book from a few minutes ago. Keep in mind we have an NFL game tonight. They had three ticket writers, two supervisors, one security guard, and no customers. None. Nil. Zero. Zilch.

The sports book manager, Tony Miller, is a long-time veteran who knows what he's doing. The direction, or I should say misdirection, has to come from somewhere above him on the organizational chart. Hilarious. I'm so happy I'm not part of that company.

The Rams and Patriots played the Thursday-night game. The final score was 24-3 Rams. That doesn't tell the story. The Pats had four trips inside the red zone and wound up with three points. Not typical of a Bill Belichick-coached team at all. Meanwhile, Cam Newton looks finished. And the Rams might be a lot better than the consensus. Their defense is formidable and their quarterback, Jared Goff, though not great, is capable.

It was a pretty evenly bet game, not much of a decision. But along with college basketball, we wound up with a slight profit.

Friday December 11, 2020

The NFL news of the week is Jalen Hurts is starting in place of Carson Wentz this week for the Eagles. Wentz, in spite of the multi-millions owed to him, forced the issue with his play on the field. He's been nothing short of terrible this season and last.

I don't know about Hurts' ability as an NFL quarterback, but I admit to being very impressed by him as a man. He was demoted at halftime of the college football championship game after leading Alabama to the championship the year before. He handled it with complete dignity. He transferred to Oklahoma where they immediately made him not only the starter, but the team captain as well. He seems like a well-centered guy. A leader of men. But I still don't know if he can play quarterback in the NFL.

Michael sat in my office for about three hours today. I'd like to think it's because he so enjoys my company, but it's more than that. He has nothing else to do. The place is dead. Hotel occupancy is about 10% for the weekend. Travel is at a minimum and the locals are watching their pennies. Besides being on high lockdown, a lot of people are running out of money. Small businesses are failing, your average worker either has his hours cut or is out of work completely.

Las Vegas had the NFR (National Finals Rodeo) and the PBR (Professional Bull Riders) every year in December for the past 30 years to save the town, but no such luck this year; both events went to Texas. Reno never could get an event to save December. I can still hear my former partner Warren Nelson saying every year in the run-up to the holiday, "I hate Christmas!" I wouldn't go that far and I always tried to hide my laughter when he went on one his tirades that could have had him visited by the ghost of Jacob Marley, but I do understand it.

Saturday December 12, 2020

Today is the annual Army-Navy game, which is great drama, though not particularly great football. Ordinarily, it's the only game of the day. With everything that has happened this year, there was a full slate scheduled, though COVID took care of a bunch of those.

Conference championship games are scheduled for this coming week. Even so, the Big 10, with Ohio State and Northwestern playing for its championship, is scrambling to get the other teams in the conference one last game. It has to be strange for some of these players who don't know if they're playing the last games of their season—or their careers. Meanwhile the NCAA hasn't decided what to do with the eligibility rules for athletes who played. A lot is up in the air at this point. Just like for the rest of us.

A couple games had playoff and/or New Year's Day bowl implications.

UCLA led by as much as 18 points in the second half. But when USC scored a touchdown with 8:02 to play, they took a 36-35 lead. UCLA came back to score a field goal with 0:52 on the clock. They thought they'd secured a 38-36 win. Evidently, no one told USC and the UCLA defense. USC went 43 yards in two plays after lousy kickoff coverage by UCLA to win 43-38. USC is undefeated and playing for a PAC-12 championship. There isn't much buzz about anyone from the PAC-12 making the college football playoff, but there is some more football to come. Regardless, USC-UCLA is the best uniform matchup in the history of football, pro or college.

I had Miami-Fla rated lower than anyone all season. My numbers just didn't add up to them being one of the top teams in the country. They hosted a pretty good North Carolina team and needed a win to get a spot in the New Year's Day bowls. They got blasted 62-26. They'll probably be in the bowl scramble with a bunch of other teams now.

Vanderbilt lost to Tennessee 42-17. However, the big story of the game was Sarah Fuller kicking two extra points for Vandy. She's the first woman to score in a Power 5 football game. Pretty cool. Of course, people made their objections known on social media, saying she really isn't deserving. After all, Vandy used a different kicker for longer field-goal attempts. So what? It's still special.

San Jose State beat Nevada to finish undefeated. They play Boise State for the Mountain West Championship. Coastal

Carolina rallied late to secure their undefeated finish. Congratulations to both teams on doing so well. Neither team entered the season with any great expectations.

The biggest consequence came in the LSU-Florida game. Florida had already clinched the SEC Eastern Division and a spot in the SEC championship game. However, they had a loss. A win over Alabama in the championship would most likely put them in the college football playoffs, even with that one loss. Their hope was to make it regardless, with a good showing against Bama, clearly the best team in the country, at least on paper.

They entered today's game as 23-point favorites over last year's college football champs, LSU. It was expected to be a cakewalk for Florida. Nope. LSU hung with them the whole way. With less than a minute to play in the game and the score tied at 34, Florida stopped LSU on third down. An LSU player lost his shoe. A Florida player picked it up and threw it. That's a penalty. LSU got a fresh set of downs and kicked a field goal with 23 seconds left. Florida got the ball and managed to try a 51-yard field goal by Evan McPherson to tie the score and put the game in overtime. McPherson is one of the best kickers in the country, but his kick bent to the left just before the goal post.

Florida head coach and noted whiner, Dan Mullen, was true to form in the press conference, pissing and moaning about the refs. Mullen drives me crazy. Get your team ready, cut the excuses, and skip the blame game. You were 23-point favorites in a huge game. Go out and win the freaking game like you're supposed to.

The COVID vaccine is here. Distribution starts tomorrow.

Sunday December 13, 2020

It was a good action day, a few good games, and one great one (from a betting perspective).

In the early set, betting was heavy on the Bucs -7 over the

Vikings and the Chiefs -7 over the Dolphins. Both favorites were clearly the better teams, so no big surprise on either. But one of our biggest players was in town and loaded up on both those sides.

The Bucs were coming off a bye. They'd been priced for perfection by the public with Tom Brady at quarterback and the highly respected Bruce Arians as coach. They were a bit disappointing this season. The thought was the bye week would cure a lot of their ills.

The Bucs were good, not great, and the beneficiaries of two highly questionable pass-interference penalties in the end zone that led directly to 10 points. Meanwhile, the Vikings kicker, Dan Bailey, entered the game as the sixth most accurate kicker in NFL history. He missed three field goals and an extra point. The Bucs won 26-14, covering the number and putting us behind early.

The Chiefs did everything they could to lose their game. Patrick Mahomes threw three interceptions, compared to two all season. They also fell behind 10-0 early, definitely opening the door to a possible upset. But they were up 23-14 late in the game with the Dolphins driving. Since the Dolphins needed two scores, they kicked a field goal, cutting the lead to 6, 23-17. They failed on the onside-kick attempt, the Chiefs ran out the clock, and we were fine with the final margin of less than seven points.

In the late-afternoon slate, the biggest win for us was the Eagles upsetting the Saints. The public bet the Saints up from -7 to -8.5 before we got some money back on the Eagles. There was also a lot of money line and teaser exposure on the Saints. The Eagles outright win, 24-21, behind new starter Jalen Hurts, was a thing of beauty.

The Sunday night game was one of the best-bet games of the season. We opened the Steelers -2.5 over the Bills on Monday morning in a key AFC matchup. However, on Monday night, the Steelers looked lousy in losing to Washington and the Bills looked terrific in beating the 49ers. When we reopened the game Tuesday morning, the money poured in on the Bills. We were as high as the Bills -2.5 until some money came back in on the Steelers. If you're keeping track, that's a five-point move. Pretty goddamn big in the NFL, especially against a team that was 11-1.

Games right around pick 'em in the NFL wind up in a lot of teasers. We wrote a ton of business on the game and once they kicked off, we didn't really need either side. But if the game fell out of the teaser bracket, it would be a score for us.

The Bills won 26-15, beating all the Steelers teasers (9-points max) and even polishing off anyone who teased the total down from 48 to go over 42. We were having an okay day going into that late game, but beating the teasers made it a very good day.

Three years ago, I broke down the teasers for Michael to show him how they were big losers for the year. The 21 potential teaser options have varying odds. We were a loser on 14 of the 21. It needed to be fixed. Badly. I changed the odds and convinced him our handle wouldn't suffer, except to change a loser into winner for us. Kudos to him for supporting me. We're now in our third year of the change and the difference to our bottom line is in the millions.

Sometimes you have to look at things you've been doing for years and realize that what once worked no longer does. The games are constantly changing and if you don't change along with them, it will cost you.

Monday December 14, 2020

Some games trigger a huge handle if they're between two teams that have grabbed the betting public's attention. Others create a huge handle because of the betting number. The sweet spot for a bookmaker is when you can have both working for you. Like we had tonight with the Ravens and Browns.

The Browns suddenly found themselves in a position to

catch the Steelers and win the AFC North. The Ravens, last year's number-one seed, needed to win out just to make the playoffs as the final seed in the AFC. An intriguing matchup, for sure. In the betting line, the Ravens were a 3-point favorite and had major money coming in on them. While the rest of the bookmakers in the world were at -3/-120 or some such thing, South Point, as I'm sure you know by now, posts games only at -110. When we got high enough on the Ravens -3, we would go to -3.5. And once again, we were the only place in the world that had the Browns +3.5 /-110.

I'm bold enough to say no one else does it like this. We're the last men standing. I really have no choice; Michael Gaughan and his partner Frank Toti have mandated I do it this way. But I don't fight it. When I was running my sports book all those years at Cal Neva, that's exactly the way I did it, with no mandate but my own way of preferring to do business.

In case you aren't aware, when you do things this way, when you're at -3/-110 and are the only one with that number, you do a lot of business with people betting the favorite. Conversely, when you go to +3.5/-110, you're the only one with that number, so you do a lot of business with people betting the underdog. The downside, and the reason no other book does this, is if the favorite wins by exactly 3, you push all the bets at -3 and lose all the bets at +3.5. You can get beat for a ton of money.

And if it does fall 3, you better have a boss who understands. My boss just makes fun of me when it happens. It relieves a lot of pressure. Of course, I don't want to lose, especially on big games like we were looking at tonight. With the above scenarios, we had a huge handle. One of the biggest in my tenure at South Point.

It was probably the best game of the season, back and forth for 60 minutes, until the Ravens kicked a field goal with :02 on the clock to go ahead 45-42. Yep, by exactly 3 points. We were going to get murdered.

The Ravens kicked off and the Browns started throwing the

ball back and forth, trying to bust a play a la California over Stanford in 1982. Back, forth, back forth, giving ground rather than advancing. What do you know! It wound up in the Browns' end zone for a safety and two points for the Ravens. Instead of a 45-42 final, it was now 47-42. We lost on the game, but only a little. That safety saved us a lot of money.

The phone started ringing. I heard "Hail to the Chief"[6], my ringtone for the big boss, Michael. He was happy as could be. He knew how bad the 3 was for us. Then I heard "Hey Mambo," the ringtone for my Italian friends. It was Jimmy, who usually doesn't stay up that late, but this one kept him awake and he knew how much that safety saved us. Another "Hey Mambo" was Vinny. He and I spent 15 minutes talking about the crazy outcome. My daughter texted me. One of my supervisors texted me. For a losing night, it was really an undeserved victory.

God looks out for drunks and bookmakers.

Tuesday December 15, 2020

With the chance of a 3 showing up in yesterday's football game, Twitter was awash with opinions on what I should do to alleviate that risk. All throughout the day, the tweets continued, with the Twitter mob trying to outdo one another with the weirdest "advice" you can imagine. I didn't indulge any of it with a response. I've been making odds and booking bets for more than 40 years and Michael is a billionaire. Neither one of us is stupid. Neither one of us got to where we are by giving

---

[6]I love using the ringtones to identify callers: "Hail to the Chief" for Michael. "Hey Mambo" for the Italians in my phone book. "Zorba's Dance" for the Greeks. "Hava Nagila" for my Jewish brethren. My wife gets "She Loves You." My daughter Jacque, "Let It Be." Other friends get "Bring It on Home." And if I don't know the number, "Who Are You?" Doubtful I answer those calls.

away money foolishly.

College football came through with aggressive scheduling. The SEC, ACC, and Big 10 all have championship games this weekend, but those conferences still tried to match all the teams that could still field a team against one another. Unfortunately, we have eight cancellations so far this week, but it's still a hell of a schedule for an ordinarily quiet Saturday. The NFL also has two games Saturday, so it should be a huge day of football, the kind of day I absolutely love. We'll have a full day of college basketball, too.

Wednesday December 16, 2020

I took today off. It was my last day to finish Christmas shopping, which I did.

I was on my couch watching TV when I heard "Hail to the Chief." The boss man calling. "Who do we need in the game?"

That caught me unawares. There was "the game" tonight? Notre Dame was playing Duke in a basketball game. He's Irish, so naturally a Notre Dame fan. And he has a relationship with Mike Kryzewski. Was that what he meant? "Uhm, what game?"

"The football game."

Now I was really confused. Was there a minor college bowl game on TV I'd forgotten about? "I don't know. I'm off today. I didn't know there was a game tonight."

"Raiders and Colts. It's about to start on Channel Five. I'm watching it."

I went scrambling to my computer. Was this one a COVID change I somehow wasn't aware of? No. Nothing. Finally, it dawned on me. "Michael, the Colts and Raiders played last Sunday. You're watching a rerun."

I could hear him laughing. He's probably the most good-hearted billionaire in the world. "Oh yeah," he said. "I'm right on top of things."

Thursday December 17, 2020

The line had jockeyed all day between Raiders -3 and -3.5. Naturally, all our Raiders business was at -3 and all our Chargers action was at +3.5.

The game was tied 27-27 at the end of regulation. The dreaded 3 was staring us right in the face again. Raiders by 3 was a decent-size loss. Of course, Chargers by 3 would be just fine. The Raiders got the ball first. Backup quarterback Marcus Mariota, in place of injured starter Derek Carr, led them to a field goal: 30-27 Raiders, a terrible result for us. But the Chargers still had a chance.

The Chargers rookie QB, Justin Herbert, likely Rookie of the Year, took them down the field, courtesy of a 53-yard pass that put them inside the 5-yard line. After a few botched plays, a.k.a. an Anthony Lynn special, Herbert ran the ball into the endzone himself, winning the game 33-30, getting us off the wrong 3 and giving us a nice win for the day.

Late today, we lost the Sun Belt Championship game between Louisiana-Lafayette and Coastal Carolina. Louisiana had been under the radar a lot this season, but is an excellent team. Coastal was undefeated, but certainly needed to win the conference to have a shot at a New Year's Day bowl game. The teams were announced as co-champions, which was probably fair, but it robbed us of a great game and a possible intriguing matchup with an outsider like Coastal in a big bowl game.

Friday December 18, 2020

Nice day with a good handle in both college football and basketball.

The biggest game of the day was USC vs. Oregon for the PAC-12 championship. It was pretty evenly bet until late in the day when we got a little push on USC. Oregon led most of the way and held on for a 31-24 win. Oregon played in place of Washington, which actually won the PAC-12 North, but didn't have enough players to field a team. So Oregon didn't win the division, but won the conference. Welcome to 2020.

One of the best outcomes of the night was in the MAC championship. Buffalo was 5-0 and highly impressive all season. But Ball State steadily improved during the year. We closed Buffalo a 13-point favorite and -600 on the money line. We had Buffalo money on both the pointspread and money line. Ball State beat them outright, 38-28.

When I gave Michael the results, he didn't even know Buffalo had a college team and he had no idea where Ball State could possibly be.

That's cool, Michael. You keep making the big decisions and leave this kind of crap to me. That formula seems to be working just fine so far.

Saturday December 19, 2020

In my youth, I loved a day like today—NFL, college football, and college basketball. And I have to admit, even now that I'm old, semi-senile, and decrepit, I was still anxious for today—great matchups in the colleges and almost anything is a great matchup in the NFL.

In the basketball, number-one Gonzaga played number-three Iowa to open the day. Gonzaga closed a 4.5-point favorite and led throughout, winning 99-88. I tried to watch as much as I could, but that was very little, thanks to how much business we had.

In the first two championship games of the day, Ohio State played Northwestern for the Big 10 title and Oklahoma played Iowa State for the same honors in the Big 12.

I had early information that Ohio State had big COVID problems, not enough to cancel the game, but enough to impact their performance. Ohio State was -20.5, which I thought was too high under any circumstances. So I stayed ahead of the move, which wound up with all the sharp money on Northwestern. The game closed Ohio State -16.5, but we still needed Northwestern, because I kept moving the number down. Northwestern took a 10-6 lead into the half. They never scored again, but held on to cover, with a 22-10 Ohio State victory.

Iowa State fell behind early, but rallied to lose 27-21, right on the closing number of Oklahoma -6.

Notre Dame vs. Clemson was the early-afternoon college feature. We had pretty good two-way action on the game, but as usual, we needed the 10-point underdog Notre Dame. It wasn't to be. Clemson won 34-10.

The real afternoon feature had the Bills against the Broncos (the NFL is still king, even when it's up against a college football championship game). We opened Bills -6.5, but took in Broncos money from the wise guys all week. This morning we were sitting at Bills -5.5. Forget about the rest of the week, today it was all Bills. We went to -6, then took a little +6 from some wise guys, but they were totally overcome by the public. We went to Bills -6.5. The wise guys took the dog, but not enough. We needed the Broncos. We never had a chance. The Bills beat them 48-19.

Among other games during the day, the big ones late were the Packers vs. the Panthers and Alabama vs. Florida for the SEC championship.

Both favorites were heavily bet, though the wise guys were on the underdogs all week. The Packers opened -8.5, then went to -9, then all the way down to -8, where we were when the day started. We wound up closing the Packers -10. That's a huge move in the NFL.

The Alabama game wasn't quite as bad. With lots of money both ways, we fluctuated between Alabama -16.5 and -17.5. Even though we closed the game -17, we had a ton of money in the last few minutes, so late it was useless to move the number. I easily could have gone as high as Alabama -18, but it didn't matter. They kicked off and we needed Florida.

I told Michael we needed at least one of the underdogs to

cover or it would be ugly.

The two games were going simultaneously. Both halftimes hit at once and it looked less than promising. Alabama was up 35-17. The Packers led 21-3.

Both underdogs played well in their second halfs and covered the number. But we couldn't knock out a teaser in the NFL, so we were looking at a lot of exposure. Hopefully, we could beat one of the teaser games tomorrow. We only needed one.

Nonetheless, today wound up being a pretty decent day. We'll take it and rejoin the battle tomorrow.

Sunday December 20, 2020

We were exceptionally busy this morning. I'm not sure why. The matchups weren't all that great. But you never know what will grab the public's attention. Not only were we busy writing hordes of tickets, but an unusual number of customers showed up betting $5K to $10K on games. We always have a few, but today we had a roomful. I loved it.

The only game that moved heavily was the Patriots-Dolphins. The Dolphins opened a 3-point favorite, but swung around to Patriots -2.5 by the time we closed. I couldn't understand that move at all. On Gill's show the previous Monday, I even said I liked the Dolphins at -3. The Dolphins beat Belichick pretty good, 22-12. We got out of the morning slightly ahead, but we didn't knock out any teasers. Trouble was looming.

In the afternoon, the Eagles faced the Cardinals, the Rams hosted the Jets, and in the potential game of the year and a Super Bowl preview, the Saints played the Chiefs.

The Cardinals were -6.5, so we had teasers running to them in that game. The other two games were big, but not for the teasers. (We'll get to them later.) We needed an Eagles outright win. The Eagles fell behind 16-0, but rallied in the second half to tie the game 26-26. The Cards went ahead 33-26, but the Eagles had one last chance. They threw to the endzone, but couldn't pull it off. The teaser blitz was on.

The big upset of the day, make that the year, was the Jets downing the Rams. We closed the Rams a 17.5-point favorite and +1300 on the money line. The Jets took it to them from the beginning, eventually holding on for a 23-20 win.

It was a big game for us. All week, people were throwing the Rams on the money line into their parlays, thinking it was a free winner. Well, nothing is free in this world and certainly not from a bookmaker. Even after that game, we were only slightly ahead for the day. The big game of the day, Chiefs-Saints, was still going on.

Last Monday, we opened the Chiefs as a 3.5-point favorite—another -3/+3.5-pointer. The first wave came in on the Saints +3.5. It was enough to move the number, so we went to -3. Naturally, the next wave came on the Chiefs -3, again enough to move the number, so back to -3.5 it went.

On Friday, the announcement came from the Saints that Drew Brees, out for weeks because of injury, would return to the starting lineup in place of Taysom Hill. Hill did fine as a replacement, but he's no Drew Brees, a certain Hall of Famer. I moved the Chiefs from -3.5 down to -3 with the announcement, but if this had happened on Monday and we had no action on the game, I would have gone down even further. Brees makes a lot more difference than a half-point. But since we'd already taken a ton of business, I moved that measly half-point.

We took in a lot of Saints +3 action and even though I was hesitant, I eventually had to go to Chiefs -2.5. Once again, we got Chiefs money at that price. When the dust settled, we were pretty even on the game, but having a low of -2.5 and a high of +3.5, I knew we were extremely vulnerable to a middle on the highest-volume game of the year so far.

Do I even have to tell you? The Chiefs won by 3, 32-29. It was our worst loss of the season, well into six figures.

On to Sunday night, featuring the Browns against the Giants. We opened the Browns -3.5, but midweek it was announced that starter Daniel Jones would miss the game. Veteran Colt McCoy would start in his place. I personally didn't see much difference between the two, but the betting public sure did. We went from -3.5 all the way up to -7 before we started getting money on the Giants. The wise guys took +6.5 as well, so we went to Browns -6, which the public went for. Then one of our biggest players laid the 6 on the Browns for $30,000. (He's the kind of player books kill for: tons of money and doesn't care what the numbers are. He just wants to bet.) The public continued to pound the Browns and the wise-guy money just couldn't overcome it. Even that big player came back from the pit and put another $12K on the Browns.

It was nip and tuck early, but eventually the Browns pulled away, winning 20-6. It capped off our worst day in a while. I really shouldn't complain;[7] we've been on a hell of a run for months.

The college football playoffs are set. The four teams are Alabama, Clemson, Ohio State, and Notre Dame. Some different opinions surfaced on Notre Dame vs. Texas A&M for that fourth spot, but who knows? There should be at least eight teams in the playoffs anyway and for sure this season, with all the craziness. This would have been the perfect (shortened) year to toss out tradition and give more teams a shot.

Monday December 21, 2020

A lot of money came in on tonight's game, featuring Cincinnati hosting a desperate Pittsburgh Steeler team. The public was on the Steelers, no surprise there. We were at Steelers -14

---

[7] But I will. Otherwise, they'll take away my bookmaker's card. As a group, we're the whiniest bunch around. We feel we're entitled to win every game on the board. I try not to be as bad as my brethren, but I fall victim to it, too.

most of the day, then late in the afternoon I went to -14.5. After taking some pretty good action on the Bengals +14.5, I was just about to go back to 14 when the big player I mentioned in yesterday's entry wanted $35,000 on the Steelers. Sure, no problem. Even though I was the first in town to go to 14.5, by then everyone else had followed. Pretty soon, the wise guys looking for the Bengals +14.5 could now find it anywhere. Mister Big Bettor came back and wanted another $15,000 on the Steelers. Sure, no problem. I went to -15 to get some money back on the Bengals and of course I did. When the wise guys see an unnatural number, especially in the NFL, it doesn't take long for them to pounce on it.

At kick off, we still needed the Bengals to cover, and a win would be better.

The Steelers looked terrible and lost outright, 27-17. From 11-0, they were now 11-3 and resembled a sinking ship. You always hear about a "team no one wants to play" in the playoffs. Well, the Steelers are the team everyone wants to play. They'll be there, but they'll get bounced like a tennis ball if they don't right the ship and quickly. Personally, I don't think they can.

Bowl season started today, too. It was the traditional Myrtle Beach Bowl, featuring Appalachian State vs. North Texas. I made App State -21, but the game opened -19.5. I opened -20, just to stay ahead of it, but it didn't matter. We got bet up to -22 and App State crushed North Texas 56-28. We lost on that game, but with the Bengals' win, we made a little for the day.

In our Survivor contest, we had the Titans, who won on Sunday. And ... you guessed it, the Steelers. So we're down to one live entry. I guess that's a lot better than a couple hundred others who now have none. But even if we do win, we'll likely be splitting it with a bunch of other players.

Tuesday December 22, 2020
First thing this morning, Tennessee dropped out of the

Liberty Bowl. That wasn't bad. Army was ready, willing, and able to replace them, so the Black Knights will face West Virginia. Then the Gasparilla Bowl went down. It's a true classic, but featured two teams, UAB and South Carolina, that have no business being at a bowl game unless they buy a ticket.

In the Potato Bowl, money showed on Nevada over Tulane. Tulane opened -3 and closed pick 'em. I overrated Tulane all year and liked them in this game. Nevada took the lead from the start and never relinquished it. I still have a spot in my heart for Nevada and the program made a nice comeback this year. Their quarterback, Carson Strong, is getting mentioned as having NFL potential. Head coach Jay Norvell has done a hell of a job. The bad news is now he's on the radar for some bigger jobs.

Later was an unusually good game for this early in the bowl season: Central Florida vs. BYU in the Boca Raton Bowl. BYU was the runaway winner, beating a very good UCF 49-23.

The NBA opened today with a light schedule. The Golden State Warriors play the Brooklyn Nets and the Clippers play the Lakers. The NBA knows how to emphasize drama, particularly on opening night. The Warriors face Kevin Durant, who signed with the Nets after winning championships with the Warriors. The Clippers and Lakers will play for early bragging rights in the City of Angels, though with the Lakers as defending champions and 17 championships under their belt, their bragging rights will last a lot longer than the result of one game, no matter who wins.

Wednesday December 23, 2020

We had a couple of nondescript bowl games today. Georgia Southern hammered Louisiana Tech 38-3 in the New Orleans Bowl and Memphis downed Florida Atlantic 25-10 in the Montgomery Bowl. I have to admit, I didn't watch a single play of either game. It was my day off and I had last-minute Christmas chores to attend to.

I wasn't totally absent from the sports book, however. I approved the reverse-teaser, ties win, and half-point cards like I do every Wednesday.

Later I got a call that the Houston Rockets had to postpone their game today against the Oklahoma City Thunder. They didn't have the required eight players available to start. Of course, COVID was involved, with players not following the required protocols. Their star, James Harden, was among them; there's a video of him at a strip club last night. A big no-no. He was fined $50,000, the only player fined so far. It has to be embarrassing for the Rockets.

Speaking of players making idiotic moves, it was revealed that after the Washington What-The-Fucks game on Sunday, their quarterback, Dwane Haskins, hosted a party in a hotel room with, uhm, let's call them strippers. Needless to say, the pictures taken showed the participants without masks doing what people do at such a soiree. I don't mind Daniel Snyder's team looking foolish, but it's nothing personal.

Thursday December 24, 2020

A typically slow Christmas Eve: one bowl game, the New Mexico Bowl, which of course was played in Texas, featuring Hawaii and Houston. Hawaii beat them 28-14. We had a nice little win.

Christmas Day is always a big for the NBA. We, along with everyone else, posted the lines today. And in what has become an annual tradition, bettors want to void their tickets when they find out the games are tomorrow and not today. Every freaking year. Oy.

Friday December 25, 2020

We helped Las Vegas sports bettors have a very Merry Christmas.

In the NFL game, the wise guys were firmly on the Vikings +7 or higher, but the public was all over the Saints. To make a long story short, if not for the smart money pounding the Vikings and under, we would have gotten murdered when the Saints beat them 52-33.

The NBA was way way worse. There were five games, all with big public teams. Not only did all five favorites win, but we never had a prayer in any one of the games. At least it spared me from torturing myself by trying to root us in.

So we did our community service by putting money in so many people's pockets. But somewhere in my mind I hear the echo of Warren Nelson's words: "I hate Christmas!"

Saturday December 26, 2020

Three NFL games, three college football games, a full college basketball schedule, and a big day in English soccer. Yeah, we were busy.

Georgia State beat Western Kentucky and Louisiana beat Texas San Antonio in their bowl games. In the FBC Mortgage Bowl, Liberty beat Coastal Carolina 37-34, in what was an actual big game. A few years ago, it would have been unthinkable for these two to be in a big bowl. Coastal was down most of the game, tied it late, then lost on a blocked field goal in overtime. Great game, but nothing like the late NFL game between the Raiders and Dolphins.

The Raiders led 16-13 entering the 4th quarter. With four minutes to play, the Dolphins tied it. Twenty-four seconds later, the Raiders connected on a 75-yard pass, then missed the extra point. Forty-two seconds after that, the Dolphins scored on a 59-yard pass and made their extra point to take a 23-22 lead.

The Raiders got the ball, kicked a field goal, and led 25-23 with 19 seconds left on the clock. No worries, Dolphins fans. Ryan Fitzpatrick hit Mack Hollins with a 41-yard completion, while having his head twisted so badly that a hoot owl would be envious. With the added face-mask penalty, the Dolphins were in position for a 44-yard field goal. Bingo. The Dolphins win 26-23.

In the betting world, the Raiders covered and the game went over, neither of which was good for us. For the Dolphins, they put themselves in position for the playoffs. Wow. What a coaching job by Brian Flores. They were the worst team in the NFL at the beginning of last year. Now they're one win away from the playoffs.

In the other NFL action, the 49ers upset the Cardinals 20-12 and the Bucs went out to a 34-0 lead at halftime over the Lions before winning 47-7. Tom Brady didn't even play the second half. The Lions were so inept, Blaine Gabbert threw two touchdown passes in his first six attempts in relief of Brady.

The results didn't look so great, but we squeezed out a small win for the day. Even Michael was impressed. We had a nice mix of action and were lucky enough that a few games fell just right for us. I must be living right.

Sunday December 28, 2020

In golf tournaments, moving day is Saturday. In the NFL, moving day is Week 16. And we definitely had some moving today.

The Browns, despite 10 wins, still aren't assured a playoff berth and needed a win over the Jets to secure their spot in the tournament and even give themselves a chance to win the division. Late yesterday, six players were placed on the COVID list and will miss the game. The line went from Browns -10 to -6.5. From there we jockeyed between -6.5 and -7 until game time. The Browns lost the game 23-16, giving us a big early win.

The Steelers played the Colts, also desperate for a win to secure a playoff spot and possible division title. Early money was on the Colts. We actually opened the Steelers -2.5 before their loss on Monday night to the Bengals. After that debacle, we reopened the Colts -2 on Tuesday morning. Plenty of money came in on both teams; eventually, the Steelers closed at -2, though the action was essentially even.

The Colts were up 24-7 in the third quarter, then the Steelers stormed back with three unanswered touchdowns to win 28-24. That win, along with the Browns loss, gave the Steelers the AFC North crown. The Steelers really needed this win. Did they right the ship? I'm far from convinced.

The Bears, losers of six straight at one point in the season, were in the driver's seat for a playoff berth. They had to beat the Jaguars, with the worst record in the league. Bears won 41-17 and it cost us, but it could have been worse.

The Washington Team-Without-A-Name needed one win to top the worst division in the history of the NFL. Early in the day, it was announced that Alex Smith wouldn't start for them; rather, the nod would go to first-round bust Dwane Haskins. Big money showed on the Panthers after the announcement. How right it was. The Panthers won 20-13.

The Chiefs limped to a 17-14 win over the Falcons. They escaped overtime on a missed 39-yard Falcons field goal as time elapsed. There are some warning signs out there for the defending champions. They've now won seven straight games, but all by one score. I have a feeling someone is going to beat them in the playoffs with a big play in a big situation. Just a feeling.

The Ravens are suddenly playing some great football, winning four straight, including a win over the Giants, 27-13. Believe it or not, the 5-10 Giants can still win the NFC East. Yes. It truly is the worst division in NFL history. Now watch the eventual winner advance to the Super Bowl. It's 2020, the year of complete lunacy.

Speaking of the worst division, two other NFC East rivals, the Cowboys and Eagles, squared off with the loser eliminated from the dubious distinction of Division champion.

The public has suddenly fallen in love Jalen Hurts, who replaced the disappointing Carson Wentz as the Eagles quarterback. We opened the Eagles -1.5, but all the money pushed the line to -3. The Cowboys fell behind early, but roared back to win 37-17. After all the drama and bullshit of the Cowboys season, they're only two steps from winning the division. But hear me O Lord, please don't make us endure a Cowboys playoff run. Haven't we suffered enough already this year?

The Rams and Seahawks game was likely to determine the NFC West title. The Seahawks drew the money and got the win, 20-9. They could dangerous in the playoffs. Their defense, awful at the beginning of the year, is now playing well. And, of course, they have Russell Wilson, one of the league's best quarterbacks.

In the Sunday night game, the Packers opened -3.5 over the Titans. Early money on the Titans dropped the line to Packers -3. But Green Bay coasted to a 40-14 win. Beating them is going to take some doing.

At the end of the day, we wound up with a big win.

In the Survivor contest, we had the Bears instead of the Cardinals. With one week to go, our dreams of great riches have shriveled. A lot of contestants will wind up with perfect records. That's what it'll take to win this thing. I only hope we're one of them.

Monday December 28, 2020

Once again, thank goodness for the wise guys. The Bills were -7 over the Patriots. Public money and some sharp players moved us to -7.5. Then the wise guys came in on the Pats +7.5. They took enough to get us back to 7, but the public overpowered them. We needed the Pats at kickoff. The Bills won 38-9, showing no mercy for the former biggest bullies on the block. Even though we lost on the game, a frustrated Bill Belichick, throwing things around on the sidelines, warmed the cockles of my heart. And you can't beat warm cockles.

The Washington We're-Trying-To-Bury-Our-Past bit the bullet this morning and cut Dwane Haskins. That's one hell of a downfall. On Sunday, he started a game that could have put his team in the playoffs and by Monday, he was out. Not benched. Cut. Wow. Move over JaMarcus Russell. Dwane Haskins is the biggest bust in NFL history.

Word is coming out today that the Washington Racist-Insults coaches were vehement in their desire to pass on Haskins in the draft, insisting he wasn't the player they wanted as the face of the franchise. Nonetheless, ownership, desperate for a quarterback, took him. Guess what? Ownership got its way, the guy was terrible, and the coaching staff got fired. Take a bow, guys. Another feather in your caps. Or, should I say, headdress.

Tuesday December 29, 2020

I hate Week 17.

We opened the Browns -7 over the Steelers. Ordinarily, the Steelers would be about a 4-point favorite. But Mike Tomlin said he would rest most of his starters. Well, rational humans figured that meant Ben Roethlisberger. Today, he announced Mason Rudolf would start in place of Ben. The number jumped from -7 to -10. What were people thinking? Of course Rudolf was going to start! Sometimes this business drives me nuts.

The Bills announced that they were taking a similar route. We had sort of assumed as much when we opened the game Bills -4.5. But with the announcement, the number dropped to pick 'em.

Both the Steelers and Bills could be playing for the number-two seed in the AFC playoffs. The catch is that seed will most likely open with the Ravens, playing terrific ball right now. The number-three seed will probably open with the Browns, nowhere near as scary an opponent. So neither seems too crazy about securing number two. There is home-field advantage, but this year, it looks pretty meaningless.

Another huge game this week is the Rams vs. the Cardinals. The winner is in the playoffs and the loser is most likely out. The Rams are definitely starting John Wolford at quarterback. He has never taken a snap in the NFL and no one really remembers much about him from his days at Wake Forest. Their regular starter, Jared Goff, is out with a thumb injury that required surgery. The Rams star receiver, Cooper Kupp, is also questionable after being put on the COVID list.

The Cardinals might or might not be in better shape. Their quarterback, Kyler Murray, is questionable with a leg injury. If he does play, he figures to be compromised. Running and scrambling are a big part of his game. His backup is Chris Streveler, whom I never heard of before today. He played at South Dakota and spent some time in the CFL.

This game stays off the board until I learn more about the Cardinal situation. At least I know the name of the Rams starter. Other than that, I'm shooting in the dark like everyone else.

The Texas Bowl, pitting TCU and Arkansas, got canceled. We still have a long way to go with this virus. Globally, we're up to 82 million cases with 1.8 million dead. Nationally, it's just under 20 million cases with 338,000 dead, including more than 3,700 today. And half the country still takes it as a badge of honor not to wear a mask. Unbelievable.

Wednesday December 30, 2020

I got the word late yesterday that Florida, playing Oklahoma in the Cotton Bowl, was short at least 12 players, including the whole receiving corps. The Cotton is the first of what's being called the New Year's Bowls. They're all supposed to be big games, but facts indicate otherwise. Dan Mullen, the Florida coach, said this was more like a spring game. Unfortunately, we wind up with a lot of bowl games like that. One team cares and the other doesn't.

The game opened with Florida a 3-point favorite. I liked Oklahoma from the start, so I moved it quickly when money started to show on the Sooners. The number had gone all the way to Oklahoma -4.5 when I heard from a very reliable source exactly what was going on with the Florida team. I was home, but I called the book and told them to go to -6 on the pointspread and jack up the money line. About 10 minutes later, they called to tell me we had a flood of money on Florida. The rest of the market was still at Oklahoma -4 or -4.5. "Don't move it," I told them. "This game will be at seven by tomorrow morning."

And it did We managed to stay ahead of the move the whole way. Eventually, the number got to -8.5 before we started taking some money back on Florida. By post time, we were pretty even, but the parlays were heavy on Oklahoma. The Sooners crushed them 55-20.

Earlier in the day, Wisconsin played Wake Forest in the Mayo Bowl. (Some mayonnaise company I never heard of sponsored the game. I guess it worked. The next time I need mayonnaise, I might actually buy their product.) Wisconsin was a 10-point favorite and naturally we needed the dog. Wake went out to a 14-point lead and I thought we were in pretty good shape. Wrong. Wisconsin beat them 42-28.

For the day in college football, it was favorite and over, favorite and over. Basketball pulled us out, though, giving us a slight plus figure for our efforts.

Back to the Florida-Oklahoma game for a second. A big part of bookmaking is cutting your losses. We didn't make any money on the Cotton Bowl, but we didn't lose much, either. So in a game that moved 11 points and that side won by a million, we didn't lose. That's not too bad, if I do say so myself.

Thursday December 31, 2020

One more day. About seven billion people and I can't wait for this year to be over. It couldn't get any worse, right? Don't say that. Don't even think it. It could get a lot worse. But let's stick to sports.

Old-timers like me will tell you the bowl setup back in the day was better. We were loaded with premier matchups on New Year's Day and often had one or two on New Year's Eve as well. This year, we had three so-so games today. Tomorrow, we have two pretty good games, along with two championship semi-finals. Not bad, but it still doesn't seem like the old days. I'm sure COVID has a lot to do with it, but the excitement for the entire bowl season has been nonexistent.

In today's first game, Ball State beat San Jose State as a 9-point dog, 34-13. One customer laid -330 on Ball State, $82,000 to win $25,000. Beating him was nice.

Mississippi State held on to beat Tulsa 28-26. The big story in that game was the fight afterward, one of the biggest and ugliest football fights I can remember. I wouldn't be surprised if law enforcement got involved.

West Virginia beat Army 24-21. I was one of the first to get information on this game. Multiple Army players were being held out for unannounced reasons; however, a cheating scandal at the Academy was suspected. The number went from West Virginia -6.5 to -10. We were way ahead of the move, but obviously it backfired. It happens. I'll still take the info whenever I can get it.

One of our big pit players bet $130,000 to win a little over $70,000 on Alabama -185 to win the national championship. The prices on these futures were all over the place, but we were about average at -185. That's a pretty big bet for us to take, so I jacked up the prices on the other three teams. I'm sure I'll be rooting against Alabama, but we've already started taking action on Clemson, Ohio State, and Notre Dame. I have got 24 hours. We'll see what happens.

No, I didn't see the New Year come in. I was asleep by 10 p.m.

I'm still waiting for the auditing report for the actual bottom line, but we won about 35% more this December than we did last December. Even that number is a bit deceiving, because last December, the NFL season had been completed and we had a pretty big win on the season totals. This season ends in January. I don't think we'll do as well this year, either. But we still have a few results that will be resolved this Sunday. I think we'll make a couple bucks, but not much.

On to 2021.

Chapter Eleven
January 1-24, 2021

"I never forget a face. But in your case, I'll make an exception."
—*Groucho Marx*

January 1, 2021

Groucho wasn't talking about 2020, but it certainly fit. Anyway, we finally got here. I don't know where exactly, but flipping the calendar and leaving 2020 behind felt good.

Only four college games today, but the action was sensational.

In the Peach Bowl, one of the official New Year's Day games, Cincinnati led all the way until Georgia kicked a field with two seconds left on the clock to take the lead, 22-21. Georgia was around a 9-point favorite and we wound up with loads of teasers on Georgia, which I balanced by getting action on the Cincinnati money line. Anyone betting Georgia teasers got them down to -2.5 or -3. A 1-point Georgia win was perfect for us.

Except it wasn't to be. Georgia kicked the ball deep and Cincy downed the ball on their own 5-yard line. I could sense my perfect scenario was going to blow up in my face. On the last play of the game, the Cincy quarterback took the snap, faded back to pass, and was sacked in the endzone. Safety. Two points for Georgia, giving them a 24-21 win. So close.

In the other early game, Northwestern pounded Auburn, 35-19. Not much of a decision either way, but nice to see the Big 10 beat the SEC.

We had some big action on the two championship games: big money-line bets on Alabama, betting a lot to win a little, and decent-sized bets to win a lot on the underdog Notre Dame if they could win outright. We were balanced on the straight bets, but totally lopsided on Alabama with the little stuff.

Bama led 21-7 at the half and the favorite was looking pretty strong. I could live with it. If the little stuff is winning, at least the money is going into the right hands. Lo and behold, the second half was a snooze fest, Bama mostly sitting on its lead. Notre Dame scored a late TD after Alabama put up a touchdown and a field goal in the second half to make the final 31-14. Notre Dame covers as a 20-point dog, despite never having a chance in the world to win the game. Take note, kids. That's one reason wise guys prefer betting underdogs. Sometimes showing up and sneaking in the back door is all you need to get the dough.

I told you about the bet we took yesterday on Alabama to win it all. By raising the prices on the rest of the teams, we got some action across the board. However, the bulk of that action came in on Clemson at +300. It was understandable. They were the defending champions, had the presumed number-one pick in the NFL draft in Trevor Lawrence, and were a 7-point favorite over Ohio State. The biggest bet we took was $20,000 to win $60,000. That's a decent-sized bet, considering we were running Clemson at the best price in the world, no exaggeration.

As far as the game itself, we needed Ohio State to win or at least cover the spread. Of course, an outright Ohio State win would be a thing of beauty. Besides giving us a big win for the day, it would eliminate Clemson from the national championship. We'd do okay on Clemson, but fantastic on Ohio State.

Ohio State went 3-and-out on its first drive. Clemson came right down and scored afterward. We looked like we were in trouble, then Ohio State's offense started to click, even though they couldn't stop Clemson. The score was tied 14-14 at the end of the first quarter. Then the Ohio State defense figured out a way to stop Lawrence and the rest of the Clemson offense. You couldn't say the same about the Clemson defense. They couldn't stop Ohio State the second quarter as the Buckeyes posted 21 unanswered points, effectively deciding the game at the end of the first half. Ohio State never let them get closer than 14 as they topped Clemson 49-28. It was a nice start to the new year.

I opened Alabama -7 over Ohio State, with a total of 76, but posted a high money line, -280/+240. With the big disparity in my futures book, I wanted to stay above the market and I was a dime higher than anyone else.

Saturday January 2, 2021

COVID is dominating the news today. What else is new? It's still rampant throughout the country and getting worse. It's no surprise sports is reflecting that.

The Bengals, for one, had multiple positive tests. They play the Ravens this week in a game the Ravens must win to get to the playoffs. The NFL has announced the game will go on as scheduled. The Ravens went from -12 to -13.5. Were this a midseason game, the date probably would have moved. They don't have that flexibility now. Playing the game as scheduled is incredibly important to the NFL and on a personal level, it's important to me. Our Survivor team has the Ravens for our last pick. If we win, we at least get a piece of the prize, a couple thousand for me. But if they cancel the game, it counts as a loss and we get shit.

The Browns, another team in a do-or-die situation, closed their practice facility today because at least one coach tested positive. Their opponent, the Steelers, also have a new COVID positive in cornerback Joe Haden. At this point, the Steelers aren't doing anything different, other than saying Haden won't play. The number dropped slightly from the Browns -9.5 to -8.5.

Alvin Kamara of the Saints tested positive, which was bad enough, but the whole running-back corps for the Saints has been declared out. The Saints still have a chance to get the number-one seed in the NFC, so the game means a lot to them. The Saints went from -6.5 to -5.

Last week, the Browns played with no wide receivers. Earlier this season, the Broncos played with no quarterback. And now the Saints are playing with no running backs. This is the NFL in the time of COVID.

In related news, 16 college basketball games were canceled today. Multiple games are canceled every day; I just haven't bothered to keep up with them. But today was inordinately high. And it's not just here. Three English Premier League games got canceled this week as well.

In today's early action, Kentucky beat N.C. State 23-21 in the Gator Bowl and Ole Miss beat Indiana 26-20 in the Outback Bowl. No big action on either, but decent results nonetheless.

The Fiesta Bowl is one of the "New Year's Day" games pitting Oregon against Iowa State. Michael called me about a half-hour before kickoff to ask who we needed. Oregon, I told him. Well, things completely turned around after that. We got flooded with Oregon money and now needed Iowa State. The Cyclones jumped out to an early lead and never relinquished it. I was going to call Michael back, but I didn't want to jinx it. Instead, when he called to see how much in the hole we were, I told him we were up for the day. A nice surprise for the big guy. But it was still early.

Texas A&M played North Carolina in the Orange Bowl, the last of the "New Year's Day" games. We opened A&M -7, but North Carolina announced a bunch of players opting out to prepare for the upcoming draft. The number slowly climbed to -10 before kickoff. With about 20 minutes to go before kick, a customer laid the A&M money line at -350, $98,700 to win $28,200. Where he got those numbers, I have no idea.

North Carolina led 27-20 in the 4th quarter, but just couldn't hold them off. A&M's talent and power ground them down, scored three 4th quarter touchdowns, and won 41-27. We blew the money line and the pointspread. It was a huge swing. We had a chance to have a big day for the sports book, but just wound up with a small plus figure.

The final day of the NFL regular season is tomorrow, which will determine season wins, division winners, player props, and team matchups. Besides that, tomorrow caps off the craziest betting week of the year. Needless to say, I'm concerned.

Sunday January 3, 2020

Just as I expected, there was a cluster of moves this morning. Before I could even pour my first cup of coffee, I made three from my home office. In addition to all the rest of the bullshit, weather wreaked havoc throughout the middle of the country and the Northeast.

We were open to getting middled on 11 of the 16 games today. We escaped the morning without any serious damage. We didn't knock out all the teams that left us vulnerable to parlays in the afternoon, but we did KO a few.

One of the biggest moves of the week was on the Dolphins over the Bills. We had the Bills -2 on the parlay card, but the Dolphins closed a 3.5-point favorite. The Bills crushed them 56-26. That one knocked out a lot of cards, besides a big win on straight bets. The Dolphins are now out of the playoffs.

Money continued to pour in on the Lions. We jockeyed between Vikings -3 and -3.5 all morning, but we had the Vikings -7 on our ties-win card. Needless to say, the Lions were a big play on the card. The Vikings went up by 8 in the game a couple times, but couldn't keep that lead. They still won 37-35, but that didn't help much.

The Giants beat the Cowboys 23-19. That was no bargain for us, but now the Giants have a chance to make the playoffs if the Eagles upset Washington tonight.

The Browns beat the Steelers 24-22 to make it into the

playoffs. That was an okay result for us. The Bucs smashed the Falcons 44-27 to enhance their playoff seed. They'll play the winner of the NFC East, which will be one of the worst playoff teams ever. Good for the Bucs, but a loser for us.

The Ravens beat the Bengals 38-3 to make the playoffs and give us a piece of the Circa Survivor contest. More on that later. The Patriots beat the Jets 28-14. No one gave a shit.

In the afternoon, the Bears faced the Packers. The Packers needed the win to secure the number-one NFC seed and the Bears needed the game to get into the playoffs. The Packers opened -6, but Bears money showed and we went as low as -4, closing at -4.5. The Packers won 35-16. Even though they lost, the Bears got into the playoffs when the Cardinals lost to the Rams, 18-7.

The Rams got all the money today. We were as high as Cardinals -3.5, then moved all the way to Rams -1, before closing the game at pick 'em. It wasn't good for the day's action, but it helped with season-win totals and their matchup with the Raiders (the Cardinals as a favorite of -.5 games). Both teams finished 8-8. A win for the good guys.

The Raiders got some money today as a 2.5-point favorite over the Broncos. Not enough to move the number, but we still needed the dog +2.5. The Raiders scored with 24 seconds to play to cut the Broncos lead to 31-30. They went for the two-point conversion and the win rather going into overtime. They converted and took a 32-31 lead. The Broncos still had time and got into long field-goal range, but missed. The 1-point Raider victory was perfect for us. They failed to cover as a 2.5-point favorite, but won the game to finish 8-8 and beat the 8-8 Cardinals in the season matchup. Phew.

The Titans needed a late field goal that bounced off the right upright and then in to beat the Texans 41-38 and win the AFC South division over the Colts who struggled, but pulled away late to beat the Jaguars 28-14.

The Seahawks won the NFC West with their 26-23 win over the 49ers.

The Chiefs rested most of their starters, while the Chargers beat them 38-21. That was a bad result for us. We opened the Chargers -3.5 and closed -6.5. That one hurt, but we never had a chance, so there was nothing to sweat.

The Washington Holy-Shit-Win-and-We're-Ins and the Eagles haven't kicked off yet, but we need Holy-Shit.

Right now, between season-win totals, season team match-ups, division winners, and yes/no to make the playoffs, we're about even. I'm happy with that, mainly because our satellite at the Rampart took way more than prudent. Once it was done, I had to fix it. I did the best I could, so I consider breaking even a victory. (Actually, we're up a few thousand and if Washington wins, we'll have a decent win on our side.)

We're in pretty bad shape heading into the Sunday-night game. A Washington win makes the season-long props look a lot better, but we're stuck pretty good with no way to escape. What would help is either an Eagles win or a Washington blowout.

Well, we got neither. In fact, we got about the worst result possible. Washington won 20-14. We opened the Eagles -1 and went all the way to Washington -7 before we got any serious takeback. Voila, it landed on the worst number possible. All in all, an ugly day.

A little more about Washington-Eagles. The way the Eagles played the final quarter has some people either scratching their heads or accusing the Eagles of outright tanking. The Eagles rested a number of players. Some indicated they were ready, willing, and able to play, but were inactive nonetheless. Even Carson Wentz, the starter a few short weeks ago, didn't dress for the game.

Washington led 17-14 to start the fourth quarter and the Eagles responded by inserting backup quarterback Nate Sudfeld, who hadn't thrown a regular-season pass since 2018. Although he's been on the Eagles roster for a couple years, he hadn't dressed since Week One. It was curious, to say the least. Sudfeld's first pass was intercepted; later, he fumbled a snap from center. It's hard to blame Sudfeld. If you wanted to see him in game action, the fourth quarter of the last game of the season is an odd place to perform your discovery.

Twitter lit up with the tanking accusations. The Giants, who would've won the NFC East with an Eagles win, weren't happy. The notorious Philly press lambasted the action. Sal Palantonio, the de facto Eagles beat correspondent for ESPN, lit into Coach Doug Pederson and whoever else could be responsible for the decision for making a mockery of the spirit of competition in the NFL. The Eagles did move up three draft positions with the loss, but that doesn't seem like enough of a reason to tank. Was there something else? Some sort of grudge against the Giants? I don't know. The whole thing doesn't make a lot of sense to me or anyone else at this point.

To the NFL's credit, a lot of schedule finagling notwithstanding, not one game was missed; they played all 256 games. They were consistent and did what they had to do—intense testing and tracing and strict protocols. The rest of the country could learn from what they did. Hats off to them.

Now I hope I didn't just jinx the playoffs.

Yes, I grabbed a piece of the Circa Survivor contest, which is good news. The bad news is not one single contestant got knocked out on Sunday. Oh well. I still pick up a couple thousand. I just had visions of what it could have been at times during the season and the final result was nowhere near that.

Monday January 4, 2021

Today, I made the prices for the Super Bowl Exacta. To win the bet, you pick the team that wins and the team that loses. There can be some pretty high payouts and the opportunity of a big score has been a good enticement for bettors. I've used it the past couple years and it brings in some good action.

I hate to brag (or as my daughter likes to tell me, I hate the fact that I love to brag), but I invented this bet. I see others booking it, even naming it the same as I have, but it's my invention. I just want to set the record straight.

Time for me to start following the basketball a little more closely. And of course, the first thing to hit my radar today is COVID.

In the NBA, Kevin Durant will miss the next four games for the Nets after being exposed to the virus. He had it earlier, so he probably doesn't have it now, but that's the protocol if you're in contact with someone who has it.

Villanova coach Jay Wright contracted the virus. Villanova currently is ranked third in the country. They'll miss their next three games.

Tuesday January 5, 2021

Did I give the NFL playoffs the μάτι? (The máti. The evil eye. I know every Greek reading this will think so.)

This morning, it was announced that Cleveland Browns head coach Kevin Stefanski, along with two other coaches and two players, had COVID. One player is a receiver I never heard of, but the other is Joe Bitonio, an All-Pro guard and the Browns' best offensive lineman. That one hurts. Of course, so does losing Stefanski. He's made a huge difference in the Browns this season. He has to leave the facility and have no physical contact with the team for at least 10 days. As far as working from afar, I don't know what's allowed and what isn't.

The Steelers opened -3.5 over the Browns. (I opened it -4. I thought the number was way too low. I made the Steelers -6.5 with my power ratings.) The number started moving up, which made total sense to me, climbing to -4.5 before the news broke on Stefanski, et al. We stayed consistently ahead (at -5), so we didn't get any action. I closed the game briefly, then reopened it at -5.5. I saw it was still moving up, so again to stay ahead of it, I went to -6. The Browns beat the Steelers earlier when the Steelers benched many of their top starters, including Ben Roethlisberger. Even then, the Browns won by only 2 points. So they just beat their arch rivals, a team that has owned them for 20 years, a team that's an hour and a half down the turnpike, to get into the playoffs on the last day of the season and now they have to play them again. I hate to play amateur psychologist, but how can they beat that same team again? They won't. The Steelers will kill them.

Other games are moving, too. Wise guys took the Rams +4.5 vs. the Seahawks. There's still a question about the Rams quarterback (Goff or Wolford?), but it wasn't enough to scare the bettors. That Rams defense is still going for them.

Alex Smith isn't 100% for the Washington How-Can-This-Crappy-Team-Be-In-The-Playoffs. Coach Ron Rivera said he might rotate Smith and seldom-used Taylor Heinecke at quarterback this week. That's not a good sign for Washington. The Bucs have gone from -7.5 to -9 at my store, though I see it lower elsewhere.

Wise guys took the Titans +3.5 against the Ravens this morning. I'm not privy to their thinking, but the Ravens have been poor in the playoffs in recent years, while the Titans had an impressive playoff run last year.

Saints-Bears is the one game that hasn't moved. The Saints are still sitting at -9.5 virtually everywhere.

The Bills dropped from -7 to -6.5 over the Colts. For value seekers, I can understand it. The number looks a little high. But do you want to step in front of this Bills freight train? Not me.

In college football, Alabama has toggled between -7 and -8 after opening at -7. Good action so far, but pretty even money-wise.

The NCAA announced the entire college basketball tournament will be held in and around Indianapolis. There are plenty of colleges and hoops courts there. Considering everything, it's probably a good idea.

DeVonta Smith, the wide receiver from Alabama, won the Heisman Trophy tonight. We didn't book it this year because of COVID. The books that did opened Smith anywhere from 50/1 to 75/1. They closed it around -600 to -1000. I'm glad we didn't book it. We would've gotten clobbered.

Thursday January 7, 2021

No matter what has happened in the world around us, I've done my best to write about any and all situations in terms of how they affect sports and/or betting. Yesterday, however, the United States Capitol was overrun. And today, it's taking every ounce of my willpower not to wade into this political fray.

I will say this: We woke up in a new country. Joe Biden was officially elected president by the Electoral College sometime in the middle of the night. I'm keeping my fingers crossed the attack on the Capitol is over for now and I can concentrate on sports.

All the football games scheduled for this weekend are still on. And we're starting to see some serious action on the games.

I opened the Colts as 7-point underdogs against the Bills. It was bet down to +6.5 are still attracting money. The Bills are a 6-point favorite now. There has also been a lot of money-line action on the Colts.

No shortage of money on the Rams so far. We opened Seahawks -4.5. That didn't last long. Wise guys took +4.5, +4, and today +3.5. All sharp money. It's interesting, because we're still not sure about the Rams' quarterback—John Wolford, who looked pretty good last week in his first start, or Jared Goff, who led them to the Super Bowl two years ago.

The Bucs-Washington Great-We're-in-the-Playoffs-And-Now-We-Have-To-Beat-Tom-Brady game has jockeyed between Bucs -8 and -9. We're right in the middle right now at Bucs -8.5.

The Ravens-Titans is one of those games I hate. Everyone

is on the Ravens -3 and the Titans +3.5. Every time I move one side, it takes no time at all for them to come in on the other side. As long as it doesn't fall Ravens by 3, we'll be okay.

The Saints opened -9.5 over the Bears. The money had been trickling in on the Saints since the opening. We finally moved to Saints -10 today. Not one big bet, but an accumulation finally moved us.

The Steelers' number zoomed up from -4 to -6 with the news of a slew of COVID cases on the Browns. Now we're starting to see some take-back on the Browns. I'm still running -6, but some -5.5s are starting to show.

My Uncle Jack would have been 93 today. I still miss him. He would be glad to know we talk about him at virtually every lunch when the boys get together.

Besides what's going on in Washington (politically, not the football team), we had over 4,000 deaths from COVID yesterday. A new record.

Friday January 8, 2021

We have pretty good action on the props we put up on all six of today's NFL playoff games. A prop I put up a while ago (Chiefs, Bills, Packers, and Saints vs. the field to win the Super Bowl) is up to -475, with the field the favorite. For the first time, I also put up an NFL Grand Salami, an over/under on the total points scored for the weekend.

Every once in a while, I think about other directions my life could have taken. I might have been a stockbroker, a sportswriter, a Ph.D. in Greek mythology or philosophy, or maybe just tuned in a bit more to my artist's heart. But even after doing this for over 40 years, I still get excited about days like we'll have this weekend. Then I realize I did, after all, find my life's work.

Unfortunately, some other things are going on in this country that can't be overlooked. We had 269,420 new cases today, a dubious new record; 14 college basketball games were canceled today; and civil unrest continues.

Saturday January 9, 2021

Man, were we busy today. Ten minutes before the first football game, we had so many people in line, it looked like Super Bowl Sunday. I have no idea how we managed to get everyone in on time, but we did.

We didn't need much the first game. The public laid -6.5 on the Bills and took the Colts +7. We had plenty of teaser action on the Bills (down to pick 'em), but I offset it with as much money-line play as I could get on the Colts. The Bills won 27-24, with a real chance to lose, which had me sweating buckets. It was a good result for us on paper. But the first game in a rotation is never as good as it looks. You're knocking out dead parlays, but aren't paying any live ones until later. Nonetheless, it's much better to start way ahead than it is way behind.

In the second game, John Wolford was announced as starting his second game at quarterback for the Rams. Some money came in on the Seahawks at that time—not a flood, but enough to change a balanced game into us needing the Rams. Wolford started, but got hurt early in the first quarter. Jared Goff, with his broken thumb, came in as Wolford's replacement. Goff can be wildly inaccurate with a perfect thumb, but he was good enough to win the game 30-20, a great result for us.

Another quarterback injury rocked the betting market just before the game. Alex Smith, who we knew wasn't 100% as he limped through practice this week, wasn't even going to dress for the Washington God-Must-Be-Punishing-Us-For-Our-Past-Racist-Names. I'd been running the Bucs high anyway, knowing I'd need the Washington I'm-Running-Out-Of-Ideas no matter what. So all I did was raise the number from Bucs -9.5 to -10. We still needed the Washington Okay-I'm-Just-About-Done at kickoff.

Tyler Heinecke played what was probably the game of his

life, keeping the game close the whole way. He finished with one touchdown, one interception, and 306 yards passing. Not fantastic numbers, but impressive given the situation. He even came back from a late collarbone injury that sent him briefly to the locker room to lead the Washington Please-Give-Us-A-Real-Name-By-Next-Season to a final touchdown. Nonetheless, the Bucs walked away with a 31-23 victory. That game cost us a bit, particularly on teasers, but we knew we were up against it needing to beat Tom Brady's team. Another game where I took some serious money-line action on the dog just to try to alleviate the teaser loss.

The football was very good for us today. Hoops were about a breakeven, with 44 college basketball games canceled today. Big day tomorrow.

Sunday January 10, 2021

In the Ravens-Titans game, we needed the Titans pretty bad. The Ravens, particularly quarterback Lamar Jackson, had a reputation of rarely overcoming a large deficit. When the Titans went out to a 10-0 lead, I thought the game was playing right into our hands. But they went into the half tied 10-10. Instead of a Titans rout, it was now a fight and the Ravens held the upper hand the rest of the game. They outgained the Titans 401 to 209. Even then, the Titans had some chances, but never could convert.

In the Bears-Saints game the Saints scored early to take a 7-0 lead. On the ensuing possession, the Bears ran a trick play and quarterback Mitch Trubisky found Javon Wims alone in the end zone. The ball went through Wims' hands like it was covered in axle grease. Had he caught that pass and tied the game at 7-7, the remainder of the game might have been played totally differently. Alas, it wasn't, and we got caught on the short end again. For the day, we managed to grind out a decent profit somehow with the two first halfs, both halftimes, and the props, but we entered the Steelers-Browns game with two losers under our belts. We were looking at a loss well into six figures with a Steelers cover. Even just an outright win would cause some serious damage via teasers and money-line parlays.

We were running the Steelers -5.5 at the time, so I jacked it up to -6 and took the money line from -300/+250 to -330/+270. That was enough for the wise guys and bargain hunters to pour in on the Browns. I probably gave away too much on the Browns' money line, but I had to alleviate the possibility of that monstrous loss. Since we were pretty even on the game, I was rooting for my hometown Steelers.

The Steelers received the opening kickoff. The first snap from center went over Ben Roethlisberger's head, into the end zone, And the Browns recovered, taking a 7-0 lead six seconds into the game. On the ensuing possession, Big Ben threw his first interception. The Browns scored another touchdown at 9:46. On the Browns next possession, I went to the bathroom and by the time I got back, they'd scored again. At the end of the first quarter, it was 28-0. I knew I'd given back too much on the Browns money line.

It was 35-10 at the half. But after the Steelers scored two third-quarter touchdowns, It was 35-23. But the Steeler defense, championship-caliber all season, was as porous as a tea strainer. The Browns prevailed 48-37 in a game that was essentially over in the first quarter.

We wound up making some money for the day, though I really don't know how—other than superior bookmaking.

Monday January 11, 2021

The college championship game is tonight. I spent the morning working on props with Lou Vargin, who runs the Monday-morning shift and is one of my key guys Then I adjusted the Super Bowl odds, including the "four teams vs. the field" and the Super Bowl Exacta.

The action was steady all day. I was working on offsetting the big futures bet we took on Alabama with a high money line on Ohio State. Of course, I didn't want to give it all away, like I did last night on the Browns. At kickoff, we still needed Ohio State for a nice sum, but Alabama crushed them, 52-24. Ohio State hung with them for about a quarter and a half, but Bama was just too much. They really are one of the best teams I've ever seen, completely unstoppable on offense. And Nick Saban has to be the best coach of all time.

The way college football is going right now, these two teams and Clemson can already be penciled in for three of the four playoff spots for next year.

By the way, this game should have been played on Friday. It's anticlimactic playing on Monday after two straight days of NFL tripleheaders. College football is terrific. But the NFL still rules the roost.

With Alabama winning and covering, and the total falling right on the number, it wasn't a very good day for us. At least NBA and college basketball were good, so that eased some of the pain.

Wednesday January 13, 2020

I made some adjustments on the Super Bowl futures. We're not in terrible shape with any of the teams left, but we're in what I would call good shape with only one team, the Chiefs. They're the favorite, so I'm not in a big sweat, but I do want to improve my position. Right now, I have them +220, which is the best price you can find by far. I'm looking for a sizable bet.

Today is the opening of the NHL season. One of the biggest changes I saw when I came back to my life's work behind the counter was the increase in hockey betting. I'm sure the Golden

Knights starting up in Las Vegas had a lot to do with it, but we get good action all the way across the board.

Big trade in the NBA today. James Harden, one of the NBA's biggest scorers, went to the Brooklyn Nets. Houston wound up with Victor Olidipo, a pretty good player, and three future first-round draft choices. Harden had been trying to force the trade since training camp. He was sick and tired of Houston's ownership, one more in a long line of players. Since 2013, the Rockets have also lost Dwight Howard, Carmelo Anthony, Chris Paul, and Russell Westbrook.

Who knows what will happen with the draft choices, but the Nets are now the favorite to win the Eastern Conference and second choice behind the Lakers to win the NBA. We're a loser on the Nets in both situations, so I'm running the price pretty low.

Donald Trump was impeached today. Again. Making him the Johnny Vander Meer of presidents.

Thursday January 14, 2021

In the NFL, Jared Goff will start this week for the Rams. It also came out that Cooper Kupp is less than 100%. It's still 48 hours to game time, but Kupp is their best offensive player. If he's not at full strength, it'll hurt the Rams. To get ahead of what I'm anticipating, I moved the Packers to -7 over the Rams. I thought we'd get to 7 eventually, anyway. I like to be first in that situation. I might be wrong, but my strategy worked just as I intended. Within minutes, one of my wise guys bet $30,000 on the Rams. He took +7 for $22,000 to win $20,000 and bet $12,500 to win $10,000, buying a half-point to +7.5. I went back to 6.5, but I still expect to need the Rams come post time.

We also took some money on the Browns +10. It had been coming in that way, so I moved the number to Chiefs -9.5.

Friday January 15, 2021

I went to Bills -3 to see what would happen. Other 3s were popping up, but with juice on the dog. Eventually, I took enough Ravens +3 to move me back to -2.5. I'm pretty sure I'll be back to 3 at some time tomorrow, but for right now I had to stop the flood.

Saturday January 16, 2021

Lots of late money showed on the Packers this morning once it was announced Cooper Kupp would be out for the Rams. Most of the wise guys were already on the Rams +7 from earlier in the week. I went there again early in the day. They pounded me pretty good at that point, forcing me back to 6.5. But of course, when the move came on the Packers, I went back to 7 quickly and was in pretty good shape with the game.

The Rams played well offensively, much better than anyone expected, and hung in with the Packers until the fourth quarter when they got finished off, losing 32-18. We did well on the game, like we always do in the first game of the rotation. But we won't know everything until the last final is put in tomorrow at around 7 p.m.

We couldn't get close to even on the Ravens-Bills game. That early big position I took, the Ravens +3, was too much to overcome. With the total of the first game flying over, we needed the second game under.

The wind played havoc with both teams and the Ravens' place kicker, Justin Tucker, hit one goal post on his first field-goal attempt and the opposite post on his next. The Ravens outgunned the the Bills in yards, first downs, and possession time, but the Bills were ahead when the biggest play of the game came with 0:58 in the third quarter. The Ravens were driving toward the Bills' end zone. A touchdown and extra point would tie the game at 10-10. Suddenly, Taron Johnson intercepted a pass in the end zone and went all the way for a pick-six. From the game about to be tied, the Bills turned the tables and stretched the lead to 14 points, huge in such a defensive-oriented game. It wound up being the last score, though the Ravens weren't giving up. Their chances were compromised when Lamar Jackson was sacked hard enough to cause a concussion. Enter Tyler Huntley, an untested rookie from Utah. He actually played well, but missed an open receiver who could have waltzed into the endzone and would have cut the lead to a single score. He drove them to the red zone once again before turning the ball over on downs. That was the Ravens' last gasp. The Bills held on for a 17-3 win.

On a personal note, I won my money-line bet on the Bills. And yes, I plan to roll it over one more time and do the same with the Packers.

Sunday January 17, 2021

Money rolled in on the Browns all morning. We went from the Chiefs -10 to -9.5 yesterday, but the steady stream continued all the way until kickoff. We closed the game Chiefs -8. We needed a Browns win or a Chiefs blowout. We got neither.

The Chiefs were extremely fortunate when, up 16-3 just before the half, Rashard Higgins reached for the goal line on a pass reception, only to fumble the ball into the end zone. When the offense does that, it's a touchback and the defense gets possession on the 20-yard line. It's a terrible rule, but it's a rule. Instead, the Browns should have had the ball, first and goal on the 1-yard line.

The Browns showed a lot of moxie and hung in there until the end. They had an even better chance when Patrick Mahomes suffered a concussion in the fourth quarter and was replaced by journeyman Chad Henne. Henne threw a terrible interception, but made up for it running for a near first down on third and long with a little more than a minute to play. Henne then converted a fourth-down pass to cinch the game for the Chiefs, 22-17. With Mahomes now questionable for next week, I didn't put up a number for the Chiefs-Bills matchup.

In the Saints-Bucs game, we had a ton of exposure on the Saints. If they covered and it went over 53, we were looking at losing $300,000. I know for some big outfits, that's a common occurrence, but it would have been a major blow for us. By the time kickoff came, all we could do was sweat the outcome.

All week long, I'd been saying on a variety of radio shows and podcasts that I'm just not crazy about the Saints. I never thought Drew Brees was in the league of Brady, Peyton Manning, and Aaron Rodgers. I even had a big bet against him when he won his only Super Bowl. (That didn't work out so well for me.) I liked the Bucs all week and now my judgment was going to be put to the test.

Brees played terribly. He threw for one touchdown and three interceptions. I didn't expect that from him, but I did expect Brady to outplay him. Brady did play well, but he was also the beneficiary of those three interceptions and another Saints turnover on a fumble. Even then, the game was tied 20-20 entering the fourth quarter, when the Bucs put 10 unanswered points on the board to walk away with a 30-20 victory.

We wound up breaking even for the day. Considering how much we won on Saturday, it was a tremendous weekend.

Monday January 18, 2021

I continued with my personal parlay after winning both of my games on Saturday. I'm betting the Packers and Bills to reach the Super Bowl. When the numbers came out, I rolled over my Packers bet and laid -190. I did the same with the Bills, taking +140. I got the best number on the Bills, but I could have laid -185 on the Packers.

Meanwhile, I put up a line for the Chiefs-Bills game when the number settled to a universal Chiefs -3. We also put up the Packers -4 over the Bucs. One of our sharp players came in late last night and took the Bucs +4. So as of this morning, we still had the Chiefs -3, and now the Packers -3.5.

The first round of props for the conference championship games were posted today, just some basic stuff like team totals and first halfs. I adjusted the Super Bowl odds and exacta and reopened the prop I had up from weeks ago with the four teams (Bills, Chiefs, Packers, and Saints) vs. the field. The field now included the Bucs, so I had to adjust for that. We'll put up many more things later in the week, but I'm still waiting for more conclusive word on Mahomes.

Money started showing on the Bills tonight. We went down to Chiefs -140 Bills +120 on the money line in the morning. I would move the Chiefs from -3 to -2.5 now, but I don't want my graveyard crew to deal with it, so I'll do it in the morning. I'm off tomorrow, but I'll be in my home office monitoring the action.

Tuesday January 19, 2021

Early this morning, a money mover for one of the big outfits bet me the Chiefs -2.5. Shit. I didn't want to do this 2.5-3 dance all week, but here it is. When the one guy played me last night, I thought this game might go to Chiefs -1.5 or -2. No such luck.

Then I was really getting overloaded on the Bucs, so I had to go to Packers -3. The rest of the market has gone to -3 with juice on the favorite or -3.5 with heavy juice on the underdog. As a result, I'm doing the 3-3.5 dance on the Packers-Bucs game as well as the 2.5-3 dance on the Chiefs-Bills. This will be a challenge. No rest for the weary. And speaking of which, we passed 400,000 COVID deaths.

Wednesday January 20, 2021

Joe Biden took the oath of office and at noon today we got a new president.

Between watching the inauguration ceremony, hearing

from my friends about the lunatics on Facebook and Twitter, and going to the doctor, I kept an eye on the football. I got a few calls today about big bets, but nothing as crazy as yesterday. Tomorrow I'll fill out the remainder of our prop menu.

Friday January 22, 2020

Action really started picking up on the NFL championship games.

I had to go to -3.5 on the Chiefs this morning, once it was announced Patrick Mahomes would definitely play. I knew one of my customers would make a big bet and he came in later, taking the Bills +3.5 for $100,000. So I went back to Chiefs -3. I'm the only 3 flat (-110) out there, so I'm getting money back on the Chiefs.

Packers continue to draw money. I went to Packers -4 and got enough big money back on the Bucs +4 to push me back down to 3.5. It didn't last long. The money kept coming in on the Packers, so back to -4 it went.

I'm in pretty good shape on both games, as long as the Packers don't win by 3 or 4 and the Chiefs don't win by 3. It's a dangerous spot to be in, but that's where we are. Still a long way to go to post time.

Hank Aaron passed away today. It was he who broke Babe Ruth's record of 714 lifetime home runs. He finished the 1973 season with 713 home runs, so it was inevitable he would break Ruth's record the following season. Racists throughout the country threatened to murder him in order to keep the record with a white man and not be broken by an African-American. It's an ugly blot on the history of baseball and the country, but Aaron handled it as gracefully as he played right field. After his career ended with a total of 755 lifetime home runs, he became a strong advocate for civil rights.

I don't know how many times I saw Aaron play, but it was a bunch. Many baseball stars stand out in my memories of attending games as a kid with my Uncle Jack, but Aaron doesn't take a back seat to any of them. RIP Hank. A life well lived.

Saturday January 23, 2021

With big bets streaming in all day, I think we'll pass the handle of last year's championship weekend.

One customer bet me the Bucs-Packers game over 52.5 when everyone else had 52, taking a half-point the worst of it. He came in a few hours later and bet over 53, this time taking a whole point the worst of it, when everyone else was still at 52. I don't know where these guys come from, but I love them.

We're looking pretty good on the futures right now. The Bucs are the worst for us, but even that isn't so bad. We still would win over $50,000 at this point. It's just that the other three teams are that much better.

UFC fans had been waiting for Dustin Poirier vs. Connor McGregor tonight. As I've written, we purposely don't book a lot of action on these fights. However, we did some good business on this card, especially the feature. In an upset, Poirier knocked out McGregor in the second round, giving us one of our infrequent UFC wins. That's nice, because we lost on everything else today.

Sunday January 24, 2021

The NFL Conference Championships are here.

Just as I was nodding off last night, one of our sharpest customers placed a $20,000 money line bet on the Bills +160. We were looking for a sizable bet at that price and that was enough to move it down a nickel. He also bet the four teams (now three) vs. the field (only the Bucs are left) -450 to win $3,000. I really needed that. That takes me off some of my Bucs futures exposure.

While I was having my first cup of tea this morning, one of the guys who bet big with us yesterday came back and put $100,000 on the Bucs +3.5. I'd just moved it, so I got lucky with that number.

By the time I walked into my office, we got another $75,000 on the Bucs +3.5. I hated to make the move to 3, but I had very little choice. From there, we moved the total up to 54, back to 53.5, up to 54, and back to 53.5, where it closed. Still, we never moved the pointspread after I went to 3. We closed the line the Packers -3, 53.5 total, and Packers -170 on the money line.

Just to tell you how nuts it was, I gave Michael the what ifs at 11:45. By the time they kicked off 15 minutes later, some of them had changed by as much as $100,000. Fantastic action.

As it wound up, the only real danger for us was the Packers winning by exactly 3. Of course, I personally needed the Packers to win in order to complete my money-line parlay for them to win the NFC.

With 2:09 to play in the game, the Packers, down 31-23, drove to the Bucs 9-yard line. On 4th and goal, they kicked a field goal to cut the lead to 31-26. Huh? Although they had three timeouts, plus the 2-minute warning, they never saw the ball again. The Bucs won it 31-26.

The story of the game was turnovers, but not how you would ordinarily think. Brady threw three interceptions, though the Packers turned them into a mere 6 points. That's as inefficient as an NFL playoff team with an all-time quarterback could possibly be; they should have turned those interceptions into a minimum of 14 points. Minimum. The Bucs played well, but certainly not great. The Packers just lacked the ability to capitalize on their numerous opportunities.

Meanwhile, I've never jumped on the "Brady is the greatest of all time" bandwagon. But now, I might have to. Besides being great, he makes everyone around him so much better—receivers, linemen, and the defense. He turned some mediocre receivers into Potential Hall of Famers. Julian Edelman and Wes Welker were very good players, but knocking on the door of Canton? Without Brady, forget about it. When Randy Moss played with Brady, they set the world on fire. Joe Montana made everyone better, too, but not for nearly as long. In other sports, I would say the same about Michael Jordan, Magic Johnson, Larry Bird, and Wayne Gretzky. But Brady is 43 and still doing it. Incredible.

South Point did well with the Packers-Bucs game, but my personal money-line parlay was shot to hell.

I'm still alive with the Bills, the team we also need at the sports book. We closed the Chiefs -3, total 55.5, and -160 on the money line. We had a tremendous result in the first game, but we're almost certain to give much of it back. The Chiefs winning by exactly 3 would be disastrous. Otherwise, we want the Bills to win to minimize the damage. If we get really lucky, the Chiefs could win by 1 or 2; we'd make a ton of money. I knew it would take a miracle, but like Jackie Gaughan once told me, "Kid, it's gotta land somewhere."

It didn't land anywhere near where I wanted it to.

The Bills scored the first 9 points of the game and I thought they were going to blow out the defending champs. Unfortunately, they didn't get on the scoreboard again until the Chiefs rattled off 21 straight points. The Bills kicked a late first-half field goal to make it 21-12. The Chiefs stretched the lead to 38-15 before the Bills made a belated futile rally to cut it to 38-24 before the final gun.

Bills quarterback Josh Allen put much of the blame on himself and no question, he didn't play well. But the defense couldn't stop Patrick Mahomes and his multitude of weapons. Mahomes was well protected by his offensive line and Allen was not. The Chiefs have enough credit to go around, just like the Bills have plenty of players and coaches to blame. The bottom line is the Chiefs are a much better team and played like it.

South Point had a fine day. My two parlays both went up in smoke, but I saw my chance and I took it. I just happened to be wrong. That's the way it goes in this racket.

I debated putting up the Super Bowl price at either Chiefs -3 or -3.5. I went with -3.5 and before I got home, we were down to -3 with money from some of my sharpest players taking the Bucs +3.5. Of course, now it looks like I'll be dancing to that -3/+3.5 tune for the next two weeks. Believe it or not, it's easier to deal with on the Super Bowl, where the alternative pointspreads get a lot of play. I put them up for this weekend's game, but the biggest bet I took was $2,000. So they aren't much help in hedging a position. But I'll figure out various numbers to offset my exposure to the game falling on 3.

All right, enough for today. I'll do the Sunday crossword puzzle, then head to bed. In the morning, I'll get up and prepare for the two-week battle in front of me.

Chapter Twelve
January 25-Febryary 9, 2021

"It's getting better all the time."
—*Paul McCartney*
"It can't get no worse."
—*John Lennon*

Monday January 25, 2021

After more action on the Chiefs -3, I went to -3.5. I have a problem when I'm running the game -3: I allow bettors to buy a half-point off the 3 for -130. Almost no one in the business allows it at any price. It's not so bad during the regular season, but in a game like this, you can get steamrolled.

Once I went to 3.5, it didn't take long for one of my big players to take it for $50,000. So back to 3 it went, but I had a serious problem on my hands. How do I stop people from buying the half-point? I had my staff change the computer and make it -135 to buy the half-point. If that doesn't stop the onslaught, I'll make it -140.

We put up the first round of routine props today. Unfortunately, we made one mistake., on the prop "Will there be a defensive or special team touchdown? Yes +250/No -300." We put it in backwards, "Yes -300/No +250." One guy bet it on his phone account +250 for $2,000 and again +240 for $2,000. He was in the book and made a couple bets at the counter, where the bets have to get approved by a supervisor. But the way the system is set up, a bet on the app goes through without approval. We caught it after the second bet, but he has action on the first two. There's nothing I can do about it. One of my best employees programmed it, so even though I'm not happy about it, there isn't a whole lot I can do to him, either—other than tell him to be more careful next time. I did close the customer's phone account. He can bet at the windows where we have to approve every bet, but he no longer has the convenience of betting from anywhere.

I'm sure many of you reading this think he did nothing wrong. Technically, he didn't. But neither did I by closing his account.

Here's a true story, just to tell you how there are different kinds of people in the world. One time we graded a golf matchup wrong. A guy came in to tell me we credited him with a winner when it was actually a loser. The difference was a little over $1,000. He was a good customer, so I told him just to keep it. For a guy like that, I'd rather he just keep the money. He's actually pretty sharp, but at least I know he'll play it back.

I've given guys breaks like that my entire career. And among Jimmy Vaccaro, Michael Gaughan and me, you're talking about three of the softest-hearted guys in the gambling business. If you stay on our good side, you'll get the benefit of the doubt every time.

But this guy today? The hell with him.

Tuesday January 26, 2021

It seems like I put up a bad prop price every year. Not a mistake in the computer, but a lousy price made by yours truly. Today, I put up "Bucs first offensive touchdown will be 1) running -110 or 2) passing -110." That was a terrible price. "Passing" should have been a big favorite. It didn't take long until it was. One guy climbed the ladder from -110 all the way up to -180.

Like I said, it was 100% my fault. It's one of those things that when I review the numbers, I'll say to myself, "Who is the idiot that put up this number? Oh yeah. It was me."

Otherwise, money continues to come in on the Chiefs -3. I don't blame them. I think that's the right side at that price. It looks like I'm eventually going to have to go to 3.5. I know if I do, wise guys will rush to the counter, elbowing each other out of the way like Joanie Weston and Baby Rocko trying to spring loose a jammer (a Roller Derby reference).

It's the one-year anniversary (that seems like the wrong word, but I don't know how else to say it) of Kobe Bryant's death. As people are remembering that tragedy, some people noticed the front page of the L.A. Times on the day following the helicopter crash. Of course, the news was dominated by Kobe's passing, but in the lower left-hand corner of the front page was a headline to a very different story: "State sees first two cases of new virus."

COVID had hit California. A remarkable irony. If we only knew then what we know now.

Wednesday January 27, 2021

The walls have been breached once again. We had to go to 3.5 this morning on the Super Bowl.

As you'd expect, the action came in pretty quick on the Bucs +3.5. Two guys bet me $50,000, two more $20,000, and a few $10,000. I'm holding fast at the 3.5, for now, anyway. A customer bet the Chiefs -3.5 for $4,000. Later, another bet me $3,000. It's a start. At least I have two customers who would rather lay -110 than -120 and have the Chiefs on his ticket. I had close to nothing on the Bucs +3. So as of this moment, I have a one-way market no matter which number I choose. Since I like the 3.5 better, I might as well use that.

We put up mostly "index" props today, where you pick the exact score or the exact number of field goals or touchdowns.

In the past, I released all the props at once; I've also done it piecemeal like this. I like this way much better. It's easier on me, plus we keep people coming in during the week.

Thursday January 28, 2021

I was just waking up when the sports book called this morning. I looked at the time on my cell phone, 6:21 a.m. From the time I went to -3.5 on the Chiefs, we'd taken a little over $200,000 on the Bucs +3.5. Now one of my regular customers was in and wanted $350,000 on the Bucs. That was just too much. I gave him $50,000 in my still uncaffeinated state and told our supervisor Joe Hohler to go back to 3. Now that I've had my tea, I think that was plenty at this stage of the game.

Just as I suspected, the money came in on the Chiefs all day. Nothing huge, but quite a few bets of several thousand each. Meanwhile, it was the same pattern as usual, with the number of tickets on the money line favoring the Bucs by a large margin.

We put up more props, but they're mostly basic variations of props we had last year. Tomorrow, we'll finalize the last of the menu with individual players and some matchups.

Friday January 29, 2021

The Super Bowl action continues as it did yesterday. If the game were played right now, we'd need the Chiefs for several hundred thousand. I'm making sure we have the best money-line price on the Bucs and whatever I have on the pointspread, it will be the best price on one side or the other. When I was at 3.5 for a while, it was easily the best price on the Bucs. No one else had +3.5 at -110. It was available at -115 or -120, but not at -110. And in this business, every penny and every half-point counts.

Now that I'm at 3 and since we do everything at -110 at South Point, we have the best price on the Chiefs. Since I'm a couple hundred thousand high on the Bucs, the money that comes in will continue on the Chiefs -3 for a while. I don't think I'll have to address any possible line changes for at least a couple of days. Meanwhile, the public will be taking the Bucs on the money line as well. I hope I'm playing this right. I think I am, but these things have a way of coming at you unexpectedly.

I talked to one local bookmaker today and he complained how slow the action was. Sure, at -115 or -120, but ours has been exceptionally strong at -110 on all straight bets. At the same time, our daily basketball and hockey action has also been well above expectations—the locals like our -110 on all straight bets on basketball as well as football.

We completed our entire prop menu today, finishing the running back, receiver, and kicker props. We also posted match-ups for a multitude of players, team yardage, the sum yardage of all made field goals, and anything else we could think of that would produce some action. We're now set until next Friday or Saturday, when we put up all those idiotic props that the media loves so much. Every newsperson around the country thinks they're cool, but you never get a bet on them unless you make a terrible mistake. And the more the media loves them, the more I hate them.

Lord Almighty, I'm getting old and crotchety.

Saturday January 30, 2021

Before I got to work today, we had a $50,000 bet on the Chiefs. We're getting close to even on the pointspread, which I knew would be a matter of time. Now I'm looking to hold the 3 as long as possible, because I've offset it with the money line (we're about $70,000 high on the Bucs) and my pointspread props.

Other than the $50,000 bet, the rest of the day was dribs and drabs with Chiefs -3 and Bucs +153, the same pattern we've seen on Super Bowls for years. Money is coming in on our props from two really sharp players. I love it when they bet early; it lets me get to the right number quickly. By next week when the public comes in to play, I know I can take some bigger bets, because the wise guys put me exactly where I need to be on a price.

Sunday January 31, 2021

Another guy came in and bet a few of the pointspread props, the Bucs -6.5 +335 and the Bucs -3.5 +240 for $3,000 a rattle on each. I'm purposely running those props high. If they win, that means I get to kill all that Chiefs -3 money. Also, if the Chiefs win by exactly 3, which would be a bad result ordinarily, these pointspread props are designed to help me.

Later, a customer bet us more than $110,000 on the props, all at $2,000 a pop. I'm 99% sure whom he's bearding for, so it's a play to be highly respected and I moved the shit out the numbers. Already, I'm getting some play the other way. I'm hoping by game time, I need the same sides he does.

Not many people care, but Nevada crushed UNLV 89-60 in college basketball. I'll make sure all these UNLV fans are reminded of it.

All in all, we had a nice day in hoops and hockey to finish out a very good month.

February 1, 2021

I got the figures for January this morning. Our handle was up slightly and the win was up 38% over last January. We've been on a pretty good roll since October. I hope we can keep it up for one more week.

I also got a report on where we are on our Super Bowl handle, year over year, with six days until kickoff. We're practically double in handle. A big part is the -110, no matter the number (usually 3) and no matter the action. When we're -3, we're the only ones with -110. And when we're at +3.5, we're the only ones with -110.

Wait a second. In case you didn't think that strategy was risky enough, today Jimmy and I were called into the office to meet with Frank and Michael. They want me to put up both numbers. That's right, giving the players the choice, at any time, to lay -3 -110 on the Chiefs or take the Bucs +3.5 -110.

I'm not crazy about it, but I'm not totally against it, either. That's essentially what we're doing now anyway. However, the difference is we can manage it. I tried to tell them if we go this route, we're at a huge risk if the game falls on 3. Aren't we at risk of that now? Yes, but only for about $300,000. If we go the -3/+3.5 route, we're looking at $2 million minimum. If they're okay with that, well then I am, too. But they have to know.

I got them to table it until Wednesday. I have a feeling they'll do it. I don't know. If I owned the place, I wouldn't. We're doing enough business already. Why put ourselves out there? But it's up to them. It's just my job to point out the risk.

Let me go on record. I'm not going back to change any of the thoughts I put down as I wrote this book. I vow not to change the spirit of anything I wrote on that particular day, whether it's about COVID, Dan Snyder, Tom Brady, or Pam if she comes to her senses in the next couple of days and shitcans me. That goes for the Super Bowl, too. If we do this -3/+3.5 thing or we just get sided like regular bookmakers in the old days, I'll write about it honestly and tell you how I felt at that time.

I just hope this game doesn't fall 3, no matter what we do.

Tuesday February 2, 2021

I talked Michael out of the -3/+3.5 line. Thank goodness. That would have been a nightmare for me to manage.

Other than that, not much to report. Except for one funny thing. A customer asked what we would take on a Super Bowl teaser. The supervisor asked how much he wanted. He refused to say; he wanted an answer from us first. The supervisor came back to ask me. Obviously, this guy was going to bet the total, not wise. With a play like that, I'd let him go pretty high.

"Fifty-thousand," I told him.

"Oh. I only wanted five thousand."

Come on, man. Just tell me what you want. We'll probably take it.

Wednesday February 3, 2021

The weather report came out today. It looks like intermittent showers in Tampa on Sunday with winds gusting up to 20 miles per hour.

More money kept showing on the under, this time under 56.5. I'm down to 56 with the total, and if they played right now, I'd need the game over. But I expect a lot of public money showing on the over from now until game time.

No crazy Super Bowl action, but one guy hit an 8-team parlay that nailed us for $75,000. That ruined our day. It happens. We'll get 'em tomorrow.

Thursday February 4, 2021

Action continues to roll in. Word came out that Mattress Mack bet $3.47 million on the Bucs +3.5 -127. I'm glad he bet it elsewhere. He's just too big for us.

Most of the big action today came in on the props. We're pretty balanced on most of them. Once we settle on a good number, which we should have by now, we can let guys fire whatever they want. One guy bet $20,000 and another $8,000 on a variety of plays. I love it. Keep it coming, fellas!

I ran the action report comparing this year to last. The average is smoothing out. We aren't double last year's pace, but we are over by 74%. Not bad.

Friday February 5, 2021

At 7 a.m., we moved the money line to a dime line. The

change was from -167/+147 to -160/+150. I've done it for the past couple years. To call it tremendously popular would be a huge understatement.

I'd been warning all the ticket writers that as of this afternoon, we'd be seeing nonstop action. From the time I came in, about 9:30 a.m., we've had lines at the windows. The kiosks too.

We ran the comparison of last year's action again and even though the curve is flattening, we're still 55% above last year's total this far out from kickoff.

Even though the wise guys are on the under, the money from all the parlays with both teams are to the over. My straight bets are $35,000 high on the under, but I still had to move the total up from 56 to 56.5; we need the under for $80,000 due to the parlay action. Do you know how many parlays it requires to swing the action that much? I don't either, but it's a shitload.

Time to head home. I love this, but it's also wearing me out. In 50 hours or so, it will all be over.

Saturday February 6, 2021

We're still well ahead of last year's pace, though the curve has certainly plateaued. As of this morning, we're 29% ahead of last year at this time.

I had a glass of Metaxa last night to calm my nerves and try to get some sleep. I had another glass in the middle of the night.

This is my 41st Super Bowl as a bookmaker and I still get stressed. It's always the little things. The graveyard switched my dime money line to a 20-cent line. I would have caught it myself, but the computer that connects to our betting system from home was on the fritz. Of course it was. Thankfully, Joe Hohler caught and corrected it.

We put up one prop, one of those stupid cross-sport bets I hate, that moved five times. Evidently, we made some kind of mistake, so I took it off. Then one guy—I'm guessing some spoiled rich trust-fund douche bag—insulted me on Twitter. I should ignore it, but it rubbed me the wrong way.

To top it off, one of my supervisors told me I have an employee refusing to wear a mask. This guy has been nothing but a pain in my ass for a couple years. Now I have to address it the day before the Super Bowl.

The game? You mean, the thing that I should be worried about and nothing else? That's fine. I can handle that. It's the other little shit that should take care of itself that gets to me.

More bullshit. I was joking with one of my absolute favorite employees and she took offense. I feel terrible about it. I really love this young lady and she does a great job. I feel like a dark cloud has been hovering over me the last two days.

The lines to get to the betting windows look like a Sunday morning. There's plenty of competition in town, but it looks like we're holding our own against the other books. The props got most of the action today. A couple of real sharp guys just bet into our numbers, but I don't think I have to sweat their action too much. Our numbers are solid and we're well balanced on most of them.

One well-known bettor came in about 5:30 and bet $149,700 in props, all at $2,000 each. He's got me strung out on some exact scoring props, but other than that, I'm rooting for him in many others. He's super sharp and I like him.

Pam and I dined at Michael's with Vinny Magliulo and his wife, Lee. Great dinner as always, but the company was even better. I needed a night like this after the past few days.

One more sleep and it's Super Sunday. If I can sleep, that is.

Super Bowl Sunday February 7, 2021

The game hadn't even started and I was already stuck $5K. I'm always going to tails and the coin toss came up heads. I hope that's not an omen. We wrote over $46,000 on the coin toss. WTF is wrong with people? Who would bet good money on this stupid shit?

I never thought I'd go back to 3.5 on the game, but after I took $300,000 to win $200,000 on the Chiefs money line, I had to risk it in order to get some back on the Bucs. I marked down the time that I moved, 2:43. By 2:48, five minutes later, I'd taken in $150,000 on the Chiefs +3.5. That's exactly what I wanted to offset the big money-line bet. My advantage: heH was laying -150 and I got to book back the hedge at -110. The disadvantage was I opened myself up to a 3-point middle. Yin and yang. I didn't want to do it unless that was what I needed to do. And I needed to.

I also got steamed on the under, going from a high of 57 as recently as yesterday to closing 55 today. That's a pretty big move. Originally, the move was based on some possible bad weather, but they showed the stadium and weather was not an issue. Nonetheless, the money continued to come in on the under.

We need the Bucs and over. However, the ideal scenario is the Chiefs to win by exactly 1 or 2 and the game stays under. That's a pretty slim margin, but it's gotta land somewhere.

The game has started. From here, I'll be writing in real time.

Halfway through the first. Still no score.

With 5:10 to play in the first quarter, the Chiefs get on the board with a 48-yard field goal.

Under a minute to play in the first quarter, Brady throws a touchdown to Gronk. Surprisingly, we made money on that. I figured it would cost us. But I sit here and sweat every prop. We have about 300 of them. I'll mention a few, but for the rest, I'll let the chips fall where they may and take a look at the end.

The Bucs had a fourth and goal from the one. They gave the ball to Chris Jones, who I need to beat in a bunch of props, and he couldn't get in. I have mixed feelings. I need the Bucs, but not with this guy scoring. I can't believe they didn't let Brady, the greatest quarterback sneaker in history, just take from center and bull his way into the endzone.

All right. Let's see if the Bucs can hold them and get the ball back in good field position.

Bucs get it back at the Chiefs 40-yard line. Gotta score here. Brady throws a pass that gets tipped and intercepted. Wait. Defensive holding. First and 10 Bucs from the 27-yard line. Fourth and five, another Chiefs penalty. Next play, Brady hits Gronk for another touchdown; 14-3 Bucs.

The Chiefs drive to the Bucs 17-yard line, then settle for a field goal with a little more than a minute left in the half.

Bucs get the ball back. The Chiefs call some questionable timeouts. I'm not sure I'd give Tom Brady extra time. Brady drives them down to the 1-yard line, then hits Antonio Brown with a touchdown pass. The Bucs will go into the half with a 21-6 lead. The Chiefs allowed that to happen with inadvisable timeouts. Things like that have plagued Andy Reid his whole career.

We opened the halftime with the Chiefs -7 and a total of 28. They bet us the Chiefs and over. We closed Chiefs -7.5, 28.5 total. If I were in a vacuum, I'd have opened it Chiefs -3.5. I'm not that confident in a Chiefs comeback.

The Chiefs get the ball to open the second half. They drive to the Bucs 35-yard line and settle for a 52-yard Butker field goal, cutting the Bucs lead to 21-9.

Bucs go 74 yards, capped by a Fournette touchdown run from the 27-yard line. Bucs lead 28-9. Fournette was never touched, as the Bucs dominate the line of scrimmage.

A Mahomes' pass gets tipped and intercepted. Bucs get the ball at the Chiefs 45-yard line. They drive deep into Chiefs' territory, but fumble a shotgun snap that Brady recovers after a big loss. Nonetheless, Succop hits a 52-yard field goal to put the Bucs up 31-9.

Chiefs drive to the 11-yard line and go for it on fourth down. Bucs hold them and get the ball with 12:32 to play in the game.

Bucs chew up clock and punt, pinning the Chiefs at their own 7 with 8:02 to play. Chiefs drive to the Bucs 27, but fail to convert on 4th down. Bucs take over with 3:58 to play, but don't milk much clock, giving the Chiefs the ball back with 3:30 to play. Mahomes gets intercepted in the end zone.

Bucs win it 31-9.

It takes forever to grade the props and, of course, the computer is overburdened with the number of bets. Finally, the results are in.

We win $535,000 and some change. Accounting might make some adjustments, but that's the figure I give Michael and he's elated. And like I've said throughout this book, when Michael is happy, I'm happy.

Monday February 8, 2021

As we approached game time yesterday, I started liking the Bucs. Originally, I was taking the Chiefs. But the more I looked at the entire lineup, I thought the Bucs had the better team, particularly at the line of scrimmage on both sides of the ball.

The skill-position players on the Chiefs were better, but that was it. And if I'm looking at a game in which Tom Brady, the Bucs' most important skill-position player, is considered a weak link, I have to like that team. Also, Mahomes wasn't 100% due to an injured toe, which is much more important than the average fan realizes. The Chiefs offensive line was in disarray once their premier left tackle, Eric Fisher, went down with an injury. Most of the respected handicappers I knew also favored the Bucs.

I wanted the Bucs going for me and the way the action was going, it didn't look like it would be that hard to make sure I needed them.

I haven't been betting much myself, but I thought the best value in betting the Bucs would be to take Tom Brady to win the MVP. I could have taken the Bucs +3.5 -115 or +145 or so on the money line, but Brady to win the MVP was +245. I thought if the Bucs did win, it was highly likely the MVP would go to the veteran quarterback earning his seventh Super Bowl ring. I was right. Brady was MVP and I picked up a couple bucks for my efforts.

Tuesday February 9, 2021

Nevada's Super Bowl figures were released today. The books won $12.6 million on a handle of $136.1 million. I'm glad we contributed nicely to the win. The handle was down, the lowest since 2016. Not a surprise to me, considering the effect COVID has had on travel and restrictions on how big (meaning small) our parties were permitted to be.

When I started this book and began planning how to approach it, I thought a bookmaker's season from Super Bowl to Super Bowl would be an amusing journey. In between would be the NCAA tournament, NBA and NHL playoffs, and a little baseball until we got to the playoffs and then more football. I knew there would be some curve balls, But I couldn't have foreseen Kobe Bryant's tragic death, Michael Gaughan eliminating some of the phone customers, or Jimmy Vaccaro heading back to Pittsburgh. I thought it would be the typical ups and downs of a sports betting year peppered with some funny anecdotes that didn't make my last book. I also wanted to include the medical history of my wife's recovery from her brain tumor and mine from MDS to make this book very personal.

When men make plans, God laughs.

All was well within the realm of possibility until March. The coronavirus hit and the whole world changed.

Personally, I was under quarantine between July and October 2019 with my bone-marrow transplant. Then, starting in October, I was under a semi-quarantine. I had to work in the back office, not out front where I prefer to be. I wasn't allowed to go to meetings in a small room, I wasn't supposed to go to sporting events, and I had to be careful going to restaurants. I had four semi-reasonable months before everything got shut down and, admittedly, I was more careful than most people. I had to be.

I wanted this book to reflect the emotions of the moment and I did that to the best of my ability. If a psychologist reads this book, he or she might think I'm either psychotic or, at a minimum, bipolar. Let me tell you, all gamblers and bookmakers have a little bit of one or the other in them. Actually, I'm certain I have it less than almost anyone, mainly due to the influence of Jimmy Vaccaro in my life. But this time in our history has been off-the-charts insane and even more so in the world of sports. And yeah, I've gone from extremely optimistic on some days to being ready to head to Hoover Dam for a fateful final jump on others.

Now that I'm finished with this journal, I might look back at some things in it and laugh. I hope so. Of course, it might be the maniacal laugh of a deranged lunatic in a straitjacket, but a laugh nonetheless.

We don't need a repeat of this past year. Let's all keep our fingers crossed for a better future.

Then One Year

About the Author

Chris Andrews began his "unofficial" career in sports betting when he was a kid in Pittsburgh. His uncle, Jack Franzi, is a legend among bookmakers and wiseguys. Chris launched his "official" career in the sports betting industry as a ticket writer in Las Vegas in 1979. He rose quickly through the ranks and became the director of the sports book at the Club Cal Neva in Reno at the age of 25. He's now the sports book director at the South Point in Las Vegas.

Visit
LasVegasAdvisor.com
for all the latest on gambling and Las Vegas

Free features include:

- Articles and ongoing updates on gambling.

- Real-time odds for all major sporting events.

- Sign-up and free-play bonuses.

- Question of the Day offering in-depth answers to gambling and Las Vegas-related questions.

- Active message boards with discussions on blackjack, sports betting, poker, and more!

Become a Las Vegas Advisor Member and get our exclusive dining, show, and gambling coupons and members-only discounts.

Keep up to Date on
All the Developments in Sports Betting

Go to GamblingWithAnEdge.com to access the blogs and podcasts of the world's top advantage players, including professional sports bettors who cover the subject from every conceivable angle. Get analyses of the latest online bonus offers and sign up through our links for added incentives. Track the progress of newly legalized sports betting jurisdictions and learn about new sports betting technologies as they're developed. Visit often for the latest information and opportunities in the explosion of sports betting nationwide.

Then One Day
by Chris Andrews

Chris Andrews became the youngest sports book director in the business at age 25, and 40 years later has been the top oddsmaker at several casinos in Las Vegas and Reno. Packed with classic stories from both sides of the counter, *Then One Day* offers a unique look at how a sports book director talks, thinks, and makes book—both in the "good-old-days" and today.

Sharp Sports Betting
by Stanford Wong

Wong's classic book on sports betting explains the logic and math behind solid strategies for betting sides, totals, parlays, and props, and identifies what are now referred to as "Wong teasers." The emphasis is on football.

Weighing the Odds in Sports Betting
by King Yao

King Yao conveys the fundamental concepts necessary to succeed at sports betting, then applies those principles to strategies for betting sides, totals, halves, season wins, parlay cards, sports pools, and more, while also addressing advanced concepts such as hedging, middling, and correlation plays.

Fantasy Sports, Real Money
by Bill Ordine

Compete in the daily fantasy sports game—football, baseball, basketball, hockey, even golf—using pro strategies and case studies from players who've won millions. Includes game plans for setting lineups, maximizing value with the salary cap, finding pricing inefficiencies, playing against (or avoiding) experts, identifying overlays, and more.

20/20 Sports Betting
by Logan Fields

The first book on sports betting to concentrate on the methods used by successful pros. What do they look for? How do they think? Where do the edges materialize? Football, baseball, golf, NASCAR, hockey, horse racing—name the sport and Fields tells you how to beat it.

Gambling Wizards
by Richard Munchkin

Gambling Wizards takes you into the lives and minds of some of the most successful professional gamblers of all time, including famed sports bettors Billy Walters and Stan Tomchin, and horse-betting phenom Alan Wood.

ABOUT HUNTINGTON PRESS

Huntington Press is a specialty publisher of Las Vegas- and gambling-related books and periodicals, including the award-winning consumer newsletter, *Anthony Curtis' Las Vegas Advisor.*

Huntington Press
3665 Procyon Street
Las Vegas, Nevada 89103
e-mail: books@huntingtonpress.com